teach
yourself

icelandic

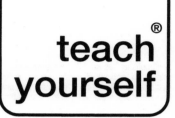

icelandic
hildur jónsdóttir

For over 60 years, more than 50 million people have learnt over 750 subjects the **teach yourself** way, with impressive results.

be where you want to be with **teach yourself**

The publisher has used its best endeavours to ensure that the URLs for external websites referred to in this book are correct and active at the time of going to press. However, the publisher and the author have no responsibility for the websites and can make no guarantee that a site will remain live or that the content will remain relevant, decent or appropriate.

For UK order enquiries: please contact Bookpoint Ltd, 130 Milton Park, Abingdon, Oxon OX14 4SB. Telephone: +44 (0) 1235 827720. Fax: +44 (0) 1235 400454. Lines are open 09.00–17.00, Monday to Saturday, with a 24-hour message answering service. Details about our titles and how to order are available at www.teachyourself.co.uk

For USA order enquiries: please contact McGraw-Hill Customer Services, PO Box 545, Blacklick, OH 43004-0545, USA. Telephone: 1-800-722-4726. Fax: 1-614-755-5645.

For Canada order enquiries: please contact McGraw-Hill Ryerson Ltd, 300 Water St, Whitby, Ontario L1N 9B6, Canada. Telephone: 905 430 5000. Fax: 905 430 5020.

Long renowned as the authoritative source for self-guided learning – with more than 50 million copies sold worldwide – the **teach yourself** series includes over 500 titles in the fields of languages, crafts, hobbies, business, computing and education.

British Library Cataloguing in Publication Data: a catalogue record for this title is available from the British Library.

Library of Congress Catalog Card Number: on file.

First published in UK 2004 by Hodder Education, 338 Euston Road, London, NW1 3BH.

First published in US 2004 by The McGraw-Hill Companies, Inc.

This edition published 2004.

The **teach yourself** name is a registered trade mark of Hodder Headline.

Typeset by Transet Limited, Coventry, England.
Printed in Great Britain for Hodder Education, a division of Hodder Headline, 338 Euston Road, London, NW1 3BH, by Cox & Wyman Ltd, Reading, Berkshire.

Hodder Headline's policy is to use papers that are natural, renewable and recyclable products and made from wood grown in sustainable forests. The logging and manufacturing processes are expected to conform to the environmental regulations of the country of origin.

Impression number   10 9 8 7 6 5 4
Year   2009 2008 2007 2006

contents

introduction

This course is intended for learners with no previous knowledge of Icelandic. Whether you're learning Icelandic on your own, or attending a class, this course is very well suited to your purposes. It is a functional course which aims to teach you to communicate in Icelandic and to use the language in a practical way. The vocabulary introduced is therefore centred around realistic everyday situations. Alongside the vocabulary from everyday life, the main grammatical structures of Icelandic are explained, so that you can create sentences of your own.

Icelandic

Icelandic is spoken in Iceland, an island in the North Atlantic Ocean between Norway and Greenland. Iceland is a relatively big country – 103,000 km^2 – but has only around 300,000 inhabitants. Icelandic belongs to the Nordic language group of the Germanic language family, together with the other Scandinavian languages, Norwegian, Swedish, Danish and Faroese. Icelandic developed from Viking Age West Norse, which was spoken in Norway and its colonies, and was brought to Iceland by the Viking settlers from Norway. In the eleventh century Icelandic began to diverge from Norwegian, but the distinction between the two languages was not fully marked until about two centuries later.

The Icelandic language has not developed greatly during the last centuries. Modern Icelandic is very similar to the Viking language and speakers of modern Icelandic can read the sagas, which were written in the thirteenth and fourteenth centuries, without any great difficulty. Icelandic can therefore be classified as a very conservative language. Hardly any dialects exist in Icelandic; this is probably due to the small size of the population, strong family ties, regular contact between different groups of people and the fact that the written language survived through the centuries. In modern Icelandic there are only two dialects, which exist among younger generations, and even these are not very different from the standard language.

Icelandic is an inflectional language, which means it has cases and endings added to the words. Some of the grammar structures are very similar to German and much of the vocabulary bears resemblance to other Germanic languages (such as the other Scandinavian languages, German and Dutch). If you already know a Germanic language, learning Icelandic will be easier for you.

How to use the book

Each unit consists of dialogues, vocabulary lists, grammar explanations and exercises. Sometimes there are additional pronunciation explanations, comments about the vocabulary and explanations in English about Iceland or Icelandic society, marked by ℹ.

At the beginning of the book there is a pronunciation guide in which the main pronunciation rules are given, but further rules will be introduced in subsequent units. More details are given in the appendix. You should study the pronunciation guide at the beginning of the book very carefully, listen to the recording and try to practise as much as you can. There are some sounds in Icelandic which do not exist in English (or related languages), so you need to pay special attention to the pronunciation.

In each unit there are a few dialogues (often two or three). Normally the dialogues are preceded by an introduction in English or Icelandic. You should read this introduction before you read the dialogues, because it gives you the context of the dialogues. All of the dialogues appear on the recording which accompanies the book. To develop a good knowledge of pronunciation, you are strongly advised to use the recording if possible.

You need to study the dialogue. The vocabulary after the dialogue gives you the meaning of the new words and phrases (words from all units can be found in the Icelandic–English vocabulary at the end of the book).

Next there are grammar explanations. Only the main grammar rules of Icelandic are described in this book. When you become more advanced you still need to consult Icelandic grammar books (see the **Taking it further** section).

At the end of each unit you will find a number of exercises. It is very important to do the exercises so that you can practise what you have learnt in the unit, both new grammar structures and new vocabulary. Try to do all the exercises both orally (to practise speaking Icelandic) and in writing (to practise writing Icelandic). The exercises are designed to practise communication and also grammar structures.

The recording that accompanies the book contains selected material from the units (marked by ▶ in the book). It contains the words in the pronunciation guide at the beginning of the book, all the dialogues, and some of the grammar explanations. The book can be used without the recording, but in that case you should try to listen to Icelandic spoken by native speakers whenever possible (e.g. on line; see the **Taking it further** section). Try also to read out loud as often as you can to increase your confidence in pronunciation. Try to use Icelandic whenever you get a chance and remember that practice makes perfect!

Abbreviations

acc.	accusative
d	has *d* in the past tense
ð	has *ð* in the past tense
dat.	dative
f.	feminine
gen.	genitive
imp.	imperative
m.	masculine
n.	neuter
nom.	nominative
past part.	past participle
pl.	plural
sing.	singular
t	has *t* in the past tense

pronunciation guide

The Icelandic alphabet has 32 letters:

Aa	Áá	Bb	Dd	Ðð	Ee	Éé	Ff
Gg	Hh	Ii	Íí	Jj	Kk	Ll	Mm
Nn	Oo	Óó	Pp	Rr	Ss	Tt	Uu
Úú	Vv	Xx	Yy	Ýý	Þþ	Ææ	Öö

As you can see, Icelandic has some letters which English doesn't have: á, ð, é, í, ó, ú, ý, þ, æ, ö. Don't worry if these seem quite foreign to you – we will go through the pronunciation of each letter later on. It is important to realize that the letters á, é, í, ó, ú and ý are separate letters from a, e, i, o, u and y, and they have their own pronunciation. The superscript mark ´ is therefore not a symbol of length or accent. So the letters a and á, for example, correspond to different sounds: a is pronounced like a in English *father* and á is pronounced like *ow* in English *down*.

We will now go through the pronunciation of each letter of the alphabet. Only the regular (i.e. usual) pronunciation will be given here; exceptions will be introduced in later units of the book and in the appendix. To explain the pronunciation, a comparison with English and other languages will be made. Phonetic symbols (within square brackets) will also be used to complement the explanations. IPA (International Phonetic Alphabet) symbols are used in the phonetic transcription except in two cases: the symbol [þ] is used instead of [θ] and the symbol [ö] instead of [œ]. In Icelandic phonetics books these two symbols are normally used instead of the IPA ones. Some of the sounds do not occur in English and it is therefore very important to listen carefully to the recording that accompanies the book. Try to practise the sounds as much as you can. In the end you will get the hang of even the 'strangest' sounds!

▶ Vowels

a [a]   is similar to *a* in English *father* and it is like French / German / Italian / Spanish **a**. Example: **sandur** (*sand*).

á [au]   like *ow* in English *down*. Example: **ást** (*love*).

e [ɛ]   like *e* in English *bed*. Example: **senda** (*send*).

é [jɛ]   like *ye* in English *yes*. Example: **ég** (*I*).

i [ɪ]   like *i* in English *hid, bid*. Example: **listi** (*list*).

í [i]   like *ea* in English *heat*. Example: **sími** (*telephone*).

o [ɔ]   like *aw* in English *law, bawd*. Example: **loft** (*air*).

ó [ɔu]   is very similar to the exclamation *oh* in English. Example: **bóndi** (*farmer*).

u [ʏ]   does not occur in English. It is produced by trying to pronounce [ɪ] (as in Icelandic **listi** or English *hid*) with rounded lips. This sound appears in German for short **ü**, like **fünf, küssen**. Example: **hundur** (*dog*).

ú [u]   like *o* in English *who*. Example: **Rússland** (*Russia*).

y [ɪ]   like *i* in English *hid, bid*. Example: **synda** (*swim*).

ý [i]   like *ea* in English *heat*. Example: **sýna** (*show*).

æ [ai]   like *i* in English *hide*. Example: **læsa** (*lock*).

ö [ö]   does not occur in English. It is produced by trying to pronounce [ɛ] (as in Icelandic **senda** or English *bed*) with rounded lips. It is quite similar to the *i* in English *bird* and *ea* in English *heard*. Example: **hönd** (*hand*).

ei [ɛi]   like *a* in English *came*. Example: **neisti** (*spark*).

ey [ɛi]   like *a* in English *came*. Example: **keyra** (*drive*).

au [öy]   see description of ö above – [y] is pronounced like [i], except that you round your lips. The sound [y] only appears in this combination [öy] in Icelandic. Example: **haust** (*autumn*). Warning: If you know German, then be really careful when you pronounce the letters **au** – they are not pronounced like German [au]!

▶ Consonants

b [b̥]   like English *b*, but with a bit more breathing; like *p* in English *spin*. Example: **bær** (*town*).

d [d̥]   like English *d*, but with a bit more breathing; like *t* in English *stop*. Example: **draumur** (*dream*).

ð [ð]   like *th* in English *father*. Example: **eða** (*or*).

f [f]   like *f* in English *father*. Example: **fá** (*get*).

g   has three main pronunciations:

    1 [g̊] When the letter **g** appears at the beginning of words, it is pronounced like English [g], but with a bit

more breathing, like *k* in English *skip*. Examples: **gata**
(*street*), **grár** (*grey*).

2 [γ] When **g** appears between vowels, or between a
vowel and **ð** or **r**, it has a guttural sound which does
not occur in English, but can be heard in Spanish in the
word **Tarragona**. Listen carefully to the recording and
try to imitate what you hear. Examples: **saga** (*story*),
sagði (*said*), **sigra** (*win*).

3 [x] When **g** appears in the middle of a word before
t or **s** it has a sound which does not occur in English,
but which can be heard in Scottish **loch**, German **ach**
and Spanish **jota**. Examples: **hægt** (*possible*), **hugsa**
(*think*).

h [h]   like *h* in English *he*. Example: **hundur** (*dog*).

j [j]   like *y* in English *yes*. Example: **já** (*yes*).

k   has three main pronunciations:
1 [kʰ] When the letter **k** appears at the beginning of
words, it is pronounced like *k* in English *kick*.
Examples: **kasta** (*throw*), **króna** (unit of money used in
Iceland).
2 [ǥ] In the middle of a word between vowels or at the
end: see description of [ǥ] above. Examples: **taka**
(*take*), **tak** (*hold*).
3 [x] When **k** appears in the middle of a word before
t or **s** it has the [x] sound: see above under the third
pronunciation of the letter **g**. Example: **rakt** (*damp*).

l [l]   like *l* in English *land*. Example: **lás** (*lock*).

m [m]   like *m* in English *mother*. Example: **mála** (*paint*).

n   has two main pronunciations:
1 [n] like *n* in English *night*. Example: **nú** (*now*).
2 [ŋ] like *n* in English *sing*. Example: **fingur** (*finger*).

p   has two main pronunciations:
1 [pʰ] when the letter **p** appears at the beginning of
words, it is pronounced like *p* in English *pen*. Example:
penni (*pen*).
2 [b̥] In the middle of a word between vowels or at the
end: see description of [b̥] above. Examples: **tapa**
(*lose*), **tap** (*loss*).

r [r]   very similar to *r* in English *brr* uttered by speakers
when shuddering with cold. It is a trill, i.e. it is rolled.
This sound appears in Scottish English and in Spanish,
as in **Tarragona**. Listen carefully to the recording and
try to imitate what you hear. Example: **rós** (*rose*).

s [s]   like *s* in English *sea*. Example: **sól** (*sun*).

| t | has two main pronunciations: |

t   has two main pronunciations:
  1 [tʰ] when the letter t appears at the beginning of words, it is pronounced like *t* in English *time*. Example: **taska** (*handbag, suitcase*).
  2 [d̥] In the middle of a word between vowels: see description of [d̥] above. Example: **gata** (*street*).
v [v]   like *v* in English *very*. Example: **vasi** (*pocket* or *vase*).
x [ǥs] **or** [xs]   It is optional whether you pronounce the letter **x** as [ǥs] or [xs]. See description of [x], [s] and [ǥ] above. Example: **buxur** (*trousers*)
þ [þ]   like *th* in English *thriller*. Example: **þurfa** (*need*).

Stress and length

▶ Stress

In Icelandic the **first syllable** of a word (e.g. **skó** in **skóli** (*school*)) is stressed (i.e. spoken with more emphasis). The only exception that need concern us here is **halló**, said when answering the telephone.

Length

Rule 1: Vowels without stress are short. Example: **skóli** – the syllable **li** is not stressed so [ɪ] is short.

Rule 2: Stressed vowels are long unless two or more consonants follow. Examples: **tala** (*speak*) – long, one consonant following, **trúa** (*believe*) – long, no consonant following, **koss** (*kiss*) – short, two consonants following.

Rule 3: Consonants are long only if they are written double *and* they come directly after the stressed vowel. Examples: **ball** (*ball*) – long **l**, **finna** (*find*) – long **n**; but **tal** (*speech*) – short **l** (not written double), **hestanna, hávaxinn** – short **n** (does not come directly after the stressed vowel). There are exceptions (namely, **pp, tt** and **kk**) which we will look at later on.

01

hæ, hvað heitir þú?
hi, what's your name?

In this unit you will learn
- how to greet people and say 'goodbye'
- how to ask someone's name and say your name
- how to ask where someone is from and say where you are from
- how to say 'yes' and 'no'
- how to thank somebody

Language points
- personal pronouns such as **ég** (*I*) and **þú** (*you*)
- common question words such as **hvað** (*what*) and **hvar** (*where*)
- word order in questions
- the verbs **að vera** (*to be*) and **að heita** (*to be called*)
- country names such as **Ísland** (*Iceland*)

▶ Greetings

Hæ! *Hi!*
Hvað segirðu? *How are you?* (lit. *What say you?*)
allt fínt *good, fine* (lit. *everything fine*)
sæll! / sæl! (to a woman) *hi*
blessaður! / blessuð! (to a woman) *hi* (lit. *blessed*)
sæll og blessaður! / sæl og blessuð! (to a woman) *hi* (lit.
  happy and blessed)
komdu sæll / komdu sæl (to a woman) *hi* (lit. *come happy*)
komdu blessaður / komdu blessuð (to a woman) *hi* (lit. *come
  blessed*)
komdu sæll og blessaður / komdu sæl og blessuð (to a
  woman) *hi* (lit. *come happy and blessed*)
sæll vertu / sæl vertu (to a woman) *hi* (lit. *be happy*)
góðan dag! / góðan daginn! *good day*
gott kvöld! / góða kvöldið! *good evening*

Pronunciation

- Be careful when you pronounce **hvað** – it is pronounced as if
  it were written **kvað**. The letters **hv** are always pronounced as
  kv.
- Be careful when you pronounce **sæll** – it is pronounced as if
  it were written **sædl**. The letters **ll** are almost always
  pronounced as **dl** if they are not followed by another
  consonant.
- Be careful when you pronounce **gott** – it is pronounced as if
  it were written **goht**. The letters **tt**, **kk** and **pp** are always
  pronounced as **ht** (or **hd**), **hk** (**hg**) and **hp** (**hb**) respectively.
  You pronounce an **h**-sound and then a short t- (/d-), k- (/g-)
  or p- (/b-) sound. The **h**-sound is (normally) a clear, ordinary

h-sound, like the one in **hundur** (*dog*). It is helpful to imagine a false boundary between the h-sound and the **t-** (/**d**-)sound; then you have an h-sound at the end of the first part, and it is easier to pronounce an [h] at the end than in the middle of a word. So when you say the word **gott**, say it in two steps: **goh –t**.

Language notes

- The question **Hvað segirðu?** (*How are you?*) is used more by younger people. It can be answered in several ways: **allt fínt** (lit. *everything fine*), **bara allt fínt** (lit. *just everything fine*), **allt ágætt** (lit. *everything OK/so-so*), **bara allt ágætt** (lit. *just everything OK/so-so*).
- **Hæ** is used more by younger people.
- **Sæl** (used to address a female) and **sæll** (used to address a male) are used less by young people (unless they are addressing older people).
- **Blessuð** (used to address a female) and **Blessaður** (used to address a male) can be used both as greetings and goodbyes. They are used between older people, although in recent years it has become trendy to use them as greetings between younger people.
- The greetings **Sæll og blessaður!**, **komdu sæll, komdu blessaður, komdu sæll og blessaður** and **sæll vertu** are used by older people.
- **Góðan daginn / Góðan dag** is used in the morning as well.

▶ Goodbyes

bless	*goodbye*
við sjáumst	*see you* (lit. *we will see each other*)
sjáumst	*see you*

> **bæ! bæ, bæ!** *bye*
> **blessaður / blessuð** (to a woman)   *goodbye*
> **vertu blessaður / vertu blessuð** (to a woman)   *bye* (lit. *be blessed*)
> **vertu sæll / vertu sæl** (to a woman)   *bye* (lit. *be happy*)

Language notes

- **Bless** is used both by older and younger people. **Bæ** is used more by younger people.
- The goodbyes **vertu blessaður** and **vertu sæll** are used by older people.

▶ Hæ, hvað heitir þú? *Hi, what's your name?*

Christof is a friend of Björn's. He's just arrived in Iceland with his girlfriend Anna. Christof and Anna have come to visit Björn and his family. Björn meets Anna for the first time.

Björn   Hæ! Hvað heitir þú?
Anna   Anna. En þú?
Björn   Ég heiti Björn.

> **hæ**   *hi*
> **hvað**   *what*
> **heitir, heiti** (from **heita**)   *are called, am called*
> **þú**   *you* (sing.)
> **en**   *but*
> **en þú?**   *and you?/how about you?*
> **ég**   *I*

Pronunciation

Be careful when you pronounce the name **Björn**. **Björn** is pronounced as if it were spelt **Björdn** or **Bjödn** – the letters **rn** are always pronounced as **rdn** or **dn** (in some common words you can choose whether to pronounce the letters **rn** as **rdn** or **dn**).

Björn   Þetta er Inga, mamma mín.
Inga   (*turning to Christof*) Sæll! Heitir þú Christof?
Christof   Já, ég heiti Christof.

þetta	*this*	mín	*my*
er (from **vera**)	*is*	já	*yes*
mamma	*mother, mum*		

Pronunciation

The letter **i** is pronounced **í** before the letters **ng**. **Inga** is therefore pronounced **Ínga**.

▶ Hvaðan ertu? *Where are you from?*

Björn doesn't know where Anna comes from, and Inga doesn't know where Christof comes from.

Björn (*turning to Anna*): Hvaðan ertu?
Anna Ég er frá Hollandi.
Inga (*turning to Christof*): Ert þú líka frá Hollandi?
Christof Nei, ég er frá Þýskalandi.

hvaðan	*where from*
ertu (ert (from **vera**) + þú)	*are you*
er (from **vera**)	*am*
frá	*from*
Hollandi (from **Holland**)	*Holland*
líka	*also*
nei	*no*
Þýskalandi (from **Þýskaland**)	*Germany*

Björn's father Kári comes home and Björn introduces Christof and Anna to him.

Björn	Þetta eru Christof og Anna.
Kári	Velkomin til Íslands!
Christof og Anna	Takk!
Kári	Eruð þið frá Þýskalandi?
Christof	Já, ég er frá Þýskalandi en Anna er frá Hollandi.

eru (from **vera**)	*are*
og	*and*
velkomin (from **velkominn**)	*welcome*
til	*to*
Íslands (from **Ísland**)	*Iceland*
takk	*thank you, thanks*
eruð (from **vera**)	*are*
þið	*you* (plural)

Pronunciation

Be careful when you pronounce **takk** – remember that the letters **kk** are always pronounced as **hk** (/hg). The easiest way to pronounce the word is to do it in two steps: **tah – k** (or **tah – g**).

Grammar

▶ The verb *að vera* (*to be*)

The verb **að vera** (*to be*) is a strong verb in Icelandic, as in most languages (including English). It has the following forms in the present tense:

að vera	*to be*
ég **er**	*I am*
þú **ert**	*you are*
hann / hún / það **er**	*he / she / it is*
við **erum**	*we are*
þið **eruð**	*you are*
þeir / þær / þau **eru**	*they are*

Language notes

- The word *to*, which accompanies the verb in the infinitive (i.e. in the dictionary form), is **að** in Icelandic.
- In the third person plural (*they*) there are three pronouns corresponding to the three genders: **þeir** is masculine, **þær** is feminine, **þau** is neuter. For two men you would therefore use **þeir**, for two women you would use **þær** and for a man and a woman you would use **þau**.

▶ Questions

Common question words in Icelandic are:

hvað	*what*
hver	*who*
hvenær	*when*
hvar	*where*

When you form questions in Icelandic you always place the verb before the noun / pronoun:

statement	question
Þú heitir Anna.	Hvað heitir þú? *What is your name?*
Your name is Anna.	(lit. *What are called you?*)
	Heitir þú Anna? *Is your name Anna?*
	(lit. *Are called you Anna?*)

The pronoun *þú* in questions

In questions you normally put the pronoun þú and the verb together:

Ert þú frá Þýskalandi?
Ertu frá Þýskalandi?   *Are you from Germany?*

If the verb form ends in -t then the þ is dropped; otherwise the þ changes to ð:

Heitir þú Anna? → **Heitirðu** Anna?   *Is your name Anna?*

If you don't put the þú and the verb together, you are effectively stressing the pronoun:

Hvað heitir **þú**?   *What's **your** name?*

▶ The verb *að heita* (*to be called*)

The verb **að heita** (*to be called*) is also a strong verb like **að vera**. It has the following forms in the present tense:

að heita	to be called
ég heit**i**	*I am called*
þú heit**ir**	*you are called*
hann / hún / það heit**ir**	*he / she / it is called*
við heit**um**	*we are called*
þið heit**ið**	*you are called*
þeir / þær / þau heit**a**	*they are called*

Note – The plural present forms of almost all strong / irregular verbs are regular; you add the regular endings **-um**, **-ið**, **-a** to the stem of the verb. Only the verb **að vera** and a few others (those which end in **á**, **o** or **u** in the infinitive, e.g. **fá** (*get*), **þvo** (*wash*), **skulu** (*shall*)) have irregular plural present forms.

Cases

There are four cases in Icelandic: **nominative** (like *I* in *I did it*), **accusative** (like *me* in *He hit me*), **dative** (like *me* in *Give it to me*) and **genitive** (like *John's* in *John's house*). All nouns in Icelandic have a particular form depending on which case they are in. We will learn more about each case later on.

Most verbs and all prepositions (words like *on*, *from*, *to*) take a particular case, i.e. the noun that follows the verb or the preposition has to be in a particular case. The preposition **frá** (*from*) always takes the dative, so the noun following this preposition must be in the dative form. The word **land** (*country*) is **landi** in the dative and words ending in -land (like **Ísland, Þýskaland, Holland**) therefore always end in -landi in the dative. We therefore say:

Ég er frá   Þýskalandi (*Germany*)
Hollandi (*Holland)*
Íslandi (*Iceland*)
Englandi (*England*)
Bretlandi (*Britain*), Stóra-Bretlandi (*Great Britain*)
Írlandi (*Ireland*)
Finnlandi (*Finland*)
Grænlandi (*Greenland*)
Frakklandi (*France*)
Póllandi (*Poland*)
Rússlandi (*Russia*)
Tékklandi (*Czech Republic*)
Ungverjalandi (*Hungary*)
Grikklandi (*Greece*)
Tyrklandi (*Turkey*)
Indlandi (*India*)
Tælandi (*Thailand*)
Eistlandi (*Estonia*)
Lettlandi (*Latvia*).

Not all country names end in **-land,** though. The following countries do not end in **-land,** and they happen to be the same in the dative form:

Svíþjóð	(*Sweden*)	Ég er frá Svíþjóð.
Sviss	(*Switzerland*)	Ég er frá Sviss.
Portúgal	(*Portugal*)	Ég er frá Portúgal.
Japan	(*Japan*)	Ég er frá Japan.
Kína	(*China*)	Ég er frá Kína.

Kanada	(Canada)	Ég er frá Kanada.
Ísrael	(Israel)	Ég er frá Ísrael.
Mexíkó	(Mexico)	Ég er frá Mexíkó.
Austurríki	(Austria)	Ég er frá Austurríki.

The following countries do not end in **-land**; they have different forms in the dative. We will learn more about these forms later.

Noregur	(Norway)	Ég er frá Noregi.
Danmörk	(Denmark)	Ég er frá Danmörku.
Ítalía	(Italy)	Ég er frá Ítalíu.
Spánn	(Spain)	Ég er frá Spáni.
Belgía	(Belgium)	Ég er frá Belgíu.
Búlgaría	(Bulgaria)	Ég er frá Búlgaríu.
Ameríka	(America)	Ég er frá Ameríku.
Bandaríkin	(United States)	Ég er frá Bandaríkjunum.
Ástralía	(Australia)	Ég er frá Ástralíu.
Rúmenía	(Romania)	Ég er frá Rúmeníu.
Kórea	(Korea)	Ég er frá Kóreu.

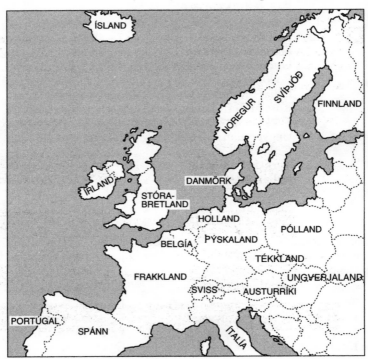

Evrópa *Europe*

Brasilía	(Brazil)	Ég er frá Brasilíu.
Argentína	(Argentina)	Ég er frá Argentínu.
Suður-Afríka	(South Africa)	Ég er frá Suður-Afríku.

Try to learn the names of the countries listed above. Can you say which country you come from? How about your foreign friends – can you say where they come from?

Practice

▶ 1 You go into a small corner shop to buy a few things. The shop assistant greets you and asks you some questions:

Shop assistant	Góðan daginn!
You	(*Use an equivalent phrase.*)
Shop assistant	Hvaðan ertu?
You	(*Say you're from England.*)
Shop assistant	Hvað heitirðu?
You	(*Say your name is Suzanna and ask 'How about you?'*)
Shop assistant	Ég heiti Eiríkur.

▶ 2 You are called Jon and your friend is Markus. You are from Sweden. You start talking to a woman on the bus and she asks you the following questions. Answer in Icelandic.

a Hvað heitið þið?
b Eruð þið frá Englandi?

3 List the countries mentioned in this newspaper advertisement.

Þýskaland		Sviss	
Verð frá	**32.845** kr.	Verð frá	**32.605** kr.
Noregur		**Pólland**	
Verð frá	**35.275** kr.	Verð frá	**32.515** kr.
Finnland		**Svíþjóð**	
Verð frá	**32.635** kr.	Verð frá	**33.665** kr.

Takmarkað sætaframboð!

4 Say where these people are from.

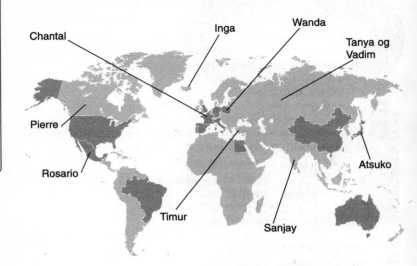

Example: Wanda er frá Póllandi.

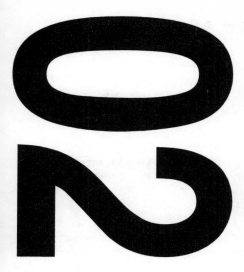

02

hvaða tungumál talarðu?

which language(s) do you speak?

In this unit you will learn
- how to use the courtesy word **fyrirgefðu** (*excuse me*)
- how to say which language(s) you speak / don't speak
- how to ask someone which language(s) they speak
- how to say what your mother tongue is

Language points
- first group of regular verbs (**tala** (*speak*))
- case government of verbs
- gender of nouns
- weak declension of feminine nouns (feminine nouns ending in -a)

▶ Ég tala íslensku / I speak Icelandic

Talarðu ensku?

Nei, ég tala bara íslensku og dönsku.

Kona Fyrirgefðu, talarðu ensku?
Maður Nei, ég tala ekki ensku. Ég tala bara íslensku og dönsku.

---

kona (f.)   *woman*
maður (m.)   *man*
fyrirgefðu   *excuse me, sorry*
talarðu (**talar** (from **tala**) + **þú**)   *do you speak*
ensku (acc. from **enska**, f.)   *English*
tala   *speak*
ekki   *not*
bara   *only*
íslensku (acc. from **íslenska**, f.)   *Icelandic*
dönsku (acc. from **danska**, f.)   *Danish*

Pronunciation

Be careful when you pronounce **ekki** – it is pronounced as if it was written **ehki**. Remember that the letters **kk** are always pronounced as **hk**. The easiest way to pronounce the word is to do it in two steps: **eh – ki**.

▶ Þið talið mjög góða íslensku! *You speak Icelandic very well!*

Björn's sister, Kristín, chats to Christof and Anna.

Kristín   Þið talið mjög góða íslensku!
Christof   Takk!
Kristín   Talið þið mörg tungumál?

Christof   Móðurmál mitt er þýska, en ég tala líka ensku, spænsku
og ítölsku – og svolitla íslensku!
Kristín   Vá, það er aldeilis! En þú Anna, hvaða tungumál talar þú?
Anna   Ég tala hollensku sem móðurmál og ég tala líka ensku,
þýsku og rússnesku – og svolitla íslensku eins og Christof!

---

talið (from **tala**)   *speak*
mjög   *very*
góða (from **góður**)   *good*
mörg   *many*
tungumál (n.)   *language(s)*
móðurmál (n.)   *mother tongue*
mitt (from **minn**)   *my*
þýska (f.)   *German*
spænsku (acc. from **spænska**, f.)   *Spanish*
ítölsku (acc. from **ítalska**, f.)   *Italian*
svolitla (from **svolítill**)   *little, little bit*
vá   *wow*
það er aldeilis!   *that's impressive!*
hvaða   *which*
hollensku (acc. from **hollenska**, f.)   *Dutch*
sem móðurmál   *as a mother tongue*
þýsku (acc. from **þýska**, f.)   *German*
rússnesku (acc. from **rússneska**, f.)   *Russian*
eins og   *like*

Grammar

Group 1 regular verbs

There are two groups of regular verbs in Icelandic, called here
Groups 1 and 2. The verb **að tala** (*to speak*) belongs to Group
1 of regular verbs, which is the larger group. Regular verbs
change in a fixed way – their conjugation follows rules.
Irregular and strong verbs, however, show some variation –
their conjugation only partially follows rules. To conjugate
regular verbs you add fixed endings to the stem of the verb (i.e.
the main part of the verb). You find the stem of the verb by
leaving off the final -a, so the stem of **tala** is **tal-**. The endings in
this group of regular verbs are: singular -*a*, -*ar*, -*ar*, plural
-*um*, -*ið*, -*a*. To conjugate the verb **að tala** you therefore add
these endings to the stem **tal**:

að tala	to speak
ég tal**a**	I speak
þú tal**ar**	you speak
hann / hún / það tal**ar**	he / she / it speaks
við t**ö**l**um***	we speak
þið tal**ið**	you speak
þeir / þær / þau tal**a**	they speak

*The following rule applies in Icelandic for all types of words (verbs, nouns etc.): when there is an **a** in the stem and an ending beginning with **u** is added, then the **a** always changes to **ö**.

Once you've learnt the endings of this group, you know how to conjugate the majority of verbs in Icelandic!

Case government of verbs

As mentioned before, most verbs in Icelandic take a particular case, i.e. the noun that follows a verb has to be in a particular case. The majority of verbs take the accusative case (like *me* in English *he hit me*) and I advise you to memorize those verbs which take the dative or the genitive (very few take the genitive!).

Gender

Nouns in Icelandic are either masculine, feminine or neuter. The gender of nouns is grammatical, i.e. the gender is determined by the form of the noun and not its meaning. In some cases, however, the gender of a noun is 'natural'; often when a noun refers to a woman then that noun is feminine (**kona** (*woman*)) and when a noun refers to a man then that noun is masculine (**maður** (*man*)). This is however not always the case – for example most of the words for professionals are masculine, but are used for both men and women (e.g. **Hún er læknir** (*She is a doctor*); see Unit 8).

The endings of nouns can often help you to decide which gender the noun is:

gender	endings*	examples
masculine	-ur, -(in)n, -(i)r, -(ar)i, -i, -(l)l, -(n)n	dag**ur** (*day*), him**inn** (*sky*), lækn**ir** (*doctor*), kenn**ari** (*teacher*), sími (*telephone*), bí**ll** (*car*), stei**nn** (*stone*)

feminine	-a, (-un), (-ing)	fjölskylda (*family*), verslun (*shop*), sýning (*show, exhibition*)
neuter	(-að), **many one-syllable nouns** (nouns with one vowel) and compound nouns where the latter part is a one-syllable noun	blað (paper), land (*country*), mál (*speech*), tungumál, Ísland.

*Letters in brackets are part of the stem of the noun; letters outside brackets are the (actual) ending.

Note – These rules for endings have some exceptions, though these are few. If you don't want to learn all the endings at once, then start with the most common ones: masculine: **-ur**; feminine: **-a** (you can use the words **maður** and **kona** to help you remember!).

Weak feminine nouns

All nouns in Icelandic have four forms, one for each case (nominative, accusative, dative and genitive). For some nouns these four forms are different from each other, but for some nouns some of the forms can be identical. The process of putting nouns in their four case forms is called declension. Most feminine words in Icelandic end in -a. The declension of these words is called a weak declension: the ending *-u* is added to the stem in accusative, dative and genitive. You find the stem of nouns by leaving off the ending, here by leaving off -a:

	Italy	*woman*	*Icelandic*	*family*	*Inga*	*Anna*	
nominative	Ítalía	kona	íslenska	fjölskylda	Inga	Anna	**-a**
accusative	Ítalíu	konu	íslensku	fjölskyldu	Ingu	Önnu	**-u**
dative	Ítalíu	konu	íslensku	fjölskyldu	Ingu	Önnu	**-u**
genitive	Ítalíu	konu	íslensku	fjölskyldu	Ingu	Önnu	**-u**

In the vocabulary lists throughout the book the case will be given for weak feminine nouns if they are not in the nominative case.

The names of the languages are all feminine words ending in -a. Remember that the verb **tala** takes accusative and we therefore say:

Ég tala **íslensku**   (*I speak Icelandic*)
       ensku   (*English*)

þýsku	(German)
hollensku	(Dutch)
frönsku	(French)
spænsku	(Spanish)
ítölsku	(Italian)
rússnesku	(Russian)
dönsku	(Danish)
portúgölsku	(Portuguese)
norsku	(Norwegian)
sænsku	(Swedish)
finnsku	(Finnish)
pólsku	(Polish)
tékknesku	(Czech)
ungversku	(Hungarian)
rúmensku	(Rumanian)
búlgörsku	(Bulgarian)
grísku	(Greek)
tyrknesku	(Turkish)
eistnesku	(Estonian)
kínversku	(Chinese)
japönsku	(Japanese)
tælensku	(Thai)
kóresku	(Korean)

Language notes

- The rule we met on p. 22 also applies here: the **a** in the stem changes to **ö** if an ending beginning with **u** is added: **ítalska** becomes **ítölsku**, **franska** becomes **frönsku**, **danska** becomes **dönsku**, **portúgalska** becomes **portúgölsku**, **japanska** becomes **japönsku** (note that only the **a** in the syllable next to the ending changes), **búlgarska** becomes **búlgörsku**.
- The words for languages are all written without a capital letter.

Practice

▶ 1 You need to ask for directions and you decide to ask a man you meet in the street. You are not confident enough to communicate with him only in Icelandic so you ask in Icelandic if he speaks English.

You (Say *'Excuse me, do you speak English?'*)
Man Nei, ég tala bara íslensku og dönsku.
You (Say *'I also speak Danish!'*)

▶ 2 Listen to, or read, the dialogue again, and answer these questions.

a Hvað talar Christof mörg tungumál?
b Hvaða tungumál talar Anna?

---

hvað ... mörg *how many*

▶ 3 You meet a man called Magnus. Greet him and ask him where he comes from and which languages he speaks. Try to work out what his answers mean.

▶ 4 Can you say the following in Icelandic?

a He speaks Icelandic, Danish and Swedish.
b They don't speak English.
c Which languages does he speak?
d They only speak French.
e Does Anna also speak Icelandic?

03

mamma Björns er íslensk

Björn's mother is Icelandic

In this unit you will learn
- how to say which nationality you are
- how to refer to members of your family
- how to refer to your male and female friends, your boyfriend / girlfriend, your husband / wife

Language points
- possessive pronouns in masculine and feminine, singular, nominative (minn, mín …)
- definite articles in the nominative (-inn, -in, -ið)

▶ Þjóðerni *Nationality*

Kærasta Björns, Guðrún, og besti vinur Björns, Gunnar, hitta Christof og Önnu.

Guðrún	Hæ og velkomin til Íslands!
Christof	Takk!
Guðrún	Christof, ert þú ekki þýskur?
Christof	Jú, ég er þýskur.
Gunnar	En þú Anna, ert þú líka þýsk?
Anna	Nei, ég er hollensk.
Gunnar	Já, ertu hollensk?! Pabbi minn er Hollendingur!

---

kærasta (f.)   *girlfriend*
Björns (from **Björn**)   *Björn's*
besti (from **bestur**)   *best*
vinur (m.)   *male friend*
hitta   *meet*
þýskur   *German* (masculine form)
jú   *yes* (answer to a negative question)
þýsk (from **þýskur**)   *German* (feminine form)
hollensk (from **hollenskur**)   *Dutch* (feminine form)
pabbi (m.)   *father, dad*
minn   *my* (masculine form)
Hollendingur (m.)   *Dutchman*

Pronunciation

Be careful when you pronounce the name **Guðrún**. It is pronounced as if it were spelt **Gvuðrún** – **Guð** (*God*) and words based on **Guð** are always pronounced with **v** inserted after the **g**.

Language notes

- Note that in Icelandic there are two words for *friend*, **vinur** (*male friend*) and **vinkona** (*female friend*). *Boyfriend* and *girlfriend* are **kærasti** and **kærasta** – **kær** means *dear, beloved*.

- If you want to answer 'yes' to a negative question (a question with **ekki**) then you have to use **jú**.

Fjölskylda Björns *Björn's family*

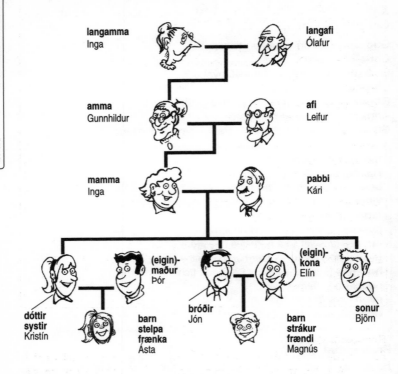

langamma Inga

langafi Ólafur

amma Gunnhildur

afi Leifur

mamma Inga

pabbi Kári

(eigin)-maður Þór

(eigin)-kona Elín

dóttir systir Kristín

barn stelpa frænka Ásta

bróðir Jón

barn strákur frændi Magnús

sonur Björn

▶ Fjölskylda Björns er mjög stór. Pabbi hans heitir Kári og mamma hans heitir Inga. Þau eru foreldrar Björns. Amma hans heitir Gunnhildur og afi hans heitir Leifur. Björn á líka langömmu og langafa – langamma hans heitir Inga (eins og mamma hans) og langafi hans heitir Ólafur. Björn á tvö systkini. Systir hans heitir Kristín og bróðir hans heitir Jón. Kristín er gift og maðurinn hennar heitir Þór. Kristín og Þór eru hjón. Þau eiga eitt barn, stelpu sem heitir Ásta. Ásta er frænka Björns. Jón er giftur og konan hans heitir Elín. Þau eiga líka eitt barn, strák sem heitir Magnús. Magnús er frændi Björns.

---

stór *big*
foreldrar (pl.) *parents*
hans *his*
amma (f.) *grandmother*

afi (m.) *grandfather*
á (from **eiga**, + acc.) *has, owns*
langamma (f.) *great-grandmother*
tvö *two*
langafi (m.) *great-grandfather*
systkini (pl.) *siblings, brothers and sisters*
systir (f.) *sister*
bróðir (m.) *brother*
gift/giftur *married*
maður (m.) *man; husband*
hennar *her*
hjón (pl.) *married couple*
barn (n.) *child*
stelpa (f.) *girl*
sem *who*
frænka (f.) *niece, cousin, aunt, female relative*
kona (f.) *woman; wife*
eitt *one*
strákur (m.) *boy*, can also mean *guy*
frændi (m.) *nephew, cousin, uncle, male relative*
dóttir (f.) *daughter*
sonur (m.) *son*

Pronunciation

Be careful when you pronounce **barn**. It is pronounced as if it were spelt **bardn** or **badn**. Remember that the letters **rn** are always pronounced **rdn** or **dn** (**dn** only in common words).

Language notes

- The words **mamma** and **pabbi** do not only correspond to 'mum' and 'dad' in English; they also mean 'mother' and 'father'. In Icelandic there are also the words **móðir** and **faðir**, but these sound formal when used.

- Sometimes the word **eiginmaður** is used for *husband*, but it is quite formal.

- Sometimes the word **eiginkona** is used for 'wife', but like **eiginmaður** it sounds formal when used.

- There is no word in Icelandic corresponding to English 'grandparents' – you have to say **afi og amma** ('grandfather and grandmother').

- **Þau eru gift** (*they are married*) has the same meaning as **Þau eru hjón** (*they are a married couple*).
- When referring to a woman being married you use **gift**. When referring to a man being married you can use either **giftur** or **kvæntur**. Many people (especially the older generation) consider it more correct to use **kvæntur**.

Grammar

Nationalities

If you've forgotten these countries' names, look at the lists in Unit 1.

Country	Adjective	Nationality
Ísland	íslenskur / íslensk	Íslendingur
England	enskur / ensk	Englendingur
Bretland	breskur / bresk	Breti
Noregur	norskur / norsk	Norðmaður
Danmörk	danskur / dönsk	Dani
Svíþjóð	sænskur / sænsk	Svíi
Finnland	finnskur / finnsk	Finni
Þýskaland	þýskur / þýsk	Þjóðverji
Frakkland	franskur / frönsk	Frakki
Spánn	spænskur / spænsk	Spánverji
Portúgal	portúgalskur / portúgölsk	Portúgali
Ítalía	ítalskur / ítölsk	Ítali
Holland	hollenskur / hollensk	Hollendingur
Austurríki	austurrískur / austurrísk	Austurríkismaður
Sviss	svissneskur / svissnesk	Svisslendingur
Belgía	belgískur / belgísk	Belgi / Belgíumaður
Írland	írskur / írsk	Íri
Grænland	grænlenskur / grænlensk	Grænlendingur
Rússland	rússneskur / rússnesk	Rússi
Pólland	pólskur / pólsk	Pólverji
Tékkland	tékkneskur / tékknesk	Tékki
Ungverjaland	ungverskur / ungversk	Ungverji
Rúmenía	rúmenskur / rúmensk	Rúmeni
Búlgaría	búlgarskur / búlgörsk	Búlgari
Grikkland	grískur / grísk	Grikki
Bandaríkin	bandarískur / bandarísk	Bandaríkjamaður

Ameríka	amerískur / amerísk	Ameríkani / Ameríkumaður
Kanada	kanadískur / kanadísk	Kanadabúi
Mexíkó	mexíkóskur / mexíkósk; mexíkanskur / mexíkönsk	Mexíkói / Mexíkani
Brasilía	brasilískur / brasilísk	Brasilíumaður
Argentína	argentínskur / argentínsk	Argentínumaður
Suður-Afríka	suður-afrískur / s-afrísk	Suður-Afríkubúi
Ástralía	ástralskur / áströlsk	Ástrali
Tyrkland	tyrkneskur / tyrknesk	Tyrki
Kína	kínverskur / kínversk	Kínverji
Japan	japanskur / japönsk	Japani
Kórea	kóreskur / kóresk	Kóreubúi
Indland	indverskur / indversk	Indverji
Tæland	tælenskur / tælensk	Tælendingur
Eistland	eistneskur / eistnesk	Eisti / Eistlendingur
Lettland	lettneskur / lettnesk	Letti / Lettlendingur

Language notes

- The masculine form of the adjective ends in **-ur** and the feminine form is the stem of the adjective (which you get by dropping the ending **-ur**). If the masculine form has a **a** in the stem, then that **a** changes to **ö** in the feminine form.
- The nationality adjectives are all written without a capital letter.
- The **a** to **ö** sound change rule does not apply when the word is in the masculine nominative singular. In the word **danskur**, for example, the ending is **-ur** but the **a** is not changed to **ö**.

Definite article

There is no indefinite article (*a, an* in English) in Icelandic. We therefore say **Björn er strákur** (*Björn is a guy*) without an article.

There is a definite article (like *the* in English) in Icelandic, which is added to the end of the noun: **maður** (*a man*), **maðurinn** (*the man*). The definite article has different forms depending on the gender, the number and the case of the noun it is added to. These are the forms in the nominative singular:

	definite article	examples	
masculine	-(i)nn	maður**inn**	*the man*
		sím**inn**	*the telephone*
feminine	-(i)n	verslun**in**	*the shop*
		kona**n**	*the woman*
neuter	-(i)ð	barn**ið**	*the child*

Tip – The masculine form has double **n** like **hann**, the feminine has one **n** like **hún** and the neuter has **ð** like **það**.

Note – If the noun ends in a vowel in the nominative then the -i- of the definite article is dropped.

Possessive pronouns (my, your ...)

The possessive pronouns (in nominative, singular, masculine and feminine) are:

	possessive pronoun	examples
first person (masculine)	minn	Þetta er pabbi minn. *This is my father.*
first person (feminine)	mín	Þetta er mamma mín. *This is my mother.*
second person (masculine)	þinn	Er þetta pabbi þinn? *Is this your father?*
second person (feminine)	þín	Er þetta mamma þín? *Is this your mother?*
third person (masculine)	hans	Þetta er pabbi hans. *This is his father.* Þetta er mamma hans. *This is his mother.*
third person (feminine)	hennar	Þetta er pabbi hennar. *This is her father.* Þetta er mamma hennar. *This is her mother.*

Tip – The masculine forms **minn/þinn** end in double **n** and have no superscript mark, like **hann**, and the feminine forms **mín/þín** end in one **n** and have a superscript mark like **hún**.

In the first person (*my*) you always use **minn / mín** and in the
second person (*your*) you always use **þinn / þín**. It depends on the
gender of the noun whether you use **minn / þinn** or **mín / þín**: if
the noun is masculine you use the masculine forms **minn / þinn** and
if the noun is feminine then you use the feminine forms **mín / þín**.

In the third person (*his*, *her*) you can use **hans** and **hennar** with
masculine and feminine nouns.

Language notes

- The possessive pronoun almost always follows the noun (not
  like in English). It can sometimes precede the noun: this gives
  it special emphasis.
- A noun followed by a possessive pronoun has to be in the
  definite form (**síminn minn, maðurinn minn, konan mín**).
  Exceptions: some words expressing family / close relations
  cannot be in the definite form: **mamma mín, pabbi minn,
  móðir mín, faðir minn, amma mín, afi minn, langamma mín,
  langafi minn, systir mín, bróðir minn, vinur minn, vinkona
  mín**. This is not true of **maður** and **kona** (see above), nor of
  kærasti and **kærasta**; these have to be in the definite form:
  kærastinn minn, kærastan mín.

Practice

1 Answer the questions as indicated.

   a   Hvað heitir mamma þín? (*Say she's called Marion.*)
   b   Hvað heitir pabbi þinn? (*Say he's called Desmond.*)
   c   Hvað heitir amma þín? En afi þinn? (*Say she's called
Gladys and he's called Terry.*)
   d   Hvað heitir bróðir þinn? En systir þín? (*Say he's called
Sean and she's called Tracy.*)

2 Pair these questions and answers.

   a   Ertu Grænlendingur?
   b   Er mamma þín þýsk?
   c   Er pabbi þinn rússneskur?
   d   Er Magnús giftur?
   e   Er Ingibjörg gift?

   i   Nei, hann er ekki rússneskur. Hann er franskur.
   ii   Nei, hún er ekki gift.
   iii   Nei, ég er Þjóðverji.
   iv   Já, hann er giftur.
   v   Nei, hún er norsk.

▶ 3 Translate the following sentences into Icelandic. If you have the recording, you could do this as an oral exercises.

a   Gunnar is from Iceland.
b   He speaks Icelandic.
c   His parents' names are Sigríður and Magnús.
d   What's his grandmother's name?
e   Björn's sister, Kristín, is married.
f   Her husband's name is Þór.

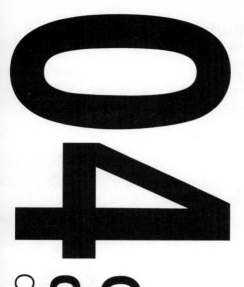

04

Christof er dökkhærður

Christof is dark-haired

In this unit you will learn
- how to describe the way somebody looks
- how to describe somebody's personality
- how to ask somebody's full name
- how to ask an Icelander what his last name is

Language points
- adjectives in the nominative
- weak declension of masculine nouns (masculine nouns ending in -i)
- genitive of strong masculine nouns (Björns, Ólafs ...)

▶ Útlit og persónuleiki *Appearance and personality*

Christof er dökkhærður og hávaxinn. Hann er hress og skemmtilegur.

Anna er líka dökkhærð og mjög grönn. Hún er frekar alvarleg og mjög heiðarleg.

Björn er ljóshærður og hávaxinn. Hann er mjög duglegur.

Guðrún er ljóshærð með sítt hár. Hún er lágvaxin og frekar þybbin. Hún er svolítið feimin.

Inga er með skollitað, stutt hár. Hún er lágvaxin og aðeins of feit. Hún er mjög gestrisin.

Kári er gráhærður. Hann er hár og grannur. Hann er mjög opinskár en samt alltaf kurteis.

dökkhærður *dark-haired*
hávaxinn *tall*
hress *fun, lively*
skemmtilegur *fun, entertaining*
dökkhærð (from **dökkhærður**) *dark-haired*
grönn (from **grannur**) *thin*
frekar *rather, a bit*
alvarleg (from **alvarlegur**) *serious*
heiðarleg (from **heiðarlegur**) *honest*
ljóshærður *blond*
duglegur *hard working, efficient*
ljóshærð (from **ljóshærður**) *blond*
með *with*
sítt (from **síður**) *long*
hár (n.) *hair*
lágvaxin (from **lágvaxinn**) *short*
þybbin (from **þybbinn**) *chubby*
svolítið *a little bit*
feimin (from **feiminn**) *shy*
skollitað *dark blond, light brown*
stutt (from **stuttur**) *short*
aðeins *a little bit*
of *too*
feit (from **feitur**) *fat*
gestrisin (from **gestrisinn**) *hospitable*
gráhærður *grey-haired*
hár *tall*
grannur *thin*
opinskár *outspoken, frank*
samt *still, yet*
alltaf *always*
kurteis *polite*

Pronunciation

The word **svolítið** is normally pronounced **soldið**.

▶ Hvað heitirðu fullu nafni? *What's your full name?*

Anna asks Björn and Guðrún about their names.

Anna	Björn, hvað heitirðu fullu nafni?
Björn	Ég heiti Björn Kárason.
Anna	En þú Guðrún, hvað heitir þú fullu nafni?
Guðrún	Ég heiti Guðrún Björk Ólafsdóttir.

---

fullu (from **fullur**)   *full*
nafni (from **nafn**, n.)   *name*

Pronunciation

Be careful when you pronounce **fullu** and **nafni**. They are pronounced as if they were written **fudlu** and **nabni**. Remember that the letters **ll** are almost always pronounced **dl**. The letters **fn** are always pronounced **bn** (this combination of **f** and **n** is not very common though).

▶ Kristín Káradóttir er dóttir Kára
Kristín Káradóttir is Kári's daughter

Björn heitir fullu nafni Björn Kárason og Kristín systir hans heitir fullu nafni Kristín Káradóttir, af því að pabbi þeirra heitir Kári. Björn Kárason þýðir að Björn er sonur Kára og Kristín Káradóttir þýðir að Kristín er dóttir Kára.

---

heitir fullu nafni   *his full name is*
af því að   *because*
þeirra   *their*
þýðir (from **þýða**)   *means*
að   *that*
Kára (gen. from **Kári**)   *Kari's*

Language note

• The phrase **af því að** (*because*) is very common in Icelandic. We can use it with words that we've learnt: **Ég tala íslensku, af því að ég er frá Íslandi** (*I speak Icelandic, because I'm from Iceland*).

i It is very common for Icelanders to have nicknames. These are formed from the first name and normally contain a double consonant and end in **-i** for men and **-a** for women. Normally the nickname is shorter than the first name but this is not always the case (e.g. the nickname **Nonni** for **Jón**). Examples: **Sigríður** – **Sigga**, **Kolbrún** – **Kolla**, **Sólveig** – **Solla**, **Sigurður** – **Siggi**, **Guðmundur** – **Gummi**, **Karl** – **Kalli**.

Icelandic surnames are normally formed by adding **-son** or **-dóttir** to the first name of the father. Some people have other surnames, such as **Möller** or **Nordal**, but this is not very common. When you address Icelanders you only use their first name. Surnames are very seldom used. Even in the telephone book names are arranged according to first names! Note that you can say **Hún heitir Kristín** and **Hún heitir Kristín Káradóttir** but you cannot say **Hún heitir Káradóttir** (this sentence is wrong). If you want to say that somebody's called something by their last name you have to say **Hún er Káradóttir**.

If you want to ask somebody what his full name is you say: **Hvað heitirðu fullu nafni?** If you want to ask somebody what his surname is you say: **Hvers son ertu / Hvers dóttir ertu?** (lit. *Whose son are you? / Whose daughter are you?*)

Magnús Jóhannsson
– Farsími
Magnús Björgvin Jóhannsson
Magnús Björn Jóhannsson
Magnús Blöndal Jóhannsson
– Farsími
Magnús Finnur Jóhannsson
– Farsími
Magnús Gunnar Jóhannsson
Magnús J Jóhannsson
– Farsími
Magnús J Jóhannsson
– Netfang
– Farsími
Magnús Ómar Jóhannsson
– Farsími
Magnús Örn Jóhannsson
Magnús Jónasson
Magnús Jónasson
– Farsími
Magnús Jónasson
Magnús Jónasson
– Farsími
Magnús Jónasson
Magnús Jónasson
– Farsími
Magnús Jónasson
– Farsímar
Magnús B Jónasson
– Farsími
Magnús I Jónasson
Magnús Már Jónasson
Magnús R Jónasson
– Farsími

REYKJAVÍK OG NÁGRENNI
Magnús

Magnús Þór Jónasson
Magnús Jónatansson
– Farsími
Magnús S Jónsson
Magnús Torfi Jónsson
Magnús Þ Jónsson
– Farsími
Magnús Þorberg Jónsson
– Farsími
Magnús Þór Jónsson
Magnús Þór Jónsson
Magnús Þór Jónsson
Magnús Þór Jónsson
– Farsímar
Magnús Þór Jónsson
– Farsími
Magnús Þór Jónsson
Magnús Þór Jónsson
– Farsími
Magnús Jósefsson
– Farsímar
Magnús Júlíus Jósefsson
Magnús Júlíusson
– Farsími
Magnús Bess Júlíusson
Magnús Már Júlíusson
Magnús Karlsson
Magnús Karlsson
Magnús Karlsson

Extract from the Reykjavik telephone book (addresses and telephone numbers deleted).

Grammar

Adjectives

Adjectives are 'describing' or 'qualifying' words. They change their form (i.e. gender, case and number (singular or plural)) according to the form of the noun that they qualify. In the nominative singular the masculine form of the adjective normally ends in -**ur**, the feminine form is the **stem** of the adjective (i.e. has no ending) and the neuter form normally ends in -**t**. You find the stem of the adjective by leaving off the ending of the masculine form (the ending is normally -**ur**). There are two main groups of adjectives depending on the endings in the nominative singular.

▶ The meanings of the new adjectives in the following tables are given on page 37 and below. On the recording you can hear how **íslenskur** (*Icelandic*) and **grannur** (*thin*) sound in their masculine, feminine and neuter forms.

1 The following endings are for the first group of adjectives, to which most adjectives in Icelandic belong.

masculine	feminine	neuter
-ur, -n/-l, r, – (i.e. no ending)	– (i.e. no ending)	-t

a This is the biggest subgroup of adjectives.

masculine	feminine	neuter
-ur	– (i.e. no ending)	-t
íslensk**ur** maður	íslensk kona	íslensk**t** barn
dansk**ur** maður	dönsk kona	dansk**t** barn
alvarleg**ur** maður	alvarleg kona	alvarleg**t** barn
skemmtileg**ur** maður	skemmtileg kona	skemmtileg**t** barn
grann**ur** maður	grönn kona	grann**t** barn
feit**ur** maður	feit kona	feit**t** barn

b If the stem of the adjective ends in a consonant + -**ð/-d/-t**, then when the neuter ending -**t** is added to it, the resulting cluser of consonants is simplified to -**tt**.

masculine	feminine	neuter
-ur	– (i.e. no ending)	**-t**
ljóshærð**ur** maður	ljóshær**ð** kona	ljóshær**t** barn
stut**tur** kjóll (m., *dress*)	stutt kápa (f., *coat*)	stutt hár (n.)
svart**ur** (*black*) kjóll	sv**ö**rt kápa	svart hár

c If the stem of the adjective ends in a vowel + **-ð/-dd**, then when the neuter ending **-t** is added to it, the resulting cluster of consonants is simplified to **-tt**.

masculine	feminine	neuter
-ur	– (i.e. no ending)	**-tt**
síð**ur** kjóll	síð kápa	sít**t** hár
rauð**ur** (*red*) kjóll	rauð kápa	rau**tt** hár

d Some adjectives take the masculine endings **-n** or **-l**. These adjectives already have **n** or **l** at the end of the stem.

masculine	feminine	neuter
-n/-l	– (i.e. no ending)	**-t**
brún**n** (*brown*) kjóll	brún kápa	brún**t** hár
gamal**l** (*old*) maður	g**ö**m**u**l kona	gamal**t** barn

e If the stem of the adjective ends in a vowel, then the ending in the masculine is **-r** and the ending in the neuter is **-tt**.

masculine	feminine	neuter
-r	– (i.e. no ending)	**-tt**
há**r** maður	há kona	hát**t** barn
opinská**r** maður	opinská kona	opinská**tt** barn

f If the stem of the adjective ends in **-r** or **-s**, then there is no ending in the masculine. The masculine form and the feminine form are therefore identical.

masculine	feminine	neuter
– (i.e. no ending)	– (i.e. no ending)	**-t**
kurteis maður	kurteis kona	kurteis**t** barn
hress maður	hress kona	hress**t** barn
stór maður	stór kona	stór**t** barn

In some of the subgroups above we have an **a to ö vowel change**. We will now look in more detail at this sound change rule. The rule that we had before says that when the word has **a** in the stem then that **a** changes to **ö** when an ending beginning with **u** is added to the word. In the cases above we get this vowel change although no ending is added. The reasons for this are historical (there used to be an **-u** ending) and you just have to remember that you always get this vowel change in the feminine singular nominative. We therefore get a vowel change from **a** to **ö** in the adjectives **grannur – grönn, svartur – svört** and **danskur – dönsk**. This sound change rule is however more complex. It is called the **u-umlaut rule** in Icelandic grammar books. When **a** is the vowel in the stem and **u** is the vowel in the next syllable (or historically there was an **u** in the next syllable, like in the feminine singular nominative) then the **a** changes to **ö**. In the adjective **alvarlegur – alvarleg**, there is no **u-umlaut**, because the **a** in the stem is not in the next syllable (**e** is in the next syllable, and it 'blocks' the umlaut). If there are other vowels between the **a** in the stem and **u** (or an historical **u** which has disappeared), then they block the vowel shift.

An additional detail of this rule is that in unstressed syllables, **a** changes to **u** rather than to **ö**. This **u** can then cause another change. In the adjective **gamall – gömul**, the second **a** of the stem is in an unstressed syllable (only the first syllable is stressed in Icelandic; see the pronunciation guide) and therefore changes to **u**, because there was historically an **u** in the next syllable. The first **a** in the stressed syllable then changes to **ö**, because there is an **u** in the next syllable (**gamal-** is the stem; this becomes *gamul which becomes **gömul**).

Note that adjectives of nationality such as **japanskur – japönsk** and **italskur – itölsk** are exceptions to this additional detail: the unstresssed **a** changes to **ö** and not **u**.

This **u-umlaut vowel change rule** is a general rule in Icelandic, and applies to nouns, verbs and adjectives.

2 The following endings are for the second group of adjectives; the masculine ends in **-inn**, the feminine in **-in** and the neuter in **-ið** (these are the same endings as for the definite article – see Unit 3):

masculine	feminine	neuter
-inn	-in	-ið

masculine	feminine	neuter
hávax**inn** maður	hávax**in** kona	hávax**ið** barn
feim**inn** maður	feim**in** kona	feim**ið** barn

Notice that the adjective changes its form according to the noun it describes, both when it immediately precedes the noun and also when it follows the noun and is separated from it by a form of the verb **að vera** (*to be*). Note also that there doesn't have to be a noun present; if a person is describing him/herself then the adjective is in the masculine form if the person is a man and in the feminine form if the person is a woman.

masculine	feminine	neuter
íslensk**ur** maður	íslensk kona	íslensk**t** barn
Maðurinn er íslensk**ur**.	Konan er íslensk.	Barnið er íslensk**t**.
Ég er íslensk**ur**.	Ég er íslensk.	

Note – the form of the adjective that is given in dictionaries is the masculine form. In the vocabulary boxes in this unit and in the subsequent units we also give the masculine form of the adjective if it appears in either the feminine or the neuter in the text.

Weak masculine nouns

Most nouns that end in **-i** are masculine. The masculine nouns that end in **-i** are called weak masculine nouns (**Kári, Frakki, sími** ...) and their declension is called a weak declension: the ending **-a** is added to the stem in the accusative, dative and genitive. Remember that you find the stem of nouns by leaving off the ending, here **-i**.

nominative	Kári	Frakki	sími	kennari	**-i**
accusative	Kára	Frakka	síma	kennara	**-a**
dative	Kára	Frakka	síma	kennara	**-a**
genitive	Kára	Frakka	síma	kennara	**-a**

In the vocabulary boxes in this unit and in the subsequent units the case will be given for weak masculine nouns if they are not in the nominative case.

Genitive of strong masculine nouns

Masculine nouns that do not end in -i in the nominative are called strong masculine nouns. The genitive of a large group of these nouns is formed by adding -s to the stem of the word. Examples:

nominative	genitive
Ólafur	Ólafs (Ólaf (stem) + s)
Leifur	Leifs (Leif (stem) + s)
Björn	Björns (Björn (stem) + s)
Gunnar	Gunnars (Gunnar (stem) + s)
Einar	Einars (Einar (stem) + s)
Jón	Jóns (Jón (stem) + s)
Jóhann	Jóhanns (Jóhann (stem) + s)

Practice

▶ 1 Describe these people. You may find the following vocabulary useful:

> **ungur** *young* **sköllóttur** *bald*
> **hamingjusamur** *happy* **reiður** *angry*

a   b   c   d

2 Put the correct forms of the adjectives in the gaps.

   a Erla, systir mín, er (*fyndinn*) _____. Hún er ekki (*leiðinlegur*) _____. Hún er með (*svartur*) _____ hár.

   b Kærastinn minn heitir Einar. Hann er (*rólegur*) _____ og mjög (*traustur*) _____.

   c Katrín er (*sætur*) _____ en aðeins of (*þybbinn*) _____.

   d Langamma mín er mjög (*mjór*) _____.

   e Gunnar, bróðir minn, er (*latur*) _____ og (*þrjóskur*) _____. En hann er alltaf (*kurteis*) _____.

fyndinn	*funny*
leiðinlegur	*boring*
rólegur	*quiet*
traustur	*reliable*
sætur	*cute, good-looking*
mjór	*thin*
latur	*lazy*
þrjóskur	*stubborn*

▶ **3** Whose daughter is she? Whose son is he?

Hvers dóttir er hún?

   a Pabbi hennar heitir Atli.
   b Pabbi hennar heitir Ingi.
   c Pabbi hennar heitir Einar.
   d Pabbi hennar heitir Karl.

Hvers son er hann?

   e Pabbi hans heitir Snorri.
   f Pabbi hans heitir Albert.
   g Pabbi hans heitir Jóhann.
   h Pabbi hans heitir Guðmundur.

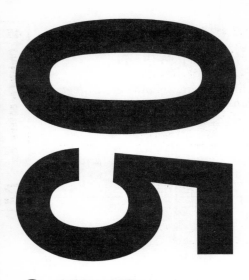

05 Christof er að lesa

lesa

Christof is reading

In this unit you will learn
- more about Iceland
- about Iceland's capital city Reykjavik
- how to make suggestions on what to do and where to go

Language points
- how to use the construction **að vera að gera eitthvað** (*to be doing something*)
- how to refer to objects / institutions / concepts by using personal pronouns
- how to use the verb **að ætla** (*to be going to, intend, plan*)
- the case government of prepositions
- how to refer to people / objects using a relative pronoun (**sem** (*who, which*))

▶ Ég er að lesa *I'm reading*

Christof er að lesa bók um Ísland.

Björn Hvað ertu að lesa? Er þetta bók um Ísland?
Christof Já.
Björn Er hún á íslensku?
Christof Já, ég er að æfa mig að lesa íslensku.
Björn Frábært!

> **lesa** (+ acc.) *read*
> **bók** (f.) *book*
> **um** (+ acc.) *about*
> **á íslensku** *in Icelandic*
> **frábært** (from **frábær**) *great*
> **ég er að æfa mig** *I'm practising* (lit. *I'm training myself*)

Pronunciation

In everyday speech the **g** in **ég** and the **ð** in **að** are dropped; for example, **ég er að lesa** is pronounced **jeralesa**.

▶ Miðbær Reykjavíkur *The centre of Reykjavik*

Björn, Christof og Anna ætla að fara að skoða miðbæ Reykjavíkur á morgun.

Christof Hvað er helst að sjá í miðbænum?
Björn Það er margt athyglisvert að sjá í miðbænum. Við verðum að skoða Alþingishúsið, Hallgrímskirkju og Háskóla Íslands. Við verðum líka að fara á Listasafn Íslands og Þjóðminjasafnið. Við skulum svo fara á kaffihús einhvers staðar. Það eru mjög mörg kaffihús í miðbæ Reykjavíkur.

> **miðbær** (m.) *city centre*
> **Reykjavíkur** (from **Reykjavík**, f.) *of Reykjavik, Reykjavik's*
> **ætla** (from **ætla**) *are going to*
> **að fara** *to go*
> **að skoða** (+ acc.) *to see*
> **miðbæ** (from **miðbær**, m.) *city centre*
> **á morgun** *tomorrow*
> **Hvað er helst að sjá í miðbænum?** *What are the main things to see in the city centre?*

það er *there is*
margt athyglisvert *many interesting things*
verðum (from verða) *have to*
Alþingishúsið (n.) *the Icelandic parliament building*
Hallgrímskirkju (acc. from Hallgrímskirkja, f.) *the church of Hallgrímur*
háskóla (acc. from háskóli, m.) *university*
Íslands (from Ísland) *of Iceland, Iceland's*
líka *also*
listasafn (n.) *art gallery*
Þjóðminjasafnið (n.) *the National Museum*
safn (n.) *museum*
við skulum (from skulu) *let's*
svo *then*
kaffihús (n.) *café*
einhvers staðar *somewhere*
það eru *there are*
mörg *many*

Pronunciation

* Be careful when you pronounce **safn** – remember that the letters **fn** are pronounced **bn**.
* Also be careful with the word **margt** – the **g** is left out in the pronunciation and it is pronounced **mart**.

▶ Háskólinn er – hann er ... *The university is – it is ...*

Björn og Christof tala saman um staði í Reykjavík.

Christof Hvar er Háskóli Íslands?
Björn Hann er við hliðina á Þjóðminjasafninu.
Christof Já, já. En hvar er Listasafn Íslands?
Björn Það er hjá tjörninni. Bíddu, ég ætla að ná í kort af Reykjavík.
Christof Já, flott.

tala saman um (+ acc.) *talk to each other / chat about*
staði (from staður, m.) *places*
við hliðina á (+ dat.) *beside*
Þjóðminjasafninu (from Þjóðminjasafnið, n.) *the National Museum*

hjá (+ dat.) *by, at*
tjörninni (from **tjörn**, f.) *small lake, pond*
bíddu (from **bíða**) *wait*
ná í (+ acc.) *get, fetch*
kort (n.) *map*
af (+ dat.) *of, from*
flott (from **flottur**) *great*

Pronunciation

Be careful when you pronounce **tjörninni** – remember that the letters **rn** are pronounced **rdn** or **dn**.

▶ Reykjavík er höfuðborg Íslands
Reykjavik is the capital of Iceland

Reykjavík er höfuðborg Íslands. Reykjavík er falleg borg. Í miðbænum er tjörn og mjög fallegur garður, sem heitir Hljómskálagarðurinn. Í Reykjavík er líka öflugt skemmtanalíf.

höfuðborg (f.) *capital*
falleg (from **fallegur**) *beautiful*
garður (m.) *park, garden*
öflugt (from **öflugur**) *great*
skemmtanalíf (n.) *nightlife* (lit. *entertainment life*)

i Iceland is a big country (103,000 km^2) but with a population of only 300,000. In the middle of the country there are glaciers, lava and sand deserts, so people only live around the coastline. As it is only possible to drive through the middle of the country in mountain jeeps owing to the rough terrain, if you want to cross from west to east of the country, for example, you have to drive along the coast.

The capital, Reykjavik, has in the region of 100,000 inhabitants. The five adjacent municipalities of Kópavogur, Hafnarfjörður, Garðabær, Seltjarnarnes and Mosfellsbær are also relatively big (by Icelandic standards!). Reykjavik and the neighbouring towns are jointly called in Icelandic **Höfuðborgarsvæðið** (*the capital area*), and close to two-thirds of the total population live here.

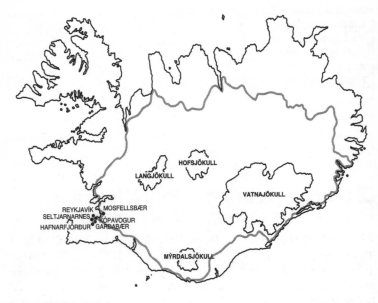

Iceland (**jökull** = *glacier*)

Grammar

Present continuous

The construction **að vera að gera eitthvað** (*to be doing something*) is very common in Icelandic. It is used to indicate a temporary action taking place at the moment of speaking. The following examples show how it is used:

Subject	**vera** in present	infinitive particle + verb in infinitive	
Ég	**er**	**að lesa**	*I'm reading*
Ég	**er**	**að skrifa**	*I'm writing*
Ég	**er**	**að tala**	*I'm speaking*
Ég	**er**	**að fara**	*I'm going*
Ég	**er**	**að borða**	*I'm eating*

▶ Replacing a noun by a pronoun

When you replace a noun which does not refer to a person with a personal pronoun, then you use the masculine, feminine or neuter form of the personal pronoun (**hann, hún, það**) depending on the gender of the noun. This is different from English, where you always use the neuter personal pronoun (**it**) to replace nouns which don't refer to people. Examples:

Er bókin (*feminine*) á íslensku? *Is the book in Icelandic?*
Já, **hún** er á íslensku.   *Yes, it is in Icelandic.*
Hvar er Háskóli (*masculine*)   *Where is the University of*
Íslands? **Hann** er í Reykjavík. *Iceland? It is in Reykjavik.*
Hvar er Listasafn (*neuter*)   *Where is the Art Gallery of*
Íslands? **Það** er í miðbænum. *Iceland? It is in the city centre.*
Er fjölskylda (*feminine*)   *Is Björn's family big?*
Björns stór? Já, **hún** er stór. *Yes, it is big.*

The regular verb *að ætla* (*to be going to*, etc.)

The verb **að ætla** (*to be going to, intend, plan*) belongs to Group 1 of regular verbs, the largest group. We've already seen one verb from this group, **að tala**, and the verb **að ætla** is conjugated in the same way. You add fixed endings (singular -**a**, -**ar**, -**ar**, plural -**um**, -**ið**, -**a**) to the stem (infinitive minus a).

að ætla	*to be going to, intend, plan*
ég ætla	*I am going to*
þú ætl**ar**	*you are going to*
hann / hún / það ætl**ar**	*he / she / it is going to*
við ætl**um**	*we are going to*
þið ætl**ið**	*you are going to*
þeir / þær / þau ætla	*they are going to*

Prepositions

Remember that all prepositions take a particular case, i.e. the noun that follows the preposition has to be in a particular case. When you learn a new preposition, learn also which case it takes. Normally a preposition always takes the same case, but there are some prepositions which can take either accusative or dative. The prepositions **í** and **á** take the accusative when there is movement involved but take the dative when there is no movement involved.

movement: í **miðbæinn** (*acc.*) *into the city centre*
position: í **miðbænum** (*dat.*) *in the city centre*

Here is a summary of the prepositions we've had so far:

- accusative: **um** *about*
- dative: **frá** *from*, **af** *of, from*, **við hliðina á** *beside*, **hjá** *by, at, with*, **með** *with* (can also take the accusative)
- genitive: **til** *to*
- **í; á** *in(to); at, in(to), on(to)*

  movement: accusative
  position: dative

How to say 'who, which'

The relative pronoun **sem** means *who* or *which*, i.e. you use **sem** for referring both to persons and to things. This is one grammar point that is easier in Icelandic than English!

Stelpan, sem er ...   *The girl who is ...*
Garðurinn, sem er ...   *The garden which is ...*

'There is / are'

If a sentence begins with *There is / are* you translate it into Icelandic with **Það er / eru.**

Það eru mörg kaffihús í   *There are a lot of cafés in the*
miðbæ Reykjavíkur.   *centre of Reykjavik.*

If, however, a noun referring to a place appears before *there is / are* then you don't use **það** in the translation into Icelandic.

Í miðbæ Reykjavíkur eru   *In the centre of Reykjavik*
mörg kaffihús.   *there are many cafés.*

Practice

▶ 1 You are chatting with Anna. Reply to her questions.

Anna   Hvað ertu að gera?
You   (*Say you're reading a book.*)
Anna   Hvað eru Christof og Björn að gera?
You   (*Say they're chatting about Reykjavik.*)
Anna   Hvar er Háskóli Íslands?
You   (*Say it's in Reykjavik.*)

2 Translate the first line of this advertisement.

Hvað ertu að lesa?

Metsölubækur með 50% afslætti.

>> Bara í dag og á morgun! <<

3 Translate the following sentences into Icelandic.
  a Anna and Inga are having a chat.
  b What's the book called?
  c It's called *Ísland á morgun*.
  d Where is the art gallery?
  e It's in Reykjavik.
  f What are you reading?
  g I'm reading a book about Italy.

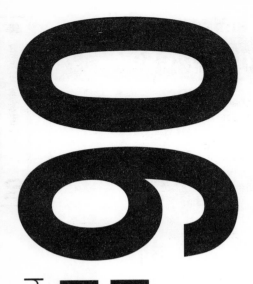

06

hann fer
klukkan tvö:
he leaves at two o'clock

In this unit you will learn
- how to ask somebody what their telephone number is and to say what your telephone number is
- how to say what time it is (whole hours) and to ask the time
- how to say what year it is
- about the Icelandic currency
- say where you live

Language points
- cardinal numbers
- gender of compound words

▶ Christof talar í símann *Christof speaks on the telephone*

Christof er að tala í símann. Hann vill fá upplýsingar um flug til Akureyrar.

Kona	Flugfélag Íslands, góðan dag.
Christof	Góðan daginn. Hvenær er fyrsta flug til Akureyrar á morgun?
Kona	Það er klukkan 7 í fyrramálið.
Christof	Hvenær þarf ég að mæta út á flugvöll?
Kona	Ekki seinna en klukkan 6.
Christof	Já, já, ókei. Takk kærlega!
Kona	Það var ekkert!

---

símann (acc. from **sími**, m.) *the telephone*
vill (from **vilja**) *wants*
fá (+ acc.) *get*
upplýsingar um *information about*
flug (n.) *flight*
til Akureyrar (from **Akureyri**) *to Akureyri*
Flugfélag Íslands *Air Iceland* (lit. *airline of Iceland*)
hvenær *when*
fyrsta *first*
klukkan 7 *at 7 o'clock*
í fyrramálið *tomorrow morning*
þarf (from **þurfa**) *need*
mæta *show up*
út á flugvöll (from **flugvöllur**, m.) *at the airport* (lit. *out on / at airport*)
ekki seinna en *not later than*
ókei *OK*
takk kærlega *thanks very much, thanks a lot*
var (from **vera**) *was*
ekkert *nothing*

▶ Björn talar við Önnu *Björn speaks to Anna*

Björn	Hvenær farið þið til Akureyrar?
Anna	Snemma í fyrramálið – klukkan 6 eða 7.
Björn	Hvenær komið þið svo aftur til Reykjavíkur?
Anna	Eftir viku.

tala við (+ acc.)   *talk to*
farið (from **fara**)   *go*
snemma   *early*
eða   *or*
komið (from **koma**)   *come*
svo   *then*
aftur   *again*
eftir (normally + acc.)   *after*
viku (acc. from **vika**, f.)   *week*

Pronunciation

In questions the **ð** ending of second person plural verbs is lost and the pronoun **þið** is pronounced **ði**: **farið þið** is therefore pronounced **fariði** and **komið þið** is pronounced **komiði**.

▶ Hvað er símanúmerið hjá Erlu?
What's Erla's telephone number?

Christof ætlar að hitta Erlu, vinkonu Björns, sem býr á Akureyri. Hann ætlar líka að hitta Snorra, frænda Björns, sem býr á bóndabæ rétt hjá Akureyri.

Christof Hvað er símanúmerið hjá Erlu?
Björn Heimasíminn er 4617776 og gsm-síminn er 8934456.
Christof Og hvað er heimilisfangið?
Björn Það er Vesturgata 41.
Christof En hvað er síminn hjá Snorra?
Björn Heimasíminn hjá honum er 4624713 og gemsanúmerið er 8674983.

bóndabæ (from **bóndabær**, m.)   *farm*
rétt hjá (+ dat.)   *near, close to*
símanúmer (n.)   *telephone number*
gsm-sími (m.)   *mobile*
heimilisfang (n.)   *address*
Vesturgata (f.)   *West Street*
heimasíminn (m.)   *the home number* (lit. *the home telephone*)
gemsanúmer (n.)   *mobile number*

Language notes

- Note that the preposition **hjá** (*at, by, with*) takes the dative (see Unit 5). After this preposition the words **Erla,** a weak feminine noun, and **Snorri,** a weak masculine noun, are therefore used in their dative forms: **Erlu** and **Snorra.** Note also that the verb **hitta** (*meet*) takes the accusative (like most verbs). After this verb the words **Erla** and **vinkona** (*female friend*), weak feminine nouns, are therefore used in their accusative forms: **Erlu** and **vinkonu;** and the words **Snorri** and **frændi** (*male relative*), weak masculine nouns, are also used in their accusative forms: **Snorra** and **frænda.**

- Note that you can say both **Hvað er <u>síminn</u> hjá Erlu?** and **Hvað er <u>símanúmerið</u> hjá Erlu?** You can also say **Hvert er símanúmerið hjá Erlu?**, but this is used mainly by older people.

- There are three words for *a mobile phone* in Icelandic: **gsm-sími, gemsi** and **farsími.** In everyday speech the word **gemsi** is normally used (at least by younger people).

▶ Akureyri er stærsti bærinn á Norðurlandi *Akureyri is the biggest town in the north*

Norðurhluti Íslands er kallaður Norðurland. Akureyri er stærsti bærinn á Norðurlandi. Austurhluti Íslands er kallaður Austurland og stærsti bærinn þar heitir Egilsstaðir. Suðurhluti Íslands er kallaður Suðurland og stærsti bærinn þar er Selfoss. Höfuðborgin Reykjavík er á Suðvesturlandi. Vesturhluti Íslands skiptist í Vesturland og Vestfirði. Stærsti bærinn á Vesturlandi heitir Akranes og stærsti bærinn á Vestfjörðum heitir Ísafjörður.

---

norðurhluti Íslands   *the northern part of Iceland*
er kallaður   *is called*
Norðurland   lit. *northern land*
stærsti   *biggest*
bærinn (m.)   *town*
austurhluti Íslands   *the eastern part of Iceland*
Austurland   lit. *eastern land*
þar   *there*
suðurhluti Íslands   *the southern part of Iceland*
Suðurland   lit. *southern land*
vesturhluti Íslands   *the western part of Iceland*
skiptist í   *is divided into*
Vesturland   lit. *western land*
Vestfirði (from **Vestfirðir**, pl.)   lit. *western fjords*
á Vestfjörðum (from **Vestfirðir**, pl.)   lit. *in the western fjords*

▶ Points of the compass

norður

norðvestur   norðaustur

vestur   **austur**

suðvestur   suðaustur

suður

ℹ️ There is no railway system in Iceland. If you want to travel around you therefore have to go by private car, bus or air. The bus system is very good and efficient (in winter, though, there are fewer destinations). Flying is also a good option. The main domestic airlines in Iceland are **Flugfélag Íslands** and **Íslandsflug**.

Grammar

▶ Cardinal numbers

The cardinal numbers *one*, *two*, *three* and *four* have separate forms for all three genders (this applies also to all numbers that end with 1, 2, 3 or 4, e.g. 2$\underline{1}$, 3$\underline{2}$, 9$\underline{3}$, 67$\underline{4}$ etc.).

masculine	feminine	neuter
1 einn (maður – *man*)	ein (kona – *woman*)	eitt (hús – *house*)
2 tveir (menn – *men*)	tvær (konur – *women*)	tvö (hús – *houses*)
3 þrír	þrjár	þrjú
4 fjórir	fjórar	fjögur

Pronunciation

- The letters **nn** are pronounced as **dn** when preceded by a letter with a superscript mark (í, ý, é, á, ú, ó) or by a diphthong (the letters **æ, ei, ey, au**): **einn** (*one*, masc.), **Spánn** (*Spain*). Otherwise the letters **nn** are pronounced as long **n**: **inni** (*barrel*). There is, however, an exception to this rule: If **nn** is part of the definite article it is always pronounced as long **n**: **kránni** (*the pub*, dative).

Tip – **Einn** has double **n** like **hann** (though it's pronounced differently), **ein** has one **n** like **hún**; **tveir** ends in **eir** like **þeir**; **tvær** ends in **ær** like **þær** and **tvö** has an **ö** sound like **þau** (au is pronounced [öy]).

Don't worry here about the plural forms of the nouns – we will learn about them later on.

The other cardinal numbers have only one form for all three genders.

Hundred, *thousand* and *million* are nouns and therefore they are of a particular gender and have plural forms. The noun **hundrað** is neuter (like all nouns whose stems end in -**að**, Unit 2) and therefore we use the neuter form of the numbers *one*, *two*, *three* and *four* when they are followed by **hundrað**; **þúsund** is neuter and therefore we use the neuter form of the numbers *one*, *two*, *three* and *four*; **milljón** is feminine and therefore we use the feminine form of the numbers *one*, *two*, *three* and *four*.

	singular	plural
hundred	hundrað (n.)	hundruð
thousand	þúsund (n.)	þúsund
million	milljón (f.)	milljónir

0 núll		7 sjö
1 einn, ein, eitt		8 átta
2 tveir, tvær, tvö		9 níu
3 þrír, þrjár, þrjú		10 tíu
4 fjórir, fjórar, fjögur		11 ellefu
5 fimm		12 tólf
6 sex		13 þrettán

14	fjórtán	30	þrjátíu
15	fimmtán	40	fjörutíu
16	sextán	50	fimmtíu
17	sautján	60	sextíu
18	átján	70	sjötíu
19	nítján	80	áttatíu
20	tuttugu	90	níutíu

100	(eitt) hundrað
200	tvö hundruð
1.000	(eitt) þúsund
2.000	tvö þúsund
1.000.000	(ein) milljón
2.000.000	tvær milljónir

21	tuttugu og einn (f. ein, n. eitt)
432	fjögur hundruð þrjátíu og tveir (f. tvær, n. tvö)
1.990	eitt þúsund níu hundruð og níutíu
1990	nítján hundruð og níutíu (used for years)

Notice that you only use one **og**:

430	fjögur hundruð og þrjátíu
438	fjögur hundruð þrjátíu og átta

We will now have a look at when you should use the masculine, feminine and neuter forms of the numeral:

- If the number indicates how many items there are, it comes before the noun and agrees with it: **tveir menn, tvær konur, tvö hús.**

- If the number identifies a particular item in a series – a year, a chapter, a house, an hour of the day – it follows the noun (if any) and is **neuter**: **(árið) nítján hundruð níutíu og tvö** (*the year 1992*); **kafli eitt** (*chapter one*); **Vesturgata eitt** (*number 1, Vesturgata*); **klukkan eitt** (*one o'clock*).

- If the number is just a digit, used for counting in general or in giving a telephone number, the **masculine** is used: 1, 2, 3, 4: **einn, tveir, þrír, fjórir; símanúmerið mitt er 5524317 fimm, fimm, tveir, fjórir, þrír, einn, sjö.**

▶ Telling the time

You use the neuter form of the numbers *one*, *two*, *three* and *four* when saying what time it is.

- To ask what time it is you use **Hvað er klukkan?** (lit. *what is the clock?*).

- To ask what time something will take place, you use **Klukkan hvað ...?** (lit. *the clock what?*).

- To say *it's 4 o'clock* you use **Klukkan er fjögur** (lit. *the clock is 4*).

- To say what time something takes place, i.e. to say *at 4 o'clock*, you use **Klukkan fjögur**.

Hvað er klukkan?	*What's the time?*
Klukkan er fjögur.	*It's four o'clock.*
Klukkan hvað ætlar Anna að fara? Hún ætlar að fara klukkan fjögur.	*What time is Anna leaving? She's leaving at four o'clock.*

Saying what your phone number is

- To say what your telephone number is you say
  Símanúmerið mitt er... / Símanúmerið hjá mér er...
  Síminn minn er... / Síminn hjá mér er ....
  The preposition **hjá** takes the dative so we have to use the dative form of **ég**, which is **mér**. The noun **símanúmer** is neuter and we therefore have to use the neuter form **mitt** of the possessive pronoun.

- To ask somebody else what their telephone number is you say
  Hvað er símanúmerið þitt? / Hvað er símanúmerið hjá þér?
  Hvað er síminn þinn? / Hvað er síminn hjá þér?
  Here we have to use the dative form of **þú**, which is **þér** (we will learn the other forms of the personal pronouns later on); **þitt** is the neuter form of the possessive pronoun.

- If you want to ask somebody what another person's telephone number is you say (using the name **Anna** as an example)
  Hvað er símanúmerið hjá Önnu?
  Hvað er síminn hjá Önnu?
  The name of the person has to be in the dative form. So far we have only learnt the declension of feminine nouns ending in **-a** and of masculine nouns ending in **-i** so these are the ones we can use at the moment.

Hvað er símanúmerið þitt?	**Símanúmerið mitt er ...**
Hvað er símanúmerið hjá þér?	**Símanúmerið hjá mér er ...**
Hvað er síminn þinn?	**Síminn minn er ...**
Hvað er síminn hjá þér?	**Síminn hjá mér er...**
Hvað er símanúmerið hjá Önnu?	**Símanúmerið hjá Önnu er ...**
Hvað er síminn hjá Önnu?	**Síminn hjá Önnu er ...**

ℹ The Icelandic currency

The Icelandic currency is the Icelandic **króna**. The singular form is **króna** and the plural form is **krónur**. The noun **króna** is feminine (like almost all words ending in **-a**) so with it you use the feminine form of the numbers *one*, *two*, *three* and *four*.

> **ein króna**
> **tvær krónur**
> **þrjár krónur**
> **fjórar krónur**

Notice that if the amount ends in 1 (e.g. 21, 331 …) then you use the singular form **króna** although the amount is higher than one **króna**. (This is true of all other nouns, so you would say **21 maður, 331 maður** etc.)

> **tuttugu og ein króna, þrjú hundruð þrjátíu og ein króna**

Both **króna** and **krónur** are abbreviated **kr.**

You can also use the word **kall** instead of **krónur** in spoken language. It is a masculine word which is only used in the singular. It is most common to use **kall** with 5 kr., 10 / 20 / 30 / 40 … kr., 100 / 200 … kr. and 1.000 / 2.000 … kr.

> **fimmkall, tíkall, fimmtíukall, hundraðkall, þúsundkall,**
> **tvö þúsundkall**

Note that if the amount is 1.100 kr. you can say either **eitt þúsund og eitt hundrað krónur** or **ellefu hundruð krónur**.

The strong verb *að búa* (*to live*)

The verb **að búa** (*to live*) is a strong verb – its conjugation only partially follows rules. Notice that the plural is regular, i.e. you add the regular endings **-um**, **-ið**, **-a** to the stem (you find the stem by leaving out the **-a** of the infinitive).

að búa	*to live*
ég bý	*I live*
þú býrð	*you live*
hann / hún / það býr	*he / she / it lives*
við bú**um**	*we live*
þið bú**ið**	*you live*
þeir / þær / þau bú**a**	*they live*

Prepositions and place names

Cities and towns

To say that you live in a particular city or town, you use the prepositions **í** or **á**. For all foreign cities you use **í**:

Ég bý í **London, Róm, Berlín, París, Amsterdam, Osló, Helsinki, Kaupmannahöfn** (*Copenhagen*)...

For Icelandic towns and cities you use either **í** or **á**:

Ég bý í **Reykjavík, Kópavogi, Hafnarfirði, Garðabæ, Mosfellsbæ, Borgarnesi** (from **Borgarnes**).

Ég bý á **Seltjarnarnesi, Akureyri, Egilsstöðum** (from **Egilsstaðir**), **Ísafirði** (from **Ísafjörður**), **Akranesi** (from **Akranes**), **Sauðárkróki** (from **Sauðárkrókur**).

All towns ending in **-eyri** and most towns ending in **-fjörður** take the preposition **á** (**Hafnarfjörður** is the main exception).

Note that the prepositions **í** and **á** take the dative here (position).

Streets

To say that you live in a particular street you use the preposition **á** and the dative form of the street name (again dative because there is no movement involved). Common street endings in Icelandic are: **-gata** (f., *street*) and **-vegur** (m., *street, road*). We know the dative form of the weak feminine noun **gata**, which is **götu**, and the dative form of **vegur** is **vegi**. Here are some examples:

Ég bý á **Vesturgötu** 5 (dat. from **Vesturgata**), **Laufásvegi** 5 (dat. from **Laufásvegur**).

Note that the street number always appears after the street name.

Compound words

The gender of compound words is always determined by the last word of the compound.

símanúmer *telephone number* (n.)   **sími** (m.), **númer** (n.)
flugvöllur *airport* (m.)   **flug** (n.), **völlur** (m.)

Note also that the first word in a compound is very often in the singular accusative or genitive form.

Practice

▶ 1 Say, then write out, the following times in words.

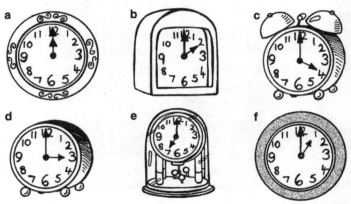

▶ 2 Say, then write out, the answers to the following calculations in words. If you have the recording you could try this exercise as mental arithmetic!

a	2 + 3 = 5	**f**	2 + 16 = 18
b	4 − 1 = 3	**g**	2 + 13 = 15
c	1 + 12 = 13	**h**	4 + 15 = 19
d	3 + 14 = 17	**i**	18 − 8 = 10
e	5 + 15 = 20	**j**	10 − 8 = 2

plús *plus*	**mínus** *minus*	**eru** *equals*

▶ 3 Listen to the recording, and write down the years that you hear. Try writing them in figures and words.

▶ 4 Answer the following questions in Icelandic, saying, then writing out the appropriate telephone numbers in words. (Note that **símanúmer / sími** is abbreviated to **s.**)

a Hvað er símanúmerið hjá Önnu?
b Hvað er símanúmerið hjá Ingu?
c Hvað er síminn hjá Ástu?
d Hvað er síminn hjá Kára?
e Hvað er síminn hjá Atla?

| Anna, s: 5643056 | Inga, s: 4318941 |

| Ásta, s: 5502031 | Kári, s: 4539478 | Atli, s: 5643223 |

5 Write out the reduced prices shown in the advertisement below.

	Áður	Nú
Bolur	2.980 kr.	**1.990 kr.**
Buxur	4.990 kr.	**2.990 kr.**
Buxur	5.996 kr.	**3.990 kr.**
Kápa	15.995 kr.	**9.990 kr.**
Mussa	6.995 kr.	**5.990 kr.**

MORGAN
KRINGLUNNI
Sími 533-1720

áður *before*	**buxur** *trousers*
nú *now*	**kápa** *woman's coat*
bolur *top*	**mussa** *blouse*

6 Answer the following questions in Icelandic, using the placenames in parentheses.

a Hvar býrðu? (**London**)
b Hvar býr Erla? (**Akureyri**)
c En Björn? (**Reykjavík**)

d Hvar býr Christof? (**Berlín**)
e Hvar býr fjölskylda Christofs? (**München**)
f Hvar búa mamma og pabbi Erlu? (**Ísafjörður**)

7 Write out in words the numbers in these advertisements from *Morgunblaðið*, one of Iceland's main newspapers.

---

símbréf (n.), **fax** (n.)   *fax*
netfang (n.), **e-mail** (n.)   *e-mail address, e-mail*
heimasíða (f.)   *home page*
opið á sunnudag   *open on Sunday*
frá ... til   *from ... to*
klukkan is abbreviated to **kl.**

---

a

𝔐𝔬𝔯𝔤𝔲𝔫𝔟𝔩𝔞𝔡𝔦𝔡

BRÉF
TIL BLAÐSINS

Kringlunni 1 103 Reykjavík ● Sími 569 1100
● Símbréf 569 1329 ● Netfang bref@mbl.is

b

Stórhöfði 33 ● Reykjavík
Sími: 577 4100 - Fax: 577 4101

www.altak.is

c

NOTAÐU TÆKIFÆRIÐ

... gefðu þér góðan tíma
í fríinu

mira

OPIÐ á sunnudag frá kl. 13 - 16

BÆJARLIND 6 200 KÓPAVOGI SÍMI: 554 6300
e-mail: mira@mira.is www.mira.is

d

PIPAR OG SALT
Klapparstíg 44
S: 562 3614

e

SÍMI
569 5100
FAX
569 5251

Skýrr hf

HEIMASÍÐA   www.skyrr.is
NETFANG   skyrr@skyrr.is

ÖRUGG
MIÐLUN
UPPLÝSINGA

07

sjáumst í kvöld klukkan hálfníu

see you tonight at half past eight

In this unit you will learn
- the names of days of the week
- expressions referring to parts of the day
- how to say what time it is

Language points
- the verb **að fara** in the present tense
- the verb **að vera** in the past tense
- how to express the future

▶ Sunnudagur til sigurs *Sunday for victory*

Here is a rhyme to help you learn the days of the week.

Sunnudagur til sigurs,
mánudagur til mæðu,
þriðjudagur til þrautar,
miðvikudagur til moldar,
fimmtudagur til frama,
föstudagur til fjár,
laugardagur til lukku.

---

sunnudagur *Sunday* (from **sunna** – old word for *sun*)
sigurs (from **sigur**, m.) *victory*
mánudagur *Monday* (from **máni** – old word for *moon*)
mæðu (gen. from **mæða**, f.) *distress, trouble*
þriðjudagur *Tuesday* (from **þriðji** – *third*)
þrautar (from **þraut**, f.) *hardship, trial*
miðvikudagur *Wednesday* (from **mið** – *middle* and **vika** – *week*)
moldar (from **mold**, f.) *earth, soil*
fimmtudagur *Thursday* (from **fimmti** – *fifth*)
frama (gen. from **frami**, m.) *distinction, fame* (old meaning),
career (today's meaning)
föstudagur *Friday* (from **fasta** – *fast*, i.e *not eating*)
fjár (from **fé**, pl. n.) *money*
laugardagur *Saturday* (from **laug** – *warm spring*, i.e. *washday*)
lukku (gen. from **lukka**, f.) *luck*

Note – The days of the week are all masculine, and are written without a capital letter.

▶ Christof hringir í Erlu *Christof rings Erla*

Christof og Anna ætla að hitta vinkonu Björns, Erlu, sem býr á Akureyri. Þau ætla að fara á tónleika í Akureyrarkirkju.

Erla   Halló?
Christof Já, er þetta Erla?
Erla   Já, þetta er hún.
Christof Hæ! Þetta er Christof.
Erla   Já, hæ!
Christof Hvað segir þú?

Erla   Bara allt fínt!
Christof Klukkan hvað eru tónleikarnir í kvöld?
Erla   Þeir byrja klukkan hálfníu.
Christof Við sjáumst í kvöld!

---

hringja *ring*
ætla (Group 1 regular) *are going to*
að hitta (+ acc.) *to meet*
sem *who, which*
tónleikar (pl. m.) *concert*
í Akureyrarkirkju *in the church of Akureyri*
Hvað segir þú? *How are you?* (lit. *what say you?*)
bara *just*
allt (from **allur**) *everything*
fínt (from **finn**) *great*
klukkan hvað *(at) what time*
í kvöld *this evening*
byrja (Group 1 regular) *start*
klukkan hálfníu *at 8.30*

Pronunciation – The prefix **hálf-** (*half*) is not stressed. In **hálfníu** the stress is on **níu**.

▶ Christof og Anna bíða eftir Erlu
Christof and Anna wait for Erla

Christof og Anna bíða eftir Erlu fyrir utan Akureyrarkirkju.

Christof Fyrirgefðu, hvað er klukkan?
Kona   Hún er að verða hálfníu; hún er 25 mínútur yfir 8.
Christof Takk kærlega!
Kona   Það var ekkert!

---

bíða eftir (+ dat.) *wait for*
fyrir utan (+ acc.) *outside*
hún er að verða *it's almost*

Note – The preposition **fyrir utan** can also be used as an adverb. Adverbs do not have to be followed by a noun in a particular case, so we can have the sentence **Christof bíður fyrir utan** (*Christof waits outside*).

Grammar

▶ The days of the week, starting with Sunday

nominative	accusative	
sunnudagur	á sunnudaginn	on (this/last) Sunday
mánudagur	á mánudaginn	on (this/last) Monday
þriðjudagur	á þriðjudaginn	on (this/last) Tuesday
miðvikudagur	á miðvikudaginn	on (this/last) Wednesday
fimmtudagur	á fimmtudaginn	on (this/last) Thursday
föstudagur	á föstudaginn	on (this/last) Friday
laugardagur	á laugardaginn	on (this/last) Saturday

Hvaða dagur er í dag?	*What day is it today?*
Það er mánudagur./	*It's Monday./*
Í dag er mánudagur.	*Today is Monday.*
Christof fer á mánudaginn.	*Christof is going/*
	leaving on Monday.
Christof fór á mánudaginn.	*Christof went/left on Monday.*

Parts of the day

	Past ←	Today →	Future
í fyrradag	**í gær**	**í dag**	**á morgun**
the day before	*yesterday*	*today*	*tomorrow*
yesterday	**í gærkvöldi**	**í kvöld**	**annað kvöld**
	last night	*tonight*	*tomorrow night*
	í gærmorgun	**í morgun**	**í fyrramálið**
	yesterday	*this morning*	*tomorrow*
	morning		*morning*

dagur (m.)	*day*	**kvöld** (n.)	*evening*

▶ What time is it?

- full hours (see Unit 6) (Remember the numerals 1–4 and 21–4 are used in neuter form.)

  Klukkan er eitt, tvö. *It's one o'clock, two o'clock.*

- half hours. In Icelandic you have to think 'half to *or* before the next hour'.

Klukkan er ... hálfeitt (*half before one*) (12.30),
hálffjögur (*half before four*) (3.30), hálfellefu (*half before eleven*) (10.30) etc.

- quarter hours

    Klukkan er ... **korter yfir** (*quarter past*) sjö (7.15), korter yfir átta (8.15), korter yfir níu (9.15).

    Klukkan er ... **korter í** (*quarter to*) tíu (9.45), korter í ellefu (10.45), korter í tólf (11.45)

- minutes

    Notice that the numerals 1–4, 21–4, etc. are in the feminine form before **mínúta** (*minute*), which is feminine.

    Klukkan er tuttugu og þrjár mínútur **yfir** eitt (1.23) (*or*: eitt tuttugu og þrjú).
    Klukkan er tvær mínútur í tvö (1.58) (*or*: eitt fimmtíu og átta).

    Hvað er klukkan? Klukkan / Hún er fimm. *What time is it? It's five o'clock.*
    Klukkan hvað ætlarðu að fara? *What time are you going?*
    Klukkan hvað ætlarðu að hitta Önnu? *What time are you going to meet Anna?*
    Klukkan fimm. *At five.*
    (Notice that no preposition is used in Icelandic).

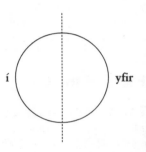

You use the feminine form of the numeral only when it is followed by **mínúta / mínútur**; otherwise you use the neuter form: Klukkan er **tvær** (fem.) mínútur í **tvö** (neuter).

The strong verb *að fara* (to go, leave)

The verb **að fara** (*to go*) is a strong verb.

að fara	to go
ég fer	I go
þú ferð	you go
hann / hún / það fer	he / she / it goes
við för**um**	we go
þið far**ið**	you go
þeir / þær / þau fara	they go

Language notes

- Remember that the plural present forms of almost all strong verbs are regular; you add the regular endings **-um, -ið, -u** to the stem of the verb.
- Remember also the **a** to **ö** sound change rule.

The future

The future is often expressed by using the verb **að ætla**.

Hvað ætlarðu að gera á morgun?	*What are you going to do tomorrow / What are you doing tomorrow?*
Ég ætla að hitta Önnu annað kvöld.	*I'm going to meet Anna tomorrow evening.*
Við ætlum að fara á tónleika á morgun.	*We're going to a concert tomorrow.*

The present tense of verbs can also often be used to express the future. In this case there is normally a time phrase, such as **á morgun**, included in the sentence.

Example:

Ég fer á morgun.	*I will go tomorrow.*

The strong verb *að vera* (to be) in the past tense

The strong verb **að vera** ('to be') has the following forms in the past tense (present tense forms are included as well):

að vera	*to be*
ég er / var	*I am / was*
þú ert / varst	*you are /were*
hann er / var	*he is / was*
við erum / vor**um**	*we are / were*
þið eruð / vor**uð**	*you are / were*
þeir eru / vor**u**	*they are / were*

Language note

- In the plural past tense the endings are regular (**-um, -uð, -u**), but what comes before the endings is irregular.

Practice

▶ 1 Answer the following questions in Icelandic. Your answers should be whole sentences.

a Hvenær ætlarðu að hitta Önnu? (*tomorrow evening*)
b Hvenær ætlarðu að hitta Erlu? (*tomorrow*)
c Hvenær ætlarðu að hringja í Láru? (*on Friday*)
d Hvenær ætlarðu að fara til Íslands? (*on Monday*)
e Klukkan hvað byrja tónleikarnir í kvöld? (*at 8.30 p.m.*)
f Klukkan hvað ætlarðu að fara á morgun? (*at 3.15 p.m.*)
g Klukkan hvað ætlarðu að hitta Dóru í fyrramálið? (*at 9.20 a.m.*)
h Klukkan hvað ætlið þið að fara annað kvöld? (*at 8.45 p.m.*)

2 Read the newspaper clippings and work out which days and parts of days are mentioned.

a

Á MORGUN

Á morgun. Fyrsta umferð í spurningakeppni Kvenfélagsins Baldursbrár fer fram annaðkvöld, sunnudagskvöldið 20. október, og hefst kl. 20.30. Liðin sem taka þátt að þessu sinni eru frá Aksjón, Norðlenska, Karlakór Akureyrar-Geysi, Trillukörlum, Skákfélagi Akureyrar og Brekkuskóla. Keppnin fer fram í safnaðarsal Glerárkirkju. Ágóði rennur í söfnun til kaupa á steindum glugga í Glerárkirkju, en hann verður vígður annan sunnudag í aðventu.

Í DAG

Í dag. Kvenfélagið Baldursbrá heldur bingó í dag, laugardaginn 19. október kl. 14 í safnaðarsal Glerárkirkju. Margt góðra vinninga er í boði, s.s. flugfar milli Akureyrar og Reykjavíkur svo dæmi sé tekið.

b

c

KYNNINGAR:

í dag	á morgun
fimmtudag	**föstudag**
kl. 14-18	**kl. 14-18**
LYFJA Lágmúla	LYFJA Smáralind
LYFJA Laugavegi	LYFJA Smáratorgi

d **SÖFN**

BORGARBÓKASAFN Reykjavíkur: www.borgarboka-
safn.is

Aðalsafn Grófarhúsi, Tryggvagötu 15. Sími: 563 1717, fax:
563 1705. Mán.-fim. kl. 10-20, föst. kl. 11-19, laug. og
sun. kl. 13-17.

Borgarbókasafnið í Gerðubergi, Gerðubergi 3-5. Sími: 557
9122, fax: 575 7701. Mán.-fim. kl. 10-20, föst. kl. 11-19.

Bókabíll. Bækistöð í Kringlusafni, sími: 580 6200. Við-
komustaðir víðs vegar um borgina.

Foldasafn v/Fjörgyn. Sími: 567 5320, fax: 567 5356. Mán.-
fim. kl. 10-20, föst. kl. 11-19.

Kringlusafn í Borgarleikhúsi. Sími 580 6200. Mán-mið. kl.
10-19, fim. kl. 10-21, föst. kl. 11-19, laug. kl. 13-17.

Seljasafn, Hólmaseli 4-6. Sími: 587 3320. Mán. kl. 11-19,
þri.-föst. kl. 11-17. Seljasafn er lokað í júlí og ágúst.

Sólheimasafn, Sólheimum 27. Sími: 553 6814. Mán.-fim. kl.
10-19, föst. kl. 11-19.

BÓKASAFN DAGSBRÚNAR: Skipholti 50D. Safnið verður
lokað fyrst um sinn vegna breytinga.

BÓKASAFN KEFLAVÍKUR: Opið mán.-fös. 10-20. Opið
lau. 10-16 yfir vetrarmánuði.

BÓKASAFN KÓPAVOGS, Hamraborg 6a. S. 570 0450. Opið
mán.-fim. kl. 10-21; föst. kl. 10-17, lau.-sun. kl. 13-17.

BÓKASAFN SAMTAKANNA '78, Laugavegi 3: Opið mán.-
fim. kl. 20-23.

BORGARSKJALASAFN REYKJAVÍKUR, Tryggvagötu 15:
Opið mán. til föst. kl. 10-16. S. 563 1770.

3 Assuming today is Wednesday, answer the following
questions in Icelandic.

  a Hvaða dagur er í dag?
  b Hvaða dagur var í gær?
  c Hvaða dagur var í fyrradag?
  d Hvaða dagur er á morgun?

▶ **4** Take the part of Christof in this conversation.

Erla   Hæ! Hvað ertu að lesa?
Christof *Say that you're reading a book about Italy.*
Erla   Já. Hvað heitir hún?
Christof *Say it's called Italy tomorrow.*
Erla   Hmm. Ertu ekki að lesa bók um Ísland?
Christof *Say you're also reading a book about Iceland – it's
called Iceland today.*
Erla   Hvenær ferðu á morgun?
Christof *Say you'll go early* (use present tense of *go*)*, at nine
tomorrow morning.*

5 Translate these sentences into Icelandic.

  a What day is it today? It is Sunday.
  b Sorry, what time is it? It's half past two.

6 Look at the schedules of **Ríkissjónvarpið** (*State television*) and **Stöð tvö** (*Channel two*), two Icelandic TV channels, and answer these questions about their programmes. The verb **byrja** means *start*; it is a regular Group 1 verb. In your answer you should use personal pronouns (*he, she, it*) to refer to the programme in question (the gender of new words you will need is given below). The first answer is given to help you get started.

Ríkissjónvarpið

a Hvenær byrjar **Morgunstundin**? *Hún byrjar klukkan níu.*
b Hvenær byrjar **Malla mús**?
c Klukkan hvað byrjar **Lísa**?
d Klukkan hvað byrjar **Kastljósið**?
e Klukkan hvað byrjar **Þýski fótboltinn**?
f Klukkan hvað byrjar **Íslandsmótið í handbolta**?
g Hvenær byrjar **Laugardagskvöld með Gísla Marteini**?
h Hvenær byrjar **Spaugstofan**?
i Hvenær byrjar myndin **Fangaflugvélin**?

Stöð tvö

j Hvenær byrjar **Barnatími Stöðvar 2**?
k Hvenær byrjar **Oprah Winfrey**?
l Klukkan hvað byrjar **Lottóið**?
m Klukkan hvað byrjar **Ísland í dag**?
n Klukkan hvað byrjar myndin **Illskan tekur völdin**?

---

morgunstund (f.)   *morning hour*
Malla   a woman's nickname
mús (f.)   *mouse*
Lísa   a woman's name
kastljós (n.)   *spotlight*
þýski fótboltinn (fótbolti, m.)   *(the) German football*
Íslandsmótið í handbolta (Íslandsmót, n.)   *Icelandic handball championship*
laugardagskvöld með Gísla Marteini (laugardagskvöld, n.)   *Saturday night with Gísli Marteinn*
spaugstofa (f.)   *comedy programme* (lit. *joke institute*)
mynd (f.)   *film*
fangaflugvélin (flugvél, f.)   *the prisoners' aeroplane*
Barnatími Stöðvar 2 (barnatími, m.)   *Channel Two children's programme*
lottó (n.)   *lottery*
Remember that **Ísland** is neuter
illskan tekur völdin   *the evil takes over* (lit. *takes the power*)

LAUGARDAGUR 26. OKTÓBER

09.00 Morgunstundin okkar
09.02 Stubbarnir (57:90)
09.26 Malla mús (28:52)
09.33 Undrahund. Merlín (8:26)
09.43 Póstkassinn
09.45 Fallega húsið mitt (17:30)
09.53 Lísa (6:13)
09.59 Babar (51:65)
10.22 Póstkassinn
10.23 Krakkarnir í stofu 402
(32:40)
10.45 Hundrað góðverk (12:20)
11.10 Kastljósið (e)
11.35 At (e)
12.05 Geimskipið Enterprise
(3:26) (e)
12.50 Svona var það (5:27)
(That 70's Show) (e)
13.25 Þýski fótboltinn
Bein útsending.
15.30 Handboltakvöld (e)
15.50 Íslandsmótið í handbolta
Bein útsending.
17.55 Táknmálsfréttir
18.05 Forskot (34:40)
(Head Start)
18.54 Lottó
19.00 Fréttir, íþróttir og veður
19.40 Laugardagskvöld með
Gísla Marteini
20.25 Spaugstofan
20.50 Pollýanna
Bresk mynd byggð á frægri
sögu eftir Eleanor H. Porter.
22.30 Fangaflugvélin (Con Air)
Aðalhlutverk: Nicolas Cage,
Steve Buscemi, Ving Rhames
og John Malkovich. (e)
00.25 Grunaður um græsku
(Under Suspicion) (e)
02.10 Útvarpsfréttir í dagskrárlok

08.00 Barnatími Stöðvar 2
10.00 Tumi bjargar málunum
11.05 Kalli kanína
11.15 Friends I (16:24)
11.40 Bold and the Beautiful
13.35 60 mínútur
14.20 Alltaf í boltanum
14.45 Enski boltinn
17.10 Sjálfstætt fólk
Sigurður Guðmundsson
17.40 Oprah Winfrey
18.30 Fréttir Stöðvar 2
18.55 Lottó
19.00 Ísland í dag, íþróttir og v.
19.30 The Osbournes (8:10)
20.00 Spin City (10:22)
(O, ráðhús)
20.30 Spy Kids
(Litlir njósnarar)
Lengi lifir í gömlum glæðum!
Í eina tíð voru Gregorio og
Ingrid njósnarar í fremstu röð.
Síðar tóku barneignir og
venjulegt heimilishald við og
frekari áform um njósnir voru
gefin upp á bátinn. Röð
óvæntra atvika fær Gregorio
og Ingrid til að taka upp fyrri
iðju og nú slást börnin þeirra
í hópinn.
Aðalhlutverk: Antonio
Banderas, Carla Gugino,
Alan Cumming, Alexa Vega.
Leikstjóri: Robert Rodriguez.
2001.
21.55 Blow
(Í nós)
Sannsöguleg kvikmynd um
George Jung,
kókainbaróninn
sem réð ferðinni á eiturlyfja-
markaðnum í Bandaríkjunum.
Hann flutti til Kaliforníu og
ætlaði sér stóra hluti en lenti
í fangelsi. Þar kynntist
George mönnum sem komu
honum í eiturlyfjasölu fyrir

alvöru. Hann efnaðist gríðar-
lega og lífið blasti svo san-
narlega við honum.
Aðalhlutverk: Johnny Depp,
Penélope Cruz, Franka
Potente. Leikstjóri: Ted
Demme. 2001. Stranglega
bönnuð börnum.
23.55 No Looking Back
(Fram á veginn)
Claudia lifir rólegu lífi í
smábæ í Bandaríkjunum.
Unnusti hennar vill giftast
henni en hún er á báðum
áttum. Hana dreymir um að
yfirgefa krummaskuðið og
leita á vit ævintýranna. Nú er
að hrökkva eða stökkva!
Aðalhlutverk: Lauren Holly,
Edward Burns, Jon Bon Jovi.
Leikstjóri: Edward Burns.
1998.
01.30 Absence of the Good
(Illskan tekur völdin)
Rannsóknarlögreglumaðurinn
Caleb Barnes er á slóð fjölda-
morðingja. Einkalíf hans er í
rjúkandi rúst. Átta ára sonur
hans var myrtur og leit hans
að fjöldamorðingjanum snýst
ekki bara um að ljúka enn
einu sakamálinu heldur gæti
það bjargað sál hans. Aðalhlutverk: Tyne Daly, Stephen
Baldwin. Leikstjóri: John
Flynn. 1999. Stranglega
bönnuð börnum.
03.05 Tónlistarmyndbönd frá
Popp TíVí

08

ég talaði við Erlu

I spoke to Erla

In this unit you will learn
- how to ask somebody what he / she does for a living
- about occupations

Language points
- Group 2 regular verbs (**kenna** (*teach*), **þekkja** (*know*), **gera** (*do*)) in the present tense and in the past tense
- Group 1 regular verbs in the past tense (**talaði ...**)
- word order in sentences

▶ Christof, Anna og Erla fara á kaffihús
Christof, Anna and Erla go to a café

Christof, Anna og Erla fara á kaffihús eftir tónleikana.

Erla Hvað gerið þið í Þýskalandi? Eruð þið í námi eða að vinna?
Christof Ég er á fimmta ári í læknisfræði og Anna er hjúkrunarfræðingur. En hvað gerir þú?
Erla Ég er kennari. Ég kenni spænsku í menntaskólanum hérna.
Christof Hvernig þekkirðu Björn?
Erla: Við vorum saman í grunnskóla. Ég ólst upp í Reykjavík.

---

eftir (normally + acc. or dat.) *after*
tónleikana (from **tónleikar**, pl. m.) *concert*
gerið (from **gera**, Group 2 (ð.) + acc.) *do*
í Þýskalandi *in Germany*
að vera í námi *to be studying*
vinna *work*
á fimmta ári *in the fifth year*
læknisfræði (f.) *medicine*
hjúkrunarfræðingur (m.) *nurse*
kennari (m.) *teacher*
kenni (from **kenna**, Group 2 (d). + acc.) *teach*
menntaskóli (m.) *secondary school, high school*
hérna *here*
hvernig *how*
þekkir (from **þekkja**, Group 2 (t) + acc.) *know*
grunnskóli (m.) *primary school*
ólst upp (from **alast upp**) *grew up*

ℹ The Icelandic school system

school	age
leikskóli (*kindergarten*)	2–6 years
grunnskóli (*primary school*)	6–16 years (obligatory)
menntaskóli / framhaldsskóli (secondary / high school)	16–20 years
háskóli (*university*)	20 + years
tækniskóli (*polytechnic university*)	

▶ Þau halda áfram að tala saman
They continue talking

Erla   Hvað gerðuð þið í gær?
Christof Við skoðuðum miðbæinn og svo hittum við þýskan vin minn sem býr hérna.
Erla   Já, hvað er vinur þinn að gera hérna?
Christof Hann kenndi þýsku í grunnskóla í fyrra en núna vinnur hann sem þýðandi.
Erla   Hvað gerði hann í Þýskalandi?
Christof Hann var að læra heimspeki en hætti í námi og ákvað að koma til Íslands.

---

halda áfram   *continue*
gerðuð (from **gera**, Group 2 (**ð**))   *did*
skoðuðum (from **skoða**, Group 1 + acc.)   *saw, did sightseeing, looked at*
hittum (from **hitta**, Group 2 (**t**) + acc.)   *met*
þýskan vin minn (acc.)   *a German friend of mine*
hérna   *here*
kenndi (from **kenna**, Group 2 (**d**))   *taught*
í fyrra   *last year*
núna   *now*
vinnur (from **vinna**)   *works*
sem   *as*
þýðandi (m.)   *translator*
gerði (from **gera**, Group 2 (**ð**))   *did*
læra (Group 2 (**ð**))   *learn, study*
heimspeki (f.)   *philosophy*
hætti (from **hætta**, Group 2 (**t**))   *quit, stopped*
námi (from **nám**, m.)   *learning, study*
ákvað (from **ákveða**)   *decided*
að koma   *to come*

Language note
• The word **sem** can mean *who*, *which* and also *as*.

▶ Hvað starfarðu? Hvað gerirðu?
What do you do for a living?

Hann er
smiður (m.)
builder

Hann er
leigubílstjóri (m.)
taxi-driver

Hún er
ritari (m.)
secretary

Hún er
læknir (m.)
doctor

Hann er
þjónn (m.)
waiter

Hann er
kokkur (m.)
cook

- Christof er í námi. Hann er að læra læknisfræði.
  Christof is studying. He is studying medicine.
- Anna er hjúkrunarfræðingur. Hún vinnur á spítala í
  Þýskalandi. *Anna is a nurse. She works in a hospital in
  Germany.*
- Björn er lögfræðingur. Hann útskrifaðist í vor og vinnur
  núna á lögfræðistofu. *Björn is a lawyer. He graduated in the
  spring and is working now in a law firm.*
- Guðrún, kærasta Björns, er ritari. Hún vinnur á
  fasteignasölu. *Guðrún, Björn's girlfriend, is a secretary. She
  works at an estate agent's.*
- Kristín, systir Björns, er fiðluleikari í Sinfóníuhljómsveit
  Íslands. Hún kennir líka í Tónlistarskólanum í Reykjavík.
  *Kristín, Björn's sister, is a violinist in the Iceland Symphony
  Orchestra. She also teaches at the Reykjavik Music School.*
- Þór, maðurinn hennar, er leikari. Hann leikur aðallega í
  Þjóðleikhúsinu. *Thor, her husband, is an actor. He performs
  mainly at the National Theatre.*

- Jón, bróðir Björns, er myndlistarmaður. Hann lærði í Svíþjóð. *Jón, Björn's brother, is a painter. He studied in Sweden.*
- Inga er viðskiptafræðingur. Hún vinnur hjá Landsbanka Íslands. *Inga is a graduate in business administration. She works at the National Bank of Iceland.*
- Kári er dósent í sagnfræði við Háskóla Íslands. *Kári is a senior lecturer in history at the University of Iceland.*

---

spítali (m.)   *hospital*
lögfræðingur (m.)   *lawyer*
útskrifaðist (from **útskrifast**)   *graduated*
í vor   *in the spring*
lögfræðistofu (dat. from **lögfræðistofa**, f.)   *law firm*
ritari (m.)   *secretary*
fasteignasölu (dat. **fasteignasala**, f.)   *estate agent's*
fiðluleikari (m.)   *violinist*
sinfóníuhljómsveit (f.)   *symphony orchestra*
tónlistarskóli (m.)   *music school*
leikari (m.)   *actor*
leikur (from **leika**)   *acts, performs*
aðallega   *mainly*
Þjóðleikhús (n.)   *National Theatre*
myndlistarmaður (m.)   *painter*
lærði (from **læra**, Group 2 (ð))   *studied*
viðskiptafræðingur (m.)   *graduate in business administration*
Landsbanki (m.)   *National Bank*
dósent (m.)   *senior lecturer*
sagnfræði (f.)   *(the science of) history*
við Háskóla Íslands (m.)   *at the University of Iceland*

Language notes

- The verb **að vinna** is used much more than the verb **að starfa**.
- Note that professional titles often end in **-fræðingur**, which can mean *scholar, expert*. Branches of science / industry often end in **-fræði**, which can mean *science*.

læknisfræði *medicine*	læknir *doctor*
sagnfræði *history*	sagnfræðingur *historian*
viðskiptafræði *business administration*	viðskiptafræðingur *graduate in business administration*
lögfræði *law*	lögfræðingur *lawyer*
hjúkrunarfræði *nursing*	hjúkrunarfræðingur *nurse*
verkfræði *engineering*	verkfræðingur *engineer*

sálfræði *psychology* sálfræðingur *psychologist*
líffræði *biology* líffræðingur *biologist*
tölvufræði / tölvufræðingur /
  tölvunarfræði   tölvunarfræðingur
  computer science   *computer scientist*

- The professions listed above are all masculine nouns (the endings -**ir**, -**ur** are masculine endings). For most professions there is only one word which is used for both men and women, but for some professions there are two words, one used for men (normally ending in -**maður**) and one for women (ends in -**kona**).

leikari *actor* leikkona *actress*
myndlistarmaður *artist* myndlistarkona *artist*
hárgreiðlumaður *hairdresser* hárgreiðlukona *hairdresser*
afgreiðslumaður afgreiðslukona
  shop assistant   *shop assistant*

Grammar

Past tense of Group 1 regular verbs

In the past tense of Group 1 regular verbs the endings -**aði**, -**aðir**, -**aði**, -**uðum**, -**uðuð**, -**uðu** are added to the stem (infinitive minus -**a**). Remember that the **a** to **ö** sound change rule always applies. The present forms are included here as well.

að tala	*to speak*	
	present	*past*
ég	tal**a**	tal**aði**
þú	tal**ar**	tal**aðir**
hann	tal**ar**	tal**aði**
við	töl**um**	töl**uðum**
þið	tal**ið**	töl**uðuð**
þeir	tal**a**	töl**uðu**

Language notes
- The latter part of the endings in the past tense plural (underlined above) are shared by all verbs (i.e. Group 2 regular verbs, strong verbs and irregular verbs).
- The following verbs, which we have already learnt, also belong to this group: **ætla, byrja, skoða, borða, starfa.**

Present and past tense of Group 2 regular verbs

The Group 2 regular verbs are divided into three subgroups depending on the endings they have in the past tense. The verb endings in these three subgroups are however the same in the present tense. In the present tense the endings -i, -ir, -ir, -um, -ið, -a are added to the stem of the verb, and in the past tense the endings -di, -dir, -di, -dum, -duð, du (subgroup 1) / -ti, -tir, -ti, -tum, -tuð, -tu (subgroup 2) / -ði, -ðir, -ði, -ðum, -ðuð, -ðu (subgroup 3) are added to the stem.

að kenna	*to teach*	
	present	*past*
ég	kenn**i**	kenn**di**
þú	kenn**ir**	kenn**dir**
hann	kenn**ir**	kenn**di**
við	kenn**um**	kenn**dum**
þið	kenn**ið**	kenn**duð**
þeir	kenn**a**	kenn**du**

Language note

We have already learnt the verbs **þýða** and **hringja**, which belong to this subgroup.

að þekkja	*to know*	
	present	*past*
ég	þekk**i**	þekk**ti**
þú	þekk**ir**	þekk**tir**
hann	þekk**ir**	þekk**ti**
við	þekkj**um**	þekk**tum**
þið	þekk**ið**	þekk**tuð**
þeir	þekkj**a**	þekk**tu**

Language notes

- Some verbs in Icelandic (regular (mainly from Group 2), irregular (see **að vilja** (*to want*) in Unit 11) and strong) end in -ja in the infinitive. In the conjugation of these verbs the -j- from the stem only appears in the *plural present* forms. In the conjugation of the verb **að þekkja** the j disappears from the second person plural, where the ending begins with -i.

This is because of a general rule in Icelandic: **j** can never be written between **ý / ey / æ/ k / g** and **i** (here we don't write **j** between **k** and **i**). Note that this applies to the verb **hringja** from the subgroup above (it does not have **j** in the second person plural, because you never write **j** between **g** and **i**).

- We have already learnt the verbs **hitta**, **mæta** and **hætta**, which belong to this subgroup.
- If the stem of the verb ends in **-tt**, one of the **t**s is dropped when the ending is added. The present and past tense forms are therefore identical: **ég hitt-i** (*I meet*), **ég hit-ti** (*I met*).

að gera	*to do*	
	present	past
ég	geri	gerði
þú	gerir	gerðir
hann	gerir	gerði
við	gerum	gerð<u>um</u>
þið	gerið	gerð<u>uð</u>
þeir	gera	gerð<u>u</u>

Language notes
- The verb **æfa** also belongs to this subgroup.

As mentioned before, the latter part of the endings in the past tense plural of all three subgroups (underlined above) are shared by all verbs.

Tip – This is the rule for when you should use **d**, **t** or **ð** in the past tense of Group 2 verbs.

- You use the ending **d** if the stem of the verb ends in **m, n, ng, l** or **ð**. Example:
   kenn-a → kenndi
- You use the ending **t** if the stem of the verb ends in **t, k, p, s** or **d**. Example:
   hitt-a → hitti
- You use the ending **ð** if the stem of the verb ends in **r, f** or **g**. Example:
   ger-a → gerði

Note that this is the same rule that we use when we form the imperative (see Unit 12).

Word order

The (conjugated) verb in Icelandic is <u>almost</u> <u>always</u> in the second position in a sentence / clause (ignoring most conjunctions, such as **af því að, en**). Note that the verb is not necessarily the second word in the sentence, but it is the *second idea* (technically the *second syntactic constituent*).

Í gær **skoðaði** ég miðbæinn.	*Yesterday I did sight-seeing in the city centre.*
Svo **hitti** ég þýskan vin minn.	*Then I met a German friend of mine.*
Hann **kenndi** íslensku, en núna **vinnur** hann sem þýðandi.	*He used to teach Icelandic, but now he works as a translator.*
Hann er Jónsson, af því að pabbi hans **heitir** Jón.	*His name is Jónsson, because his father's name is Jón.*
Anna og Gunnar **eru** frá Íslandi, og Elín **er** líka frá Íslandi.	*Anna and Gunnar are from Iceland, and Elín is also from Iceland.*
Hvar **er** Akureyrarkirkja?	*Where is the church of Akuyreyri?*

The exception to this rule is when the verb is in the first position in questions without a question word:

Talar þú ensku?	*Do you speak English?*

Practice

▶ 1 Listen to the recording and write down the correct forms of the verbs as you hear them in the following sentences. If you don't have the recording, work out what the correct forms should be.

a (**kenna**, *present tense*) Ég _____ þýsku og íslensku.

b (**gera**, *present tense*) Hvað _____ hann?

c (**gera**, *present tense*) Hvað _____ foreldrar hans?

d (**þekkja**, *present tense*) Hvernig _____ þú Erlu?

e (**ætla**, *past tense*) Ég _____ að fara heim. (**heim** *home*)

f (**ætla**, *past tense*) Við _____ að fara heim.

g (**kenna**, *past tense*) Við _____ ensku og norsku.

h (**hitta**, *past tense*) Hvenær _____ þær Önnu?

▶ **2** Björn's friend Magnús asks you some questions. The text on pages 81–2 will help you!

Magnús	Hvað gerir Inga?
You	*(Say that she's a graduate in business administration and works in the National Bank of Iceland.)*
Magnús	Er Christof að vinna?
You	*(Say 'no, he's studying medicine'.)*
Magnús	Er Björn hjúkrunarfræðingur?
You	*(Say 'no, he's a lawyer'.)*
Magnús	Er Kristín sellóleikari (*cellist*)?
You	*(Say 'no, she's a violinist'.)*
Magnús	Vinnur Guðrún hjá bílasölu (*car salesroom*)?
You	*(Say 'no, she works in an estate agency'.)*
Magnús	Er Kári dósent í læknisfræði?
You	*(Say 'no, he's a senior lecturer in history'.)*

3 Find fifteen occupations in this wordsearch.

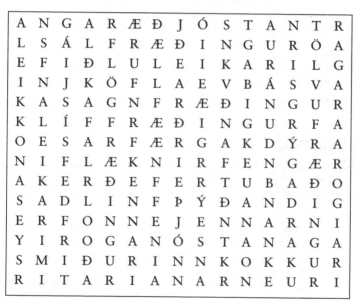

```
A  N  G  A  R  Æ  Ð  J  Ó  S  T  A  N  T  R
L  S  Á  L  F  R  Æ  Ð  I  N  G  U  R  Ö  A
E  F  I  Ð  L  U  L  E  I  K  A  R  I  L  G
I  N  J  K  Ö  F  L  A  E  V  B  Á  S  V  A
K  A  S  A  G  N  F  R  Æ  Ð  I  N  G  U  R
K  L  Í  F  F  R  Æ  Ð  I  N  G  U  R  F  A
O  E  S  A  R  F  Æ  R  G  A  K  D  Ý  R  A
N  I  F  L  Æ  K  N  I  R  F  E  N  G  Æ  R
A  K  E  R  Ð  E  F  E  R  T  U  B  A  Ð  O
S  A  D  L  I  N  F  Þ  Ý  Ð  A  N  D  I  G
E  R  F  O  N  N  E  J  E  N  N  A  R  N  I
Y  I  R  O  G  A  N  Ó  S  T  A  N  A  G  A
S  M  I  Ð  U  R  I  N  N  K  O  K  K  U  R
R  I  T  A  R  I  A  N  A  R  N  E  U  R  I
```

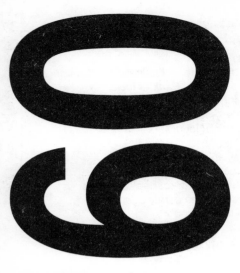

09

við sjáumst um helgina

I'll see you at the weekend

In this unit you will learn
- to talk about what you're going to do and what you did

Language points
- the strong verb **að fara** in the past tense
- declension of personal pronouns
- the verb construction **vera búinn að gera eitthvað**
- declension of strong feminine nouns (**höfn, Reykjavík, Akureyri, Danmörk ...**)
- declension of the feminine definite article
- adverbs of place (**inn, inni ...**)

▶ Christof, Anna og Erla hittast aftur
Christof, Anna and Erla meet again

Erla Hæ! Gaman að sjá ykkur!

Anna Sömuleiðis!

Erla Hvað gerðuð þið í dag?

Christof Við fórum að skoða hús Davíðs Stefánssonar.

Erla Já, er það? Davíð er uppáhaldsskáldið mitt!

Anna Svo löbbuðum við niður að höfn.

Erla Já, það er mjög fallegt niðri við höfnina.

---

gaman *nice*
að sjá (+ acc.) *to see*
ykkur (acc. from **þið**) *you*
sömuleiðis *likewise*
fórum (from **fara**) *went*
hús (n.) *house*
Davíð Stefánsson an Icelandic poet
er það? *really?* (lit. *is it?*)
uppáhalds- *favourite*
skáld (n.) *poet*
mitt (n.) *my*
löbbuðum (from **labba**, Group 1) *walked*
niður að (+ dat.) *down to*
höfn (dat., f.) *harbour*
niðri við höfnina *down by the harbour*

▶ Sjáumst um helgina! *See you at the weekend!*

Erla Hvað ætlið þið að gera á morgun?

Christof Ég ætla að heimsækja Snorra og Anna ætlar að kíkja í búðir.

Erla Jæja, ég þarf víst að fara aftur að kenna. Við sjáumst um helgina áður en þið farið suður.

Anna Já, við gerum það.

---

um helgina (from **helgi**, f.) *at the weekend*
heimsækja (+ acc.) *visit*
kíkja *have a look*
búðir (pl. from **búð**, f.) *shop*

jæja   *well*
þarf (from þurfa)   *have to, need*
víst   *probably*
áður en   *before*
við gerum það   *we'll do that* (lit. *we'll do it*)

▶ Christof talar við Björn í símann
Christof talks to Björn on the telephone

Christof hringir í Björn. Kristín, systir Björns, svarar í símann.

Kristín   Já, halló?
Christof   Hæ, þetta er Christof.
Kristín   Nei, hæ!
Christof   Er Björn heima?
Guðrún   Já, bíddu aðeins, ég ætla að kalla á hann.

...

Björn   Blessaður! Hvernig líkar þér á Akureyri?
Christof   Mjög vel. Í gær skoðuðum við hús Davíðs Stefánssonar og Lystigarðinn og svo fórum við auðvitað í sund!
Björn   Ertu búinn að hafa samband við Erlu?
Christof   Já. Við hittum hana bæði í fyrradag og í gær.
Björn   Já, hvað gerðuð þið?
Christof   Í fyrradag fórum við á tónleika í Akureyrarkirkju og svo í gær borðuðum við hádegismat saman.
Björn   Ertu búinn að heimsækja Snorra?
Christof   Nei, ég ætla að fara til hans á morgun.

svarar (from svara, Group 1) í símann   *answers the telephone*
heima   *at home*
aðeins   *a little bit*
kalla á (+ acc.)   *call (somebody)*
Hvernig líkar þér á A.?   *How do you like it in A.?*
vel   *well*
Lystigarðinn (from Lystigarður, m.)   *park, botanic garden*
auðvitað   *of course*
fórum í sund   *went swimming*
sund (n.)   *swim, swimming*
að hafa samband við (+ acc.)   *contact*
samband (n.)   *contact, connection, relationship*
bæði ... og   *both ... and*
gerðuð (from gera, Group 2 (ð))   *did*
hádegismat (from hádegismatur, m.)   *lunch*

saman   *together*
ertu búinn að heimsækja   *have you visited*
til hans   *to his place* (lit. *to him*)
hans (gen. from **hann**)   *to him, his*

Grammar

The strong verb *að fara* (to go) in the past tense

Strong verbs feature a vowel change and no ending in the first person singular in the past tense. The strong verb **að fara** has the following forms in the past tense (present tense forms are included as well):

að fara *to go, leave*		
	present	*past*
ég	fer	fór
þú	ferð	fórst
hann	fer	fór
við	förum	fórum
þið	farið	fóruð
þeir	fara	fóru

Language notes

- Remember that in the plural present tense of strong verbs the rule is: stem + regular endings (**-um, -ið, -a**) (except that **a** in the stem becomes **ö** if the ending begins with **u**). (The verb **að vera** and a few others are exceptions.)
- Remember that in the plural past tense the endings are regular (**-um, -uð, -u**), but what comes before the endings is irregular.

Declension of personal pronouns

	first person	**second person**	**third person**		
			m.	**f.**	**n.**
nom.	ég (*I*)	þú (*you*)	hann (*he*)	hún (*she*)	það (*it*)
acc.	mig	þig	hann	hana	það
dat.	mér	þér	honum	henni	því
gen.	mín	þín	hans	hennar	þess

	first person	**second person**	**third person**		
			m.	**f.**	**n.**
nom.	við (*we*)	þið (*you*)	þeir (*they*)	þær (*they*)	þau (*they*)
acc.	okkur	ykkur	þá	þær	þau
dat.	okkur	ykkur	þeim	þeim	þeim
gen.	okkar	ykkar	þeirra	þeirra	þeirra

Note – It isn't too difficult to learn the declension of personal pronouns in the plural. The first and second person are declined in the same way, except that the form begins with **o** in the first person and **y** in second person. In the third person the accusative forms in feminine and neuter are the same as the nominative forms, so you don't have to learn new forms. The dative and genitive forms are the same for all three genders.

Saying that you've done something

The verb construction **vera búin(n) að gera eitthvað** means *have finished doing something*, *have done something* or *have already done something*. The word **búin(n)** is formed from the verb **að búa** (which can mean among other things *prepare, make*). It has the same endings as an adjective ending in **-inn** in the masculine, nominative:

masculine	**feminine**	**neuter**
bú**inn**	bú**in**	bú**ið**

Maðurinn er bú**inn** að hitta Erlu.
The man has (already) met Erla.

Konan er bú**in** að lesa bókina.
The woman has finished reading the book.

Barnið er bú**ið** að borða.
The child has finished eating.

Declension of strong feminine nouns

We have already seen the declension of weak feminine nouns, i.e. feminine nouns that end in **-a** in nominative (Unit 2). Feminine nouns that do not end in **-a** in the nominative are called strong feminine nouns and they have no ending in the nominative. Their declension is as follows:

nom.	borg	Akureyri	Svíþjóð	höfn	helgi	bók	Kristín
	city		Sweden	harbour	weekend	book	
acc.	borg	Akureyri	Svíþjóð	höfn	helgi	bók	Kristínu -/-u
dat.	borg	Akureyri	Svíþjóð	höfn	helgi	bók	Kristínu -/-u
gen.	borgar	Akureyrar	Svíþjóðar	hafnar	helgar	bókar	Kristínar -ar

Language notes

- Most strong feminine nouns are declined like **borg**.
- In strong feminine nouns that have **ö** in nom. sing., the **ö** changes to **a** when an ending beginning with **a** is added.

nominative	genitive
höfn *harbour*	hafnar
biðröð *queue*	biðraðar
tjörn *pond*	tjarnar
gjöf *present*	gjafar

- The words **Akureyri** and **helgi** are without an ending in the nominative; the **i** is part of the stem and not an ending. In strong feminine nouns where the stem ends in **-i**, the **i** disappears in the genitive.

There are a few strong feminine nouns which are irregular, e.g. **systir**, **dóttir**, **Reykjavík** and **Danmörk**:

nominative	systir *sister*	dóttir *daughter*	Reykjavík	Danmörk
accusative	systur	dóttur	Reykjavík	Danmörku
dative	systur	dóttur	Reykjavík	Danmörku
genitive	systur	dóttur	Reykjavíkur	Danmerkur

Note that **vík** means *cove*, *creek*. There are quite a few place names that end in **-vík**, such as **Keflavík** (a town, site of Iceland's international airport) and **Grindavík** (a town).

Declension of the feminine definite article

nominative	-(i)n
accusative	-(i)na
dative	-(i)nni
genitive	-(i)nnar

The **i** is left out if the stem of the noun ends in a vowel.

Tip – these endings are almost the same as those for the declension of **hún**: acc. ha**na**, dat. he**nni**, gen. he**nnar**.

	Weak feminine nouns		Strong feminine nouns	
nominative	kona**n**	*the woman*	borg**in**	*the city*
accusative	konu**na**		borg**ina**	
dative	konu**nni**		borg**inni**	
genitive	konu**nnar**		borgar**innar**	

Adverbs of place

The following adverbs of place are used when movement is involved: **út** *outside*, **inn** *inside*, **niður** *down(stairs)*, **upp** *up(stairs)*.

Ég ætla að fara inn. *I'm going to go inside.*
Ég ætla að fara út. *I'm going to go outside.*

These place adverbs have the ending **-i** if there is *no movement* involved: úti, inni, niðri, uppi.

Ég er inni. *I'm inside.*
Ég er úti. *I'm outside.*

Practice

▶ 1 Complete the following sentences with the correct forms of the personal pronouns. Sentences **a–h** are on the recording.

   a Ég talaði um (hann). (**tala um** + acc. = *speak about*)
   b Við fórum til (hann).
   c Hann talaði við (hún).
   d Við ætlum að fara til (hún).
   e Talaðir þú um (ég)?
   f Hann talar bara um (þú).
   g Hún þekkir (hann).
   h Þekkir þú barnið? Nei, ég þekki (það) ekki.
   i Ég talaði við (þær).
   j Ég hugsa oft um (þið). (**hugsa um** + acc. = *think about*; **hugsa**: Group 1)
   k Inga þekkir (þeir) ekki.
   l Konurnar töluðu við (þau).
   m Ætlarðu að skrifa (við) bréf (*letter*)?

2 Look back at the text on pages 89–90 and answer the following questions about Christof using full sentences.

   Hvað var Christof búinn að gera á Akureyri þegar (*when*) hann hringdi í Björn?

   a Var hann búinn að hitta Erlu?
   b Var hann búinn að skoða hús Davíðs Stefánssonar?

c Var hann búinn að fara í Akureyrarkirkju?
d Var hann búinn að heimsækja Snorra?
e Var hann búinn að fara í sund?
f Var hann búinn að skoða Lystigarðinn?

▶ 3 Christof also speaks to Inga, Björn's mother, on the phone. Take Christof's part in the conversation.

Inga	Sæll!
Christof	*(Respond appropriately.)*
Inga	Hvernig líkar þér á Akureyri?
Christof	*(Say 'very much'; lit. 'very well'.)*
Inga	Ertu búinn að hitta Erlu og Snorra?
Christof	*(Say yes, you met Erla yesterday and you're going to visit Snorri tomorrow.)*
Inga	Hittirðu systur Erlu?
Christof	*(Say no, she is in Reykjavik now.)*
Inga	Hvað ertu búinn að skoða á Akureyri? Ertu búinn að skoða hús Davíðs Stefánssonar?
Christof	*(Confirm that you went to see it yesterday – use **skoða**.)*

4 Look at the cartoons below. Translate the text.

---

líka við + acc.   *to like (somebody)*

Ertu búin að hitta Kára?
Já, við hittumst á
þriðjudaginn.

Hvernig líkar þér við hann?
Mjög vel!

hafðirðu það ekki gott?

didn't you have a nice time?

In this unit you will learn
- how to write an e-mail
- how to talk about your holiday

Language points
- the strong verb **að koma** (*to come*) in the present and the past tense
- the irregular verb **að hafa** (*to have*) in the present and the past tense
- about the use of cases (nom., acc., dat., gen.)
- declension of strong masculine nouns (**hundur**, **bíll** ...)
- declension of the masculine definite article
- more about the case government of verbs

▶ Christof og Anna senda Birni tölvupóst *Christof and Anna send Björn an e-mail*

Hæ, hæ!

Hér er gott veður, sól og 15 stiga
hiti. Í gærkvöldi fórum við út að borða
með Erlu og í kvöld ætlum við að hitta
Snorra á kaffihúsi. Við komum aftur til
Reykjavíkur í næstu viku. Skilaðu
kveðju frá okkur til allra. Sjáumst
bráðum!

Christof og Anna

senda ((+ dat.), + acc. Group 2 (**d**))   *send*
Birni (dat. of **Björn**)   *Björn*
tölvupóst (acc. from **tölvupóstur**, m.)   *e-mail*
hér   *here*
gott (from **góður**)   *good*
veður (n.)   *weather*
sól (f.)   *sun*
stiga (from **stig**, n.)   *degrees*
hiti (m.)   *heat, warmth*
fara út að borða   *go out for dinner* (lit. *out to eat*)
komum (from **koma**)   *come*
í næstu viku   *next week*
skilaðu kveðju frá okkur   *give our regards*
skila (+ dat., Group 1)   *return*
allra (from **allir**)   *everybody*
sjáumst   *see you*
bráðum   *soon*

Note – Instead of using **tölvupóstur** people often use **e-mail** (n.).
However, it is considered 'better' Icelandic to use **tölvupóstur**.
Sometimes **tölvupóstur** is shortened to **póstur**.

▶ Christof og Anna koma aftur til Reykjavíkur *Christof and Anna return to Reykjavik*

Björn nær í Christof og Önnu á flugvöllinn.

Björn	Hæ! Gaman að sjá ykkur!
Christof	Sömuleiðis!
Björn	Höfðuð þið það ekki gott á Akureyri?
Christof	Jú, við höfðum það mjög gott.
Björn	Bíðið þið hérna, ég ætla að ná í bílinn. Ég kom á jeppanum, af því að bíllinn minn er bilaður.

---

nær í (from **ná í** + acc.)   *picks up*
á flugvöllinn   *at the airport*
gaman   *pleasant, nice*
höfðuð þið það ekki gott?   *didn't you have a nice time?*
hafa það gott   *have a nice time*
bíðið (imp. from **bíða**)   *wait*
bílinn (acc. from **bíll**, m.)   *car*
jeppanum (dat. from **jeppi**)   *jeep*
bilaður   *broken down*

▶ Björn, Christof og Anna fara heim til Björns *Björn, Christof and Anna go to Björn's house*

Björn, Christof og Anna leggja af stað heim.

Björn	Ég skal taka bakpokann þinn, Anna.
Anna	Takk! Nei, tókstu hundinn með þér?
Björn	Já, Tryggur gamli fékk að koma með.

---

leggja af stað   *go, start a journey*
skal (from **skulu**)   *shall, will*
taka (+ acc.)   *take*
bakpokann (acc. from **bakpoki**, m.)   *backpack*
tókstu (from **taka** + **þú**)   *did you take*
hundinn (acc. from **hundur**, m.)   *dog*
Tryggur   dog's name (means *loyal*)

> **gamall** *old*
> **fékk** (from **fá**) *get, be allowed*
> **fékk að koma með** *was allowed to come with me* (lit. *got to come with*)

Note – A question starting with **nei** conveys surprise.

Grammar

The strong verb *að koma* (*to come*)

að koma *to come*		
	present	*past*
ég	kem	kom
þú	kemur	komst
hann	kemur	kom
við	kom**um**	kom**um**
þið	kom**ið**	kom**uð**
þeir	kom**a**	kom**u**

Language notes

- In the plural present tense of strong verbs the rule is always: stem + regular endings (**-um**, **-ið**, **-a**), not forgetting that **a** in the stem becomes **ö** if the ending begins with **u**. There are a few exceptions to the rule, including **að vera**.
- In the plural past tense the endings are regular (**-um**, **-uð**, **-u**), but what comes before the endings is irregular.

The irregular verb *að hafa* (*to have*)

The verb **að hafa** (*to have*) is an irregular verb. There is a distinction made between irregular and strong verbs: all strong verbs feature a vowel change and have no ending in the past tense first person singular (*I*), whereas irregular verbs always have an ending in the past tense first person singular (and only some feature a vowel change). The verb has the following forms in the present and the past tense (regular endings are in bold):

að hafa	*to have*	
	present	*past*
ég	hef	hafði
þú	hefur	hafðir
hann	hefur	hafði
við	höfum	höfðum
þið	hafið	höfðuð
þeir	hafa	höfðu

Language points

- The plural forms are regular: stem + endings for Group 2 of regular verbs.
- Remember that in the plural present tense of all verbs (regular, irregular or strong) the rule is always: stem + regular endings (-**um**, -**ið**, -**a**). There are a few exceptions to this rule, including **að vera**. This verb is therefore very regular and consequently easy to memorize!
- Remember that the **a** to **ö** sound change rule (u-umlaut rule) always applies.

Declension of strong masculine nouns

We've already looked at the declension of weak masculine nouns, i.e. masculine nouns ending in -**i** in the nominative (Unit 3). Remember that those masculine nouns which do not end in -**i** are called strong masculine nouns. In the nominative they end in either -**ur**, -**l**, -**n**, -**r** or have no ending. The declension of most strong masculine nouns is as follows:

nom.	hundur	strákur	bíll	steinn	læknir	Gunnar	kór	
	dog	*boy*	*car*	*stone*	*doctor*		*choir*	
acc.	hund	strák	bíl	stein	lækni	Gunnar	kór	-
dat.	hundi	strák	bíl	steini	lækni	Gunnari	kór	-(i)
gen.	hunds	stráks	bíls	steins	læknis	Gunnars	kórs	-s

The strong masculine noun endings can also be represented as -**ur**, -(**l**)**l**, -(**n**)**n**, -(**i**)**r** (see Unit 2). The ending **l** always has another **l** immediately preceding it, but that **l** is part of the stem of the noun and not an ending. In the same way the ending **n** has another **n** immediately preceding it and the ending **r** has an **i** immediately preceding it (the first **n** and **i** are then part of the stem). It is important to know what is the stem of the noun and what is the ending, because you always add the case endings to the stem of the noun.

Tip – The words have either no ending in the dative as for **strákur**, or an -i ending as for **hundur**. The rule is: a) if the stem of a word from this group ends in one consonant, it has no ending in the dative, e.g. **strák-ur** is **strák** in the dative; b) if the stem ends in two consonants it has an -i ending in the dative, e.g. **hund-ur** is **hund-i** in the dative, unless these two consonants are -kk-, -gg- or -ng-, in which case there is no ending in the dative singular, e.g. **sokk-ur** (*sock*) is **sokk** in the dative sing., **vegg-ur** (*wall*) is **vegg** in the dative singular and **hring-ur** (*ring*) is **hring** in the dative singular. This rule has many exceptions (e.g. **stein** is **steini** in the dative) but it can be used as a guideline.

There are a few strong masculine nouns which are irregular, e.g. **maður** (whose endings are however regular), **bróðir**, **sonur**, **fjörður**, **Björn**:

nom.	maður	bróðir	sonur	fjörður	Björn
	man	*brother*	*son*	*fjord*	
acc.	mann	bróður	son	fjörð	Björn
dat.	manni	bróður	syni	firði	Birni
gen.	manns	bróður	sonar	fjarðar	Björns

Declension of the masculine definite article

nominative	-(i)nn
accusative	-(i)nn
dative	-num
genitive	-(i)ns

The **i** is left out if the stem of the noun ends in a vowel.

Tip – These endings are almost the same as for the declension of **hann**: acc. **ha<u>nn</u>**, dat. **ho<u>num</u>**, gen. **ha<u>ns</u>**.

Weak masculine nouns

nominative	kennar**inn**	*the teacher*
accusative	kennar**ann**	
dative	kennar**num**	
genitive	kennar**ans**	

Strong masculine nouns

nominative	hundur**inn**	strákur**inn**	steinn**inn**	læknir**inn**
	the dog	*the boy*	*the stone*	*the doctor*
accusative	hund**inn**	strák**inn**	stein**inn**	lækn**inn**
dative	hund**inum**	strák**num**	stein**inum**	lækn**inum**
genitive	hunds**ins**	stráks**ins**	steins**ins**	læknis**ins**

Case government of verbs

The majority of verbs take the accusative. You should memorize those verbs that take either the dative or the genitive. Note that some verbs allow double object constructions, e.g. **senda**, **kenna**.

> **Ég sendi honum tölvupóst** *I sent him an e-mail*
> **Ég kenndi honum þýsku** *I taught him German.*

Word order in double object constructions is normally: verb + dat. + acc., and the person involved is always in the dative.

> **Ég sendi Guðmundi** (dat.) **tölvupóst** (acc.). *I sent Guðmundur an e-mail.*
> **Ég sendi honum** (dat.) **tölvupóst** (acc.). *I sent him an e-mail.*
> **Ég sendi honum** (dat.) **hann** (acc.). *I sent him it.*

Use of the cases in Icelandic

Accusative case

The accusative case is mainly used:

- after verbs that require objects in the accusative: **ég hitti Ingu** (*I met Inga*), **ég kenni ensku** (*I teach English*);
- after certain prepositions: **tala um hana** (*speak about her*);
- after prepositions (**á, í**) when the subject (or object) is in motion: **fara í miðbæinn** (*go into the city centre*);
- with certain time expressions: **í dag** (*today*), **á morgun** (*tomorrow*)

Dative case

The dative case is used:

- to describe the location of somebody or something: **á Íslandi** (*in Iceland*);
- with certain time expressions: **í næstu viku** (*next week*);

- after certain prepositions: **frá Þýskalandi** (*from Germany*), **hjá mér** (*with me, at my place / home*);
- in double object constructions: **ég kenndi honum ensku** (*I taught him English*), **ég sendi honum tölvupóst** (*I sent him an e-mail*);
- after verbs that require objects in the dative: **hann hjálpaði mér** (*he helped me*).

Genitive case

The genitive case is used:

- to mark possession: **mamma Björns** (*Björn's mother*);
- after certain prepositions: **fara til Gunnars** (*go to Gunnar's*);
- in certain constructions (e.g. about age): **eins árs gamall** (*one year old*) (we will look at this later)
- after certain verbs (very few!): **ég sakna hennar** (*I miss her*).

Practice

▶ **1** Fill in the gaps with the correct forms of the verb **að koma**.

  a Ég _____ (*present tense*) á morgun.
  b Við _____ (*present tense*) á morgun.
  c _____ (*present tense*) þú á morgun?
  d Hvenær _____ (*past tense*) þú í gær?
  e Hvenær _____ (*past tense*) hann til Akureyrar?

▶ **2** Use the words in the box below to fill the gaps in this holiday message.

Ég _____ til Íslands í _____. Hér er _____ gott veður. Á morgun ætla ég að _____ Ingu, _____ Björns. Ég kem heim á _____. Sjáumst _____!

fyrradag	vinkonu	kom	mánudaginn
bráðum	mjög	heimsækja	

3 What would you say in Icelandic in the following situations?

  a You meet your friend. Greet him / her and say that you're happy to see him / her.
  b Your friend has just come back from holiday. Ask if he / she had a nice time.
  c Your friend is going on holiday. Ask him / her when he / she is coming back home.

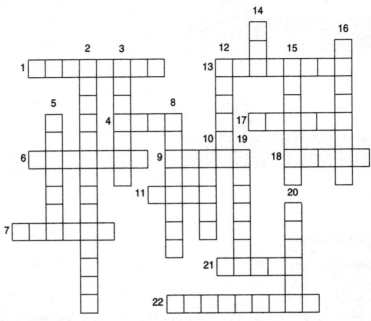

4 Krossgáta (crossword)

Lárétt (Across)

1 Ég talaði þýsku við _____ (Kristján). (tala við + acc.)
4 Þær fóru heim til _____ (Páll).
6 Við fórum í _____ (*the school*) í gær.
7 Guðrún ætlar að heimsækja _____ (Gunnar) annað kvöld.
9 Ég sendi _____ (Ólafur) tölvupóst.
11 Hvaða _____ (*man*) varstu að tala við?
13 Ert þú frá _____ (Ísafjörður)?
17–18 Hún var að tala um _____ (*brother*) _____ (Finnur).
21 Hvenær komuð þið heim (*home*) frá _____ (Björn)?
22 Við ætlum að fara til _____ (*the teacher*) annað kvöld.

Lóðrétt (Down)

2 Þekkirðu _____ (*the cellist*)?
3 Ég ætla að ná í _____ (*the jeep*).
5 Hringdirðu í _____ (*the doctor*)? (hringja í + acc.)
8 Hann er í _____ (*the school*).
10 Ætlarðu að hringja í _____ (Arnar)?
12 Hún hafði samband við _____ (Ísleifur) í gær. (hafa samband við + acc.)
14 Ég ætla að fara til _____ (*grandfather*) í fyrramálið.
15 Fórstu til _____ (Ingólfur) í gærkvöldi?
16 Ertu búinn að hitta _____ (*the secretary*)?
19 Fór hann með _____ (Ingvar)?
20 Hann ætlar að ná í _____ (*the car*).

11

Geturðu farið út í búð fyrir mig?

can you go to the shop for me?

In this unit you will learn
- about going shopping
- to ask for items of food and drink

Language points
- past participle of Groups 1 and 2 regular verbs, of the irregular verb **að hafa** (*to have*) and of the strong verb **að geta** (*can, to be able to*) in the present and the past tense
- use of the verb **að geta**
- the irregular verb **að vilja** (*to want*) in the present and the past tense
- declension of weak and strong neuter nouns
- declension of the neuter definite article

▶ Á leiðinni heim *On the way home*

Björn	Ég ætla að koma við í sjoppu á leiðinni heim – ég er svo rosalega svangur. Viljið þið eitthvað?
Anna	Já, það yrði gott að fá eitthvað að borða.
...	
Stelpa	Góðan daginn! Get ég aðstoðað þig?
Björn	Já, ég ætla að fá eina pylsu með tómatsósu og sinnepi og eina samloku með hangikjöti og salati.
Stelpa	Eitthvað fleira?
Björn	Já, ég ætla líka að fá einn poka af ostapoppi og eina flösku af sódavatni með sítrónu.
...	
Stelpa	Viltu fá poka?
Björn	Já, takk.
Stelpa	Gjörðu svo vel!
Björn	Takk fyrir.

---

koma við í (+ dat.)   *stop at*
sjoppu (acc. from **sjoppa**, f.)   *kiosk*
leiðinni (dat. from **leið**, f.)   *way, route*
heim   *home*
svo   *so*
rosalega   *terribly, extremely*
svangur   *hungry*
viljið (from **vilja**, + acc.)   *want*

eitthvað (acc.)   *something*
yrði (from **vera**)   *would be*
gott (from **góður**)   *good*
að fá   *to get*
get (from **geta**)   *can*
aðstoðað (from **aðstoða**, Group 1 + acc.)   *help, assist*
eina (acc. from **ein**)   *one*
pylsu (acc. from **pylsa**, f.)   *hot dog*
með (+ dat. or acc.)   *with*
tómatsósu (dat. from **tómatsósa**, f.)   *ketchup*
sinnepi (dat. from **sinnep**, n.)   *mustard*
samloku (acc. from **samloka**, f.)   *sandwich*
hangikjöti (dat. from **hangikjöt**, n.)   *smoked meat*
kjöt (n.)   *meat*
salati (dat. from **salat**, n.)   *salad*
fleira   *more*
poka (acc. from **poki**, m.)   *bag*
af (+ dat.)   *of*
ostapoppi (dat. from **ostapopp**, n.)   *popcorn with cheese*
flösku (acc. from **flaska**, f.)   *bottle*
sódavatni (dat. from **sódavatn**, n.)   *soda water*
sítrónu (dat. from **sítróna**, f.)   *lemon*
já takk   *yes, please*
gjörðu svo vel   *here you are,* (lit. *do so well* – see the note
   about this phrase in Unit 14)
takk fyrir   *thanks* (lit. *thanks for*)

Pronunciation

Be careful when you pronounce the word **vatn** – it is
pronounced as if it were written **vahdn**. The letters **tn** are always
pronounced as **hdn**. The easiest way to pronounce the word is
to do it in two steps: **vah – dn**.

▶ Inga biður Björn að fara út í búð
Inga asks Björn to go to the shop

Mamma Björns, Inga, er inni í eldhúsi.

Inga   Björn minn, geturðu ekki farið út í búð fyrir mig?
Björn   Jú, ekkert mál.
Inga   Það vantar fisk, mjólk, smjör, grænmeti … Bíddu, ég ætla
   að skrifa lista.

biður (from **biðja** + acc.)   *ask*
búð (f.)   *shop*
inni í (+ dat.)   *inside (of)*
eldhúsi (dat. from **eldhús**, n.)   *kitchen*
Björn minn   *Björn dear*
farið (past part. from **fara**)   *go*
fyrir (+ acc. (can sometimes take dat.))   *for*
ekkert mál   *no problem*
vantar (from **vanta**, Group 1 + acc.)   *need*
fisk (acc. from **fiskur**, m.)   *fish*
mjólk (acc., f.)   *milk*
smjör (acc., n.)   *butter*
grænmeti (acc., n.)   *vegetables*
bíddu (imp. from **bíða**)   *wait*
skrifa (Group 1)   *write*
lista (acc. from **listi**, m.)   *list*

Grammar

Past participle

The past participle is formed from verbs (English: *gone*, *spoken*, *written*) and it is used in verb constructions such as in English *I have spoken* and *I had spoken*. In Icelandic there are a few other verb constructions where it is used (see **Use of the verb að geta** below). The past participle is formed in the following way:

- Group 1 of regular verbs: stem + -að.

    talað (*spoken*), ætlað (*planned*), byrjað (*begun*)

- Group 2 of regular verbs: stem + -t. There are some exceptions as the past participle of some regular verbs of Group 2 ends in -að (e.g. að brosa (*to smile*) – past participle: brosað; að trúa (*to believe*) – past participle: trúað).

    gert (*done*), kennt (*taught*), þekkt (*known*)

- Irregular verbs: learn the participle for each verb. It ends in either -að (although some end in ð like að ná (*to get, reach*) – náð, see Unit 12), -t or -ið (sometimes stem + -að / -t); the verb að hafa (*to have*): stem + t; the verb að vilja (*to want*): stem + að.

    haft, viljað   *had, wanted*

- Strong verbs: learn for each verb; normally ends in -ið (sometimes stem + -ið). There are two exceptions, the verb að

geta (*to be able to*) – past participle: **getað** and the verb **að sjá**
(*to see*) – past participle: **séð**.

    farið, lesið, komið   *gone, read, come*

The strong verb *að geta* (to be able to, can) in the present and the past tense

að geta	*can, to be able to*	
	present	*past*
ég	get	gat
þú	get**ur**	gast
hann	get**ur**	gat
við	get**um**	gát**um**
þið	get**ið**	gát**uð**
þeir	geta	gátu
past participle: geta**ð**		

Note – Remember that in the plural present tense of of all verbs (regular, irregular or strong) the rule is always: stem + regular endings (**-um, -ið, -a**) (although the **a** to **ö** sound change rule always applies). There are a few exceptions such as the verb **að vera**. Remember also that the endings are regular (**-um, -uð, -u**) for the plural past tense of strong verbs, but what comes before the endings is irregular.

Use of the verb *að geta* (to be able to)

The verb **að geta** is always followed by the **past participle**. This is different from English, where it is followed by the infinitive.

Get ég **aðstoðað** þig?   *Can I help you?*
(past participle from **aðstoða**, Group 1 regular verbs)

Geturðu **farið** út í búð?   *Can you go to the shop?*
(past participle from **fara**, strong verb)

Geturðu **komið** með mér?   *Can you come with me?*
(past participle from **koma**, strong verb)

The irregular verb *að vilja* (*to want*) in the present and the past tense

að vilja	to want		
		present	*past*
ég		vil	vil**di**
þú		vilt	vil**dir**
hann		vill	vil**di**
við		vilj**um**	vil**dum**
þið		vilj**ið**	vil**duð**
þeir		vilj**a**	vil**du**
past participle: vilj**að**			

Language notes

- The plural present tense is regular as for all verbs (except the verb **að vera** and a few others), and the plural forms in the past tense are also regular: stem + endings for Group 2 of regular verbs.
- Remember that in the conjugation of verbs ending in -**ja** in the infinitive, the -**j**- only appears in the plural forms of the present tense (see Unit 8).
- Note that the verb **að vilja** can either take a noun / pronoun in the accusative form or it can take an infinitive without the infinitive marker.

Viltu **poka** (acc.)?	*Do you want a bag?*
Vilt þú **eitthvað** (acc.)?	*Do you want something?*
Viltu **fá** poka?	*Do you want to get a bag?*
Ég vil **fara** heim.	*I want to go home.*

Declension of weak neuter nouns

Neuter nouns that end in -**a** are called weak neuter nouns (note that nouns that end in -**a** are normally feminine, so these neuter nouns are an exception to that rule). There are only a very few weak neuter nouns and most of them denote parts of the body. Their declension is called a weak declension: they do not change their form in the singular.

nominative	aug**a** (*eye*)	hjart**a** (*heart*)
accusative	aug**a**	hjart**a**
dative	aug**a**	hjart**a**
genitive	aug**a**	hjart**a**

The words **eyra** (*ear*) and **lunga** (*lung*) are two more examples of words that are declined in this way.

Declension of strong neuter nouns

Neuter nouns that do not end in -a are called strong neuter nouns. They are often monosyllabic (with only one vowel) and they have no ending in the nominative.

nominative	hús	barn	blað	kjöt	grænmeti	
	house	*child*	*paper*	*meat*	*vegetable*	
accusative	hús	barn	blað	kjöt	grænmeti	-
dative	húsi	barni	blaði	kjöti	grænmeti	-i
genitive	húss	barns	blaðs	kjöts	grænmetis	-s

Note – If the stem of the word ends in -i then there is no -i added in the dative. If, however, the stem of the word ends in -s then -s is still added to the word in the genitive (so the word ends in double s).

Declension of the neuter definite article

nominative	-(i)ð
accusative	-(i)ð
dative	-(i)nu
genitive	-(i)ns

The **i** is left out if the stem of the noun ends in a vowel.

Weak neuter nouns

nominative	augað	*the eye*
accusative	augað	
dative	auganu	
genitive	augans	

Strong neuter nouns

nominative	húsið	barnið	grænmetið
	the house	*the child*	*the vegetable*
accusative	húsið	barnið	grænmetið
dative	húsinu	barninu	grænmetinu
genitive	hússins	barnsins	grænmetisins

Practice

▶ **1** Christof is at the kiosk. Take his part in the conversation.

Christof	(*Say 'good day'.*)
Afgreiðslukona	Góðan daginn. Get ég aðstoðað þig?
Christof	(*Say 'yes, you're going to have a sandwich with butter, smoked meat and salad'.*)
Afgreiðslukona	Eitthvað fleira?
Christof	(*Say 'yes, a bottle (use **eina flösku**) of soda water'.*)
Afgreiðslukona	Viltu poka?
Christof	(*Say 'yes, please'.*)
Afgreiðslukona	Gjörðu svo svel.
Christof	(*Say 'thank you'.*)

2 Look at the dialogues in this unit and mark the following sentences **rétt** (*true*) or **rangt** (*false*).

Á leiðinni heim

a Björn, Christof og Anna koma við í sjoppu á leiðinni heim.
b Björn vill koma við í sjoppu á leiðinni heim, af því að hann er rosalega svangur.
c Anna vill líka fá eitthvað að borða.
d Björn vill fá samloku með osti (*cheese*) og grænmeti.
e Björn vill ekki fá poka.

Inga biður Björn að fara út í búð

f Björn og mamma hans eru að tala saman.
g Það vantar bara smjör og hangikjöt.
h Björn ætlar að fara út í búð.
i Mamma Björns skrifar lista.

3 Change the sentences in the exercise above into the past. The first one has been done for you:

Example: a Björn, Christof og Anna <u>komu</u> við í sjoppu á leiðinni heim.

▶ **4** Complete the following sentences with the correct form of the verb in brackets.

a Geturðu _____ (tala) við hana?
b Ég gat ekki _____ (skrifa) listann fyrir hana.
c Getur hann ekki _____ (fara) út í búð?
d Geturðu _____ (koma) á morgun?
e Ég _____ (geta, *past tense*) ekki skrifað honum bréf.

12

Björn og Guðrún kaupa fiskibollur

Björn and Guðrún buy fishcakes

In this unit you will learn
- about shopping for food
- the names of common groceries

Language points
- the verb **að kaupa** (*to buy*) in the present and in the past tense
- the irregular verb **að eiga** (*to own, have, shall, be supposed to*)
- the irregular verb **að ná** (*to get, reach*)
- imperative (**farðu, náðu í …**)
- making suggestions using **kaupum, förum** (*let's …*)
- the declension of feminine nouns in the plural
- the declension of the feminine plural definite article

▶ Björn og Guðrún, kærastan hans, skreppa út í búð *Björn and Guðrun, his girlfriend, pop out to the shop*

> *Kaupa:*
> *brauð*
> *2 lítra af léttmjólk*
> *3 dósir af fiskibollum*
> *kartöflur*
> *smjör*
> *rækjuost*
> *1 kálhaus*
> *3 gúrkur*
> *3 paprikur*
> *4 gulrætur*
> *5 perur*
> *5 appelsínur*
> *súkkulaðiís með hnetum*

Björn Eigum við að taka kerru?
Guðrún Nei, það er nóg að taka körfu.

---

kaupa (+ acc.) *buy*
brauð (acc., n.) *bread*
lítra (acc. pl., from **lítri**, m.) *litres*
af (+ dat.) *of, from*
léttmjólk (dat., f.) *semi-skimmed milk*
dósir (acc. pl. from **dós**, f.) *can, tin*
fiskibollum (dat. pl. from **fiskibolla**, f.) *fishcakes*
kartöflur (acc. pl. from **kartafla**, f.) *potatoes*
smjör (acc. n.) *butter*
rækjuost (acc. from **rækjuostur**, m.) *soft shrimp cheese*
kálhaus (acc. from **kálhaus**, m.) *head of cabbage*
gúrkur (acc. pl. from **gúrka**, f.) *cucumbers*

paprikur (acc. pl. from **paprika**, f.)   *peppers*
gulrætur (acc. pl. from **gulrót**, f.)   *carrots*
perur (acc. pl. from **pera**, f.)   *pears*
appelsínur (acc. pl. from **appelsína**, f.)   *oranges*
súkkulaðiís (acc., m.)   *chocolate ice cream*
hnetum (dat. pl. from **hneta**, f.)   *nuts*
eigum (from **eiga**)   *shall*
taka (+ acc.)   *take*
kerru (acc. from **kerra**, f.)   *shopping trolley*
það er nóg   *it is enough*
körfu (acc. from **karfa**, f.)   *basket*

▶ Guðrún vill kaupa nammi *Guðrun wants to buy some sweets*

Guðrún   Kaupum líka smá nammi.
Björn   Ókei, farðu og náðu í það á meðan ég næ í ísinn.
Guðrún   Já, ég hitti þig við kassann.

smá   *a little*
nammi (n.)   *sweets*
farðu (far (from **fara**) þú)   *go*
náðu í (ná + þú + acc.)   *get*
á meðan   *while*
næ í (from **ná**)   *get*
kassann (acc. from **kassi**, m.)   *checkout*

Note – Remember (see Unit 7) that the future is often expressed by using the present form of verbs:

Ég **fer** á morgun.   *I'll go tomorrow.*
Ég **hitti** þig við kassann.   *I'll meet you by the check-out.*

▶ Guðrún gleymdi að ná í sjampó
Guðrun forgot to get shampoo

Björn stendur í biðröð við kassann. Guðrún kemur til hans.

Guðrún   Æi, ég gleymdi að ég ætlaði að kaupa sjampó. Ég ætla að fara og ná í það.
Björn   Já, allt í lagi – vertu bara fljót.

---

stendur (from **standa**)   *stands*
biðröð (f.)   *queue*
æi   *oh*
gleymdi (from **gleyma**, Group 2 (**d**))   *forgot*
sjampó (acc., n.)   *shampoo*
allt í lagi   *OK, all right*
vertu (**vert** (from **vera**) + **þú**)   *be*
fljót (from **fljótur**)   *quick*

Grammar

The irregular verb *að kaupa* (*to buy*) in the present and past tenses

að kaupa	*to buy*	
	present	*past*
ég	kaup**i**	keypt**i**
þú	kaup**ir**	keypt**ir**
hann	kaup**ir**	keypt**i**
við	kaup**um**	keypt**um**
þið	kaup**ið**	keypt**uð**
þeir	kaup**a**	keypt**u**
past participle: keyp**t**		

Note – Remember that the plural present tense is regular for all verbs (with a few exceptions) and here the singular present tense is also regular (stem + endings from Group 2 of regular verbs). In the past tense the endings are regular (from Group 2), but what comes before the endings is irregular.

The irregular verb *að ná* (*to get, reach*) in the present and the past tense

að ná	*to get, reach*	
	present	*past*
ég	næ	náði
þú	nærð	náðir
hann	nær	náði
við	**ná**um	ná**ðum**
þið	ná**ið**	ná**ðuð**
þeir	ná	ná**ðu**
past participle: ná**ð**		

Language notes

- The stem of some verbs ends in **á** or **o**: these verbs do not have the ending **-a** in the infinitive. The plural present tense for these verbs is regular except that they do not get the ending **-a** in the third person plural (**þeir**). Remember that the plural present of almost all strong / irregular verbs is regular, except for the verb **að vera** and a few others ending in **á** or **o** in the infinitive and the verb **að skulu** (*shall*) (see Unit 13).

- The verb **að ná** is regular in the past tense: stem + endings from Group 2 of regular verbs.

The irregular verb *að eiga* (*to own, have* etc.) in the present and the past tense

að eiga	*to own, have, shall, be supposed to*	
	present	*past*
ég	á	átti
þú	átt	átt**ir**
hann	á	átti
við	eig**um**	átt**um**
þið	eig**ið**	átt**uð**
þeir	eig**a**	átt**u**
past participle: átt		

Language notes

- The plural present tense is regular as for almost all verbs. In the past tense the endings are regular (from Group 2), but what comes before the endings is irregular.

- The verb **að eiga** has several meanings:

  1 If it is followed by a noun in the accusative form then it means *to own*, *have* or *have got*, e.g. **Átt þú bíl** (acc.)? (*Do you own / have a car?*); **Átt þú hund** (acc.)? (*Do you own / have a dog?*); **Hann á tvö systkini** (acc.) (*He's got two brothers and sisters*).

  2 **að eiga að gera eitthvað** means *to be supposed to do something*, e.g. **Ég á að fara út í búð.** (*I'm supposed to go to the shop.*), **Ég á að skrifa honum bréf.** (*I'm supposed to write him a letter.*).

  3 **Eigum við…?** or **Á ég …?** is used to suggest something and means *shall / should we / I*, e.g. **Eigum við að fara út í búð?** (*Shall we go to the shop?*), **Eigum við að fara á kaffihús?** (*Shall we go to a café?*), **Á ég að ná í þig?** (*Shall I pick you up?*), **Á ég að kaupa eitthvað fyrir þig?** (*Shall I buy something for you?*).

Imperative

The imperative is a verb form that is used to give orders, instructions or advice. In English these forms are, for example: *go* (home), *write* (to him), *read* (the book). The imperative exists in the second person singular (**þú**) and in the second person plural (**þið**).

Plural imperative

The plural imperative forms are identical with the present tense forms in the second person plural.

infinitive	imperative	
tala	Talið þið (saman)!	*Talk (to each other)!*
borða	Borðið þið (eggin)!	*Eat (the eggs)!*
koma	Komið þið!	*Come!*

There is one exception: the verb **að vera** in the imperative is **verið þið**.

The ending of the verb and the pronoun, **ið þið**, is shortened to **iði** in the spoken language; e.g. **talið þið** is pronounced **taliði**, **borðið þið** is pronounced **borðiði** and **komið þið** is pronounced **komiði**. This is normally not reflected in writing, although sometimes it can be: **Þegiði!** (from **þegja** (*shut up*). If you don't put the pronoun **þið** and the verb together, there is special emphasis on **þið**: Náið <u>þ</u>ið í Ingu og <u>við</u> náum í Ara (*You pick up Inga and <u>we'll</u> pick up Ari*).

Singular imperative

The singular imperative is formed with the infinitive of the verb / stem of the verb + **þú**, which is added to the infinitive or stem of the verb and becomes **-ðu, -du, -ddu** or **-tu**. The rules are given below.

1 The imperative of Group 1 regular verbs (end in **-aði** in the past tense, first person singular) is: **infinitive + ðu.**

infinitive	imperative	
tala	tala**ðu**!	*speak!*
borða	borða**ðu**!	*eat!*

2 In most other cases the imperative is: **stem + -ðu/-du/ -ddu/-tu**. Note that if the stem of the verb ends in **j**, then it is removed before **þú** is added.

a) **þú** becomes **-ðu** after **r, f, g** or after a **vowel**

infinitive	imperative	
gera	ger**ðu** ...!	*do ...!*
fara	far**ðu**!	*go!*
ná	ná**ðu** ...!	*get ...!*
sjá	sjá**ðu**!	*see!*

b) **þú** becomes **-du** after **l, m, n, ng**

infinitive	imperative	
koma	kom**du**!	*come!*
kenna	kenn**du**!	*teach!*
hringja	hring**du**!	*ring!*
(*j removed*)		

c) **þú** becomes **-ddu** after a **vowel + ð** (the **ð** in the stem changes to **d**)

infinitive	imperative	
bíða	bí**ddu**!	*wait!*

d) **þú** becomes **-tu** after **p, t, s, k, d** (only **-u** is added to a stem ending in **-tt**; in a stem ending in **-d** the **d** is deleted)

infinitive	imperative	
kaupa	kaup**tu**!	*buy!*
hitta	hit**tu**!	*meet!*
synda	syn**tu**!	*swim!*

Note that these rules are the same as the one we met for forming the past tense of Group 2 regular verbs (see Unit 8).

3 Irregular imperative forms:

infinitive	imperative	
vera	ver**tu**!	*be!*
þegja	þegi**ðu**!	*shut up!*

Note that you can have þú separated from the verb if there is emphasis on it. In this instance -**ðu** or -**u** is deleted from the normal imperative form:

Far <u>**þú**</u> með honum!	<u>*You*</u> *go with him!*
Tala <u>**þú**</u> við hann!	<u>*You*</u> *talk to him!*
Vert <u>**þú**</u> inni.	<u>*You*</u> *stay indoors!*

Making suggestions

When you make a suggestion to somebody to do something with you, then you can use a sentence where the verb is in the first person plural and placed at the beginning of the sentence without a subject (**við**): **Kaupum nammi** (*Let's buy some sweets*), **Förum á kaffihús** (*Let's go to the café*). This can be translated by *let's*. You can also make the suggestions by saying **Eigum við að kaupa nammi?**, **Eigum við að fara á kaffihús?**, but there is a difference in meaning (as there is in English between *Let's buy some sweets.* and *Shall we buy some sweets?*).

Plural of feminine nouns

So far we have learnt the declensions of feminine nouns in the singular (see Units 2 and 9). Now we will look at the forms of feminine nouns in the plural, first of weak feminine nouns and then of strong feminine nouns.

Weak feminine nouns

Remember that weak feminine nouns end in -**a** in the nominative singular (see Unit 2). In the plural the following endings are added to the stem: -**ur** in the nominative, -**ur** in the accusative, -**um** in the dative and either -**na** or -**a** in the genitive.

	(singular)	plural	(singular)	plural	(singular)	plural
nom.	(stelpa)	stelp**ur**	(kirkja)	kirkj**ur**	(karfa)	körf**ur**
	girl		*church*		*basket*	
acc.		stelp**ur**		kirkj**ur**		körf**ur**
dat.		stelp**um**		kirkj**um**		körf**um**
gen.		stelp**na**		kirk**na**		karf**a**

Language notes

- Remember that the **a** to **ö** sound change rule (u-umlaut rule) always applies.
- The genitive ending is **-na** unless the word ends in **-ja** (and there is no **g** or **k** immediately preceding the **j**), **-ía**, **-va**, **-ra** or **-na**: then the ending is **-a**.
- It should be pointed out that the genitive plural form of some weak feminine nouns is very seldom used and many native speakers of Icelandic have problems deciding whether to use the ending **-na** or **-a**.
- The weak feminine noun **kona** is irregular in the genitive plural:

	(singular)	plural
nom.	(kon**a**) *woman*	kon**ur**
acc.		kon**ur**
dat.		kon**um**
gen.		kven**na**

- Note that only the genitive form is irregular here: the ending **-na** is regular but what comes before the ending is irregular.

Strong feminine nouns

Feminine nouns that do not end in **-a** in the nominative singular are strong feminine nouns (see Unit 9). In the plural the following endings are added to the stem: **-ir** or **-ar** in the nominative, **-ir** or **-ar** in the accusative, **-um** in the dative and **-a** in the genitive.

	(singular)	plural	(singular)	plural	(singular)	plural
nom.	(borg) *city*	borg**ir**	(höfn) *harbour*	hafn**ir**	(helgi) *weekend*	helg**ar**
acc.		borg**ir**		hafn**ir**		helg**ar**
dat.		borg**um**		höfn**um**		helg**um**
gen.		borg**a**		hafn**a**		helg**a**

Language notes

- We saw in Unit 9 that in strong feminine nouns that have **ö** in nom. sing., the **ö** changes to **a** when an ending beginning with **a** is added. Here we also see that the **ö** in nom. sing. changes to **a** before an ending beginning with **-i**.

nominative singular	höfn	biðröð	tjörn
	harbour	*queue*	*pond*
nominative plural	hafnir	biðraðir	tjarnir
accusative plural	hafnir	biðraðir	tjarnir
genitive plural	hafna	biðraða	tjarna

- Strong feminine words end either in **-ir** or **-ar** in the nominative plural and accusative plural. When you learn a new strong feminine noun, then learn also what the plural ending is in the nominiative (which is then the same as the ending in the accusative).
- The following words are declined like **borg** (ending in **-ir** in the nominative and accusative plurals):
    þjóð (*nation*), leið (*route*), sól (*sun*), búð (*shop*), dós (*can*)
- The strong feminine nouns **systir**, **dóttir**, **bók** and **gulrót** have an irregular declension in the plural (**systir** and **dóttir** are irregular in the singular as well, see Unit 9):

	(singular)	plural	(singular)	plural
nom.	(systir)	systur	(dóttir)	dætur
	sister		*daughter*	
acc.		systur		dætur
dat.		systrum		dætrum
gen.		systra		dætra
	(singular)	plural	(singular)	plural
nom.	(bók)	bækur	(gulrót)	gulrætur
	book		*carrot*	
acc.		bækur		gulrætur
dat.		bókum		gulrótum
gen.		bóka		gulróta

- All words that end in **-rót** are declined like **gulrót**.

Declension of the definite article in the feminine plural

We've learnt the definite article in the feminine singular (see Unit 9). Now we will learn the forms of the definite article in the feminine plural.

nominative	-nar
accusative	-nar
dative	-num
genitive	-nna

When you add the definite article to feminine plural nouns **in** the dative, the -m ending is dropped.

stelpu<u>m</u> → stelpu + num
körfu<u>m</u> → körfu + num
konu<u>m</u> → konu + num
borgu<u>m</u> → borgu + num
helgu<u>m</u> → helgu + num
bóku<u>m</u> → bóku + num

Weak feminine nouns

nom.	stelpur**nar**	körfur**nar**	konur**nar**
	the girls	*the baskets*	*the women*
acc.	stelpur**nar**	körfur**nar**	konur**nar**
dat.	stelpu**num**	körfu**num**	konu**num**
gen.	stelpna**nna**	karfa**nna**	kvenna**nna**

Strong feminine nouns

nom.	borgir**nar**	helgar**nar**	bækur**nar**
	the cities	*the weekends*	*the books*
acc.	borgir**nar**	helgar**nar**	bækur**nar**
dat.	borgu**num**	helgu**num**	bóku**num**
gen.	borga**nna**	helga**nna**	bóka**nna**

Pronunciation

Note that in spoken Icelandic the **u** in the ending of the noun in the dative plural normally changes to **o** before the article, so **stelpu<u>u</u>num** is pronounced in everyday speech **stelp<u>o</u>num**, **borgunum** is pronounced **borg<u>o</u>num** etc. This is however never seen in written Icelandic.

Practice

1 Put the correct form of the verbs in the spaces. Use the present tense.

a _____ (eiga + þú) kærasta?
b _____ (eiga) þau hund?
c _____ (eiga) þið bíl?
d Ég _____ (eiga) margar (*many*) vinkonur.
e Ég _____ (ná) í ísinn.

▶ 2 You're with your friend Jóhann in the supermarket. Complete your part of the conversation.

You (*Suggest to Jóhann that you should buy pears and carrots.*)
Jóhann Jú, og líka appelsínur.
You (*Ask 'shouldn't we also buy some fish?'*)
Jóhann Jú, kaupum eitt kíló af fiski.
You (*Tell Jóhann 'I'm going to get the sweets', and ask him to get the ice cream.*)
Jóhann Já, ég næ í ísinn.

3 Look at Björn's and Guðrún's shopping list on page 114 and answer these questions.

a Keyptu þau grænmeti?
b Keyptu þau appelsínur?
c Keyptu þau hangikjöt?
d Keyptu þau brauð?
e Keyptu þau pylsur?
f Keyptu þau kjötbollur?
g Keyptu þau samlokur?

4 Give the following orders, using the verbs in brackets and the pronoun þú.

a (tala þú) við hann!
b (ná þú) í bílinn!
c (kaupa þú) bókina!
d (kalla þú) á hann!
e (fara þú) með honum!
f (hringja þú) í Ingu!

13

hvað er í matinn?

what's for dinner?

In this unit you will learn
- how to ask what's for dinner
- how to talk about laying the table

Language points
- the verb **að skulu** (*shall*) in the present tense
- the verb **að verða** (*have to*) in the present and in the past tense
- the verb **að finnast** (*to think, to feel*)
- the present perfect (**ég hef talað**) and the past perfect (**ég hafði talað**)
- the declension of masculine nouns in the plural
- the declension of the definite article in the masculine plural
- more about how to refer to objects / institutions / concepts by using personal pronouns

▶ Hvað er í matinn? *What's for dinner?*

Björn og Guðrún koma heim úr búðinni og fara inn í eldhús. Þar eru Inga, mamma Björns og Ásta, frænka Björns.

Ásta Hæ! Keyptuð þið eitthvað nammi?
Björn Já, lakkrís og súkkulaði.
Inga Ásta mín, ekki fá þér sælgæti fyrir matinn!
Ásta Nei, nei, ég geri það ekki. Hvað er í matinn?
Inga Fiskibollur.
Ásta Æðislegt, mér finnst þær svo góðar!

---

matinn (acc. from **matur**, m.) *food*
úr (+ dat.) *from*
búðinni (dat. from **búð**, f.) *shop*
þar *there*
eitthvað (here) *some*
lakkrís (acc., m.) *liquorice*
súkkulaði (n.) *chocolate*
fá þér *have* (lit. *get yourself*)
sælgæti (n.) *sweets*
ég geri það ekki *I won't do that*
æðislegt (from **æðislegur**) *great*
mér finnst (from **finnast** + acc.) *I think*
góðar (from **góður**) *good*

Language notes

• Both **nammi** and **sælgæti** mean *sweets*. The word **nammi** is used more by younger people and **sælgæti** is used more by older people.

• The word **æðislegt / æðislegur** is mainly used by the younger generation.

▶ Inga og Ásta elda matinn *Inga and Ásta cook the dinner*

Inga Jæja, ég ætla að byrja að elda matinn.
Ásta Ég skal hjálpa þér, amma.
Inga Takk, elskan mín. Náðu í tvo hnífa fyrir mig.
...
Inga Getur þú skorið tómatana og gúrkurnar?
Ásta Já. Vá, ég hef aldrei séð svona stóra tómata!
Inga Já, þeir eru ansi stórir.

elda matinn   *cook (the) dinner*
skal (from **skulu**)   *shall*
elskan (f.)   *love*
tvo (acc. from **tveir**)   *two*
hnífa (acc. pl. from **hnífur**, m.)   *knife*
skorið (past part. from **skera** + acc.)   *cut*
tómatana (acc. pl. from **tómatur**, m.)   *tomatoes*
aldrei   *never*
séð (past part. from **sjá**)   *seen*
svona   *such*
stóra (from **stór**)   *big*
tómata (acc. pl. from **tómatur**, m.)   *tomatoes*
ansi   *quite, rather*
stórir (from **stór**)   *big*

▶ Ásta leggur á borð *Ásta sets the table*

Inga   Geturðu ekki lagt á borðið fyrir mig?
Ásta   Jú, ekkert mál.
Inga   Leggðu á borð fyrir sex. Þú verður að taka diska og gaffla úr
            uppþvottavélinni.
Ásta   Á ég að leggja skeiðar á borðið?
Inga   Já, það verður ís í eftirmat.

diskur
hnífur
gaffall
skeið
glas

leggðu (from **leggja** + **þú**)   *lay, set*
fyrir sex   *for six* (short for **fyrir sex manns** *for six people*)
verður (from **verða**)   *have to*
diska (acc. pl. from **diskur**, m.)   *plates*
gaffla (acc. pl. from **gaffall**, m.)   *fork*

úr (+ dat.)   *from*
uppþvottavélinni (dat. from **uppþvottavél**, f.)   *dishwasher*
á ég   *shall I*
leggja (+ acc.)   *lay, put*
skeiðar (acc. pl. from **skeið**, f.)   *spoons*
það verður   *there will be*
í eftirmat (acc. from **eftirmatur**, m.)   *for dessert*

Grammar

The irregular verb *að skulu* (*shall, will*) in the present tense

að skulu	*shall, will*
ég skal	*I shall*
þú skalt	*you shall*
hann / hún / það skal	*he / she / it shall*
við skul**um**	*we shall*
þið skul**uð**	*you shall*
þeir / þær / þau skul**u**	*they shall*

Language notes
- The plural present tense of all verbs (regular, irregular and strong) is regular, except for the verbs **að vera**, **að skulu** and a few others (ending in **á** or **o** in the infinitive – see **að ná** in Unit 12).
- The verb **að skulu** does not have past tense forms.
- The verb **að skulu** can mean either *shall* or *will*, e.g. **ég skal gera það á morgun** can mean *I will do it tomorrow* or *I shall do it tomorrow*. In the first person plural it can also mean *let's*, e.g. **við skulum fara heim**: *let's go home*.

The strong verb *að verða* (*to have to*) in the present and the past tense

að verða *to have to*		
	present	*past*
ég	verð	varð
þú	verður	varðst
hann	verður	varð

við	verð**um**	urð**um**
þið	verð**ið**	urð**uð**
þeir	verð**a**	urð**u**

Language note

- The verb **að verða** can have other meanings. Besides *have to* it can also mean *become, turn,* or *will be.*

Hún vill verða lögfræðingur.	*She wants to become a lawyer.*
Hún verður fimmtíu ára á morgun.	*She turns fifty tomorrow.*
Það verður ís í eftirmat.	*There will be ice cream for dessert.*
Búðin verður opin á sunnudaginn.	*The shop will be open on Sunday.*

The strong verb *að finnast* (*to think / feel*) in the present and past tense

Some verbs have a subject in the dative or the accusative. These verbs are called impersonal verbs and in the present and past tense they have only one form for all persons. The subject used with the verb **að finnast** is always in the dative.

að finnast *to think, feel*		
dative	*present*	*past*
mér	finnst	fannst
þér	finnst	fannst
honum / henni / því	finnst	fannst
okkur	finnst	fannst
ykkur	finnst	fannst
þeim / þeim / þeim	finnst	fannst

Language notes

- Note that some verbs end in -**st** in the infinitive. Most of these verbs (not the verb **að finnast** though) are reciprocal verbs, i.e. the action of the verb involves two people doing the same thing to each other.

| að sjást: Við sjáumst á morgun. | (lit. *We'll see each other tomorrow.*) |
| að hittast: Þær hittust í miðbænum. | (lit. *They met each other in the town centre.*) |

- Note that in a sentence with the verb **að finnast** you do not use another conjugated verb (i.e. a verb which is not in the infinitive form) in the sentence. In the following examples, the English verbs (underlined) are not used in Icelandic.

Mér finnst fiskibollur góðar.	*I think fishcakes <u>are</u> good.*
Mér finnst leiðinlegt að **fara í skólann.**	*I think <u>it is</u> boring to go to school.*

The present perfect ('I have spoken') and the past perfect ('I had spoken')

The present perfect is formed by using the verb **að hafa** in the present tense and the past participle of the relevant verb.

ég hef talað	*I have spoken*
ég hef skrifað	*I've written*
ég hef haft	*I have had*
ég hef komið	*I have come*

Note that the present perfect is not used as frequently in Icelandic as in English. In many cases where you use the present perfect in English, you would use the construction **vera búin(n) að gera eitthvað** in Icelandic.

Ég er búin(n) að tala við **Önnu og hún ætlar að …**	*I have spoken to Anna and she's going to …*
Ertu búin(n) að heimsækja **Önnu?**	*Have you visited Anna yet?*

(See also past participle adjectives in Unit 14: **hún er farin heim** – *she's gone home.*)

Normally when you use the present perfect in Icelandic you also use words such as **aldrei, aldrei áður** (*never before*), **oft, oft áður** (*often before*), **einhvern tíma** (*ever*) in the sentence.

Ég hef <u>aldrei</u> séð hann <u>áður</u>.	*I've never seen him before.*
Ég hef <u>oft</u> séð hann <u>áður</u>.	*I've often seen him before.*
Hefurðu <u>einhvern tíma</u> farið til Þýskalands?	*Have you ever been to Germany?*

The past perfect is formed by using the verb **að hafa** in the past tense and the past participle of the relevant verb.

ég hafði talað	*I had spoken*
ég hafði skrifað	*I had written*
ég hafði haft	*I had had*
ég hafði komið	*I had come*

Plural of masculine nouns

We have already learnt the declensions of masculine nouns in the singular (see Units 4 and 10). Now we will learn the forms of masculine nouns in the plural, first of weak masculine nouns and then of strong masculine nouns.

Weak masculine nouns

Weak masculine nouns end in -i in the nominative singular (see Unit 4). In the plural the following endings are added to the stem: -**ar** in the nominative, -**a** in the accusative, -**um** in the dative and -**a** in the genitive.

(sing.)	(sími)	(afi)	(Breti)	(skóli)	
	telephone	*grandfather*	*Briton*	*school*	
	plural	**plural**	**plural**	**plural**	
nom.	símar	afar	Bretar	skólar	-**ar**
acc.	síma	afa	Breta	skóla	-**a**
dat.	sím**um**	öf**um**	Bret**um**	skól**um**	-**um**
gen.	síma	afa	Breta	skóla	-**a**

Note – Remember that the **a** to **ö** sound change rule (u-umlaut rule) always applies.

Strong masculine nouns

All masculine nouns that do not end in -i in the nominative singular are strong masculine nouns (see Unit 10). Most strong masculine nouns have the same endings in the pural as weak masculine nouns: -**ar** in the nominative, -**a** in the accusative, -**um** in the dative and -**a** in the genitive.

(sing.)	(hundur)	(gaffall)	(læknir)	(steinn)	
	dog	*fork*	*doctor*	*stone*	
	plural	**plural**	**plural**	**plural**	
nom.	hund**ar**	gaffl**ar**	lækn**ar**	stein**ar**	-**ar**
acc.	hund**a**	gaffl**a**	lækn**a**	stein**a**	-**a**
dat.	hund**um**	göffl**um**	lækn**um**	stein**um**	-**um**
gen.	hund**a**	gaffl**a**	lækn**a**	stein**a**	-**a**

Language notes

• In all words ending in -(**al**)**l** (notice that the **al** in brackets is part of the stem, and that the second **l** is the actual ending), the **a** in the last syllable is dropped before an ending beginning with a vowel. For the word **gaffall** all the endings in the plural begin with a vowel; the second **a** is therefore dropped in the plural. In the singular, however, one case ending begins with a vowel, so the **a** is dropped only once:

gaffall (nom.)
gaffal- (acc.; no ending is added)
gaffl-i (dat.)
gaffal-s (gen.)

Note that the rule above also applies to the adjective **gamall** (*old*; see Unit 16).

• In the word **læknir**, as in other words ending in -(i)r, the **i** of the stem is dropped before the plural endings are added.

Some strong masculine nouns have an irregular declension in the plural; the most common ones are **maður**, **bróðir** and **sonur** (they are also irregular in the singular, see Unit 10):

	(singular)	plural	(singular)	plural	(singular)	plural
nom.	(maður)	menn	(bróðir)	bræður	(sonur)	synir
	man		*brother*		*son*	
acc.		menn		bræður		syni
dat.		mönn**um**		bræð**rum**		son**um**
gen.		mann**a**		bræð**ra**		son**a**

Declension of the definite article in the masculine plural

We've learnt the declension of the definite article in the masculine singular (see Unit 10). Now we will learn the forms of the definite article in the masculine plural.

nominative	-nir
accusative	-(i)na
dative	-num
genitive	-nna

Note – The **i** in the accusative is dropped when it is preceded by a vowel.

Weak masculine nouns

nominative	símar**nir**	*the telephones*	skólar**nir**	*the schools*
accusative	síma**na**		skóla**na**	
dative	símu**num**		skólu**num**	
genitive	síma**nna**		skóla**nna**	

Strong masculine nouns

nominative	hundar**nir**	gafflar**nir**	steinar**nir**	menni**rnir**
	the dogs	*the forks*	*the stones*	*the men*
accusative	hunda**na**	gaffla**na**	steina**na**	menn**ina**
dative	hundu**num**	göfflu**num**	steinu**num**	mönnu**num**
genitive	hunda**nna**	gaffla**nna**	steina**nna**	manna**nna**

Language notes

- As with feminine nouns in the plural, the **m** in the ending of the noun in the dative is dropped before the article is added, e.g. símu<u>m</u> → símu + num; hundu<u>m</u> → hundu + num; mönnu<u>m</u> → mönnu + num.
- Note that in the nominative plural of the noun **menn** you add **ir** before you add the definite article: nom.pl. menn → **menn + ir + nir**.

Pronunciation

- As with definite feminine nouns in the plural, the **u** in the ending of the masculine noun in the dative plural changes normally in speech to **o** before the article, so **skólunum** is pronounced in everyday speech **skólonum**, **hundunum** is pronounced **hund<u>o</u>num** etc. Note that this is never written.

Using pronouns

When you use a pronoun to replace a noun, the pronoun has to be in the same gender and number as the noun it is replacing. However, the case of the pronoun depends on its function in the sentence, and so it it won't always be in the same case as the noun it is replacing.

Hvar er gúrkan (**feminine singular**)? **Hún** er á borðinu.
Where is the cucumber? It is on the table.
Hvar eru gúrkurnar (**feminine plural**)? **Þær** eru á borðinu.
Where are the cucumbers? They are on the table.
Hvar eru gúrkurnar (**feminine plural, <u>nom</u>.**)? Ég borðaði
þær (<u>acc</u>.). *Where are the cucumbers? I ate them.*

Hvar er tómaturinn (**masculine singular**)? **Hann** er hérna.
Where is the tomato? It is here.
Hvar eru tómatarnir (**masculine plural**)? **Þeir** eru hérna.
Where are the tomatoes? They are here.
Hvar eru tómatarnir (**masculine plural, <u>nom</u>.**)? Ég borðaði
þá (<u>acc</u>.). *Where are the tomatoes? I ate them.*

Hvar er blaðið (**neuter singular**)? Það er hérna.
Where is the newspaper? It's here.
Hvar eru blöðin (**neuter plural**)? Þau eru hérna.
Where are the newspapers? They're here.
Hvar eru blöðin (**neuter plural, <u>nom.</u>**)? Ég sá þau
(**<u>acc.</u>**) ekki. *Where are the newspapers? I haven't seen them.*

Don't worry here about the neuter plural form **blöðin** – we will
learn the plural of neuter nouns and the neuter definite article in
the next unit.

Practice

▶ 1 Answer Björn's questions in Icelandic. Don't worry about
the forms of the adjective **góður** (*good*) – we'll learn the
declension of adjectives in Unit 15. In your answers use the
same form of the adjective that is used in the questions.

Björn	Finnst þér fiskur góður?
You	(*Say 'yes', you think that fish is good.*)
Björn	Finnst þér fiskibollur góðar?
You	(*Say 'no', you don't think that fishcakes are good.*)
Björn	Finnst þér brauð með smjöri og osti gott?
You	(*Say 'yes', you think bread with butter and cheese is good.*)
Björn	Finnst þér sælgæti gott?
You	(*Say 'yes', you think sweets are very good.*) (*Use* rosalega – 'extremely'.)
Björn	Finnst þér grænmeti gott?
You	(*Say 'no', you don't think that vegetables are good.*)

2 Answer the following in Icelandic, first with 'yes', then with
'no'.

a Hefurðu einhvern tíma (*ever*) lesið bók eftir (*by*) Halldór
Laxness? (Use **aldrei** (*never*) in your 'no' answer.)

b Hefurðu einhvern tíma farið til Þýskalands? (Use **aldrei**
and **oft** (*often*) in your answers.)

c Hefurðu einhvern tíma komið til Íslands? (Use **oft** in your
'yes' answer.)

d Hefurðu einhvern tíma hitt Íslendinga? (Use **oft** in your
'yes' answer.)

e Hefurðu lesið bók um Ísland?

▶ 3 Answer the following questions, replacing the nouns with
personal pronouns.

a Hvar eru tómatarnir? _____ eru á borðinu.

b Hvar eru bílarnir? _____ eru fyrir framan húsið.

c Hvar eru dósirnar? _____ eru inni í eldhúsi.

d Náðirðu í hundana? Nei, ég náði ekki í _____.

e Borðaðirðu gúrkurnar? Nei, ég borðaði _____ ekki.

f Skoðaðirðu bílana? Nei, ég skoðaði _____ ekki.

4 Change the nouns in the following sentences into the plural.

    a Ég hitti kennarann í gær.

    b Ég keypti hníf.

    c Ég fór að hitta strákinn í gær.

    d Hann þekkir ekki manninn.

    e Töluðu þau við lækninn?

    f Keypti hann bílinn?

    g Þekktirðu lögfræðinginn?

14 takk fyrir mig

thanks for the meal

In this unit you will learn
- mealtime etiquette

Language points
- the verb **að fá** (*to get*) in the present and in the past tense
- the reflexive pronouns (*myself, yourself …*)
- the expression **að fá sér eitthvað** (lit. *to get yourself something*)
- about past participles being used as adjectives
- the declension of neuter nouns in the plural
- the declension of the definite article in the neuter plural
- the declension of numerals

▶ Maturinn er tilbúinn! *Dinner is ready!*

Inga er búin að elda matinn.

Inga	Jæja, maturinn er til. Gjörið þið svo vel.
Christof	Takk.

(Allir nema Inga setjast við borðið.)

Inga	Hvað viljið þið að drekka? Það er til mjólk, kók, appelsínusafi, eplasafi…
Björn	Ég ætla að fá kók.
Ásta	Já, ég líka.
Inga	En þú Christof, hvað má bjóða þér að drekka?
Christof	Kók væri fínt. Get ég nokkuð fengið vatnsglas líka?
Inga	Já, auðvitað. Guðrún, hvað vilt þú?
Guðrún	Smá mjólk, bara hálft glas.

…

Christof	Íslenska vatnið er ofsalega gott! Það er þægilegt að geta drukkið vatn beint úr krananum!
Inga	Já, það er mjög þægilegt. Þarftu ekki alltaf að kaupa vatn á flöskum í Þýskalandi?
Christof	Jú, ég geri það alltaf. Það eru margir heima sem sía vatnið, en mér finnst bara síað vatn ekki nógu gott á bragðið.

---

maturinn er til   *dinner is ready*; here **til** is short for **tilbúinn**
  (*ready*)
gjörið þið svo vel   *please go ahead*
allir   *everybody*
nema   *except*
setjast   *take a seat, sit down*
við (normally + acc.)   *at*
drekka (+ acc.)   *drink*
það er til   *we have*, lit. *it exists*
kók (n.)   *coke*
appelsínusafi (m.)   *orange juice*
eplasafi (m.)   *apple juice*
hvað má bjóða þér?   *what would you like?* (lit. *what can you
  be offered?*)
væri   *would be*
nokkuð   untranslatable; see below
fengið (past part. from **fá** + acc.)   *get*
vatnsglas (acc. n.)   *glass of water*
smá mjólk   *a little milk*
hálft (from **hálfur**)   *half*
íslenska vatnið (**vatn**, n.)   *the Icelandic water*
ofsalega   *really, extremely*

gott (from **góður**)   *good*
þægilegt (from **þægilegur**)   *convenient*
drukkið (past participle from **drekka**)   *drink*
beint   *straight, directly*
úr (+ dat.)   *from*
krananum (from **krani**, m.)   *tap*
alltaf   *always*
á flöskum (dat. pl. from **flaska**, f.)   *in bottles*
margir   *many people*
sía (+ acc., Group 1)   *filter*
mér finnst   *I think*
síað (from **síaður**)   *filtered*
ekki nógu gott á bragðið   *doesn't taste good enough* (lit. *not enough good on the taste*)

Language notes

- When you say *here you are / please go ahead* you use **gjörðu svo vel** if you're addressing one person (**þú**) and **gjörið þið svo vel** if you're addressing more than one person (**þið**). The verb **að gjöra** is an old verb for *to do* and is only used in the combination **gjörðu / gjörið þið svo vel**. The literal meaning of **gjörðu / gjörið þið svo vel** is *do so well*. Note that **gjörið þið** is pronounced in everyday speech **gjöriði**.

- The word **nokkuð** in the question **Get ég nokkuð fengið vatnsglas?** makes the question polite. If you're asking if you can get or borrow something or if you are asking somebody to do something for you, then adding **nokkuð** can often make the question more polite.

> Geturðu nokkuð rétt   *(See below.)*
> mér smjörið?
> Geturðu nokkuð náð í   *Can you pick up Ari for me?*
> Ara fyrir mig?

Note that **nokkuð** can have other meanings.

▶ Geturðu nokkuð rétt mér smjörið?
Can you pass me the butter?

Allir byrja að borða.

Christof (*turning to Inga*) Geturðu nokkuð rétt mér smjörið?
Inga   Já, gjörðu svo vel.
Christof Takk.

Björn   Pabbi, geturðu rétt mér salatið?
Kári   Hérna.

…

Inga   Christof, viltu ekki fá þér meira?
Christof   Jú, ég fæ mér kannski tvær bollur í viðbót.
Inga   Viltu ekki fá þér tvær kartöflur líka?
Christof   Jú, takk.
Inga   Guðrún mín, vilt þú ekki fá þér meira?
Guðrún   Nei, takk. Ég er orðin svo södd – ég er alveg að springa!

---

rétt (past part. from **rétta**, Group 2 (**t**), + dat. and acc.)   *hand*
gjörðu svo vel   *here you go*
salat (n.)   *salad*
hérna   *here*
fá þér   *have*, lit. *get yourself*
meira   *more*
fæ (from **fá** + acc.)   *get*
kannski   *maybe*
bollur   *balls* (here *cakes*, short for: **fiskibollur** – *fishcakes*)
í viðbót   *in addition*
jú takk   *yes, please*
orðin (from **verða**)   *become*
södd (from **saddur**)   *full*
alveg   *just, absolutely*
springa   *explode*

Note – The verb **að rétta** is one of those verbs which take two objects, one in the dative form and one in the accusative form. In the question **Geturðu rétt mér smjörið?** (*Can you pass me the butter?*) the pronoun **mér** is in the dative form and the word **smjörið** is in the accusative form.

Hann rétti Guðmundi (*dat.*)   *He passed Guðmundur*
  bókina (*acc.*)   *the book.*
Réttu honum (*dat.*)   *Pass him the apple.*
  eplið (*acc.*).

▶ Takk fyrir mig *Thanks for the meal*

Allir standa upp frá borðinu.

Christof   Takk fyrir mig!
Inga   Verði þér að góðu.
Christof   Það var gott að fá íslenskar fiskibollur aftur!

standa upp	*stand up*
frá borðinu	*from the table*
takk fyrir mig	*thanks for the meal*
verði þér að góðu	*you're welcome*

Note – In response to **Takk fyrir mig**, which means literally *Thanks for me*, you reply (to one person) **Verði þér að góðu**. In response to **Takk fyrir okkur**, which means literally *Thanks for us*, you reply (to more than one person) **Verði ykkur að góðu** (lit. *be you to good*).

▶ Ávextir *Fruit*

bananar   vínber   pera   epli   jarðarber   appelsína

Inga   Fáið ykkur endilega ávexti.
Christof   Takk, ég er bara orðinn svo saddur.
Inga   Ég læt ávaxtaskálina vera hérna á borðinu, þið getið fengið ykkur seinna í kvöld ef þið viljið.

fáið ykkur	lit. *get yourselves*
endilega	*by all means*
ávexti (acc. pl. from **ávöxtur**, m.)	*fruit*
ég er bara orðinn svo saddur	*I'm just so full*
læt (from **láta** + acc.)	*let*
ávaxtaskálina (acc. from **ávaxtaskál**, f.)	*fruit bowl*
þið getið fengið ykkur	*you can get yourselves (some)*
seinna	*later*
ef	*if*

Grammar

The strong verb *að fá* (*to get*) in the present tense and the past tense

að fá	*to get*		
		present	*past*
ég		fæ	fékk
þú		færð	fékkst
hann		fær	fékk
við		fá**um**	feng**um**
þið		fá**ið**	fengu**ð**
þeir		fá	feng**u**
past participle: feng**ið**			

Language notes
- Remember that those verbs which end in **á** in the infinitive do not have the ending -**a** in the third person plural (**þeir**) present tense (but are otherwise regular in the present plural).
- The endings in the plural past tense are regular as for all strong / irregular verbs, but what comes before the endings is irregular.

Reflexive pronouns

A reflexive pronoun is a pronoun such as *myself* which refers back to the subject of a sentence. For example, in the sentence *He made himself a cup of tea*, the reflexive pronoun *himself* refers back to *he*. In Icelandic the reflexive pronouns in the first person and second person are identical to the personal pronouns. The reflexive pronoun in the third person is the same for singular and plural: accusative **sig**, dative **sér**, genitive **sín** (it is declined like **ég** and **þú**). Here is a list of all the reflexive pronouns (reflexive pronouns are not used in the nominative):

	first person	second person	third person		
			m.	f.	n.
nominative	(ég)	(þú)	–	–	–
accusative	mig	þig	sig	sig	sig
dative	mér	þér	sér	sér	sér
genitive	mín	þín	sín	sín	sín

nominative	(við)	(þið)	–	–	–
accusative	okkur	ykkur	sig	sig	sig
dative	okkur	ykkur	sér	sér	sér
genitive	okkar	ykkar	sín	sín	sín

Accusative

æfa sig (*train (oneself)*)

ég æfi **mig**
þú æfir **þig**
hann æfir **sig**
hún æfir **sig**
það (barnið) æfir **sig**

við æfum **okkur**
þið æfið **ykkur**
þeir æfa **sig**
þær æfa **sig**
þau æfa **sig**

raka sig (*shave (oneself)*, Group 1 of reg. verbs)

ég raka **mig**
þú rakar **þig**
hann rakar **sig**

við rökum **okkur**
þið rakið **ykkur**
þeir raka **sig**

Dative

þvo sér (*wash (oneself)*)

ég þvæ **mér**
þú þværð **þér**
hann þvær **sér**
hún þvær **sér**
það þvær **sér**

við þvoum **okkur**
þið þvoið **ykkur**
þeir þvo **sér**
þær þvo **sér**
þau þvo **sér**

Genitive

hefna sín (*avenge oneself*, Group 2 of reg. verbs (d))

ég hefni **mín**
þú hefnir **þín**
hann hefnir **sín**
hún hefnir **sín**
það hefnir **sín**

við hefnum **okkar**
þið hefnið **ykkar**
þeir hefna **sín**
þær hefna **sín**
þau hefna **sín**

Note – Note the difference in meaning between **Gunnar rakaði sig** (**sig** = Gunnar) (*Gunnar shaved himself*) and **Gunnar rakaði hann** (**hann** ≠ **Gunnar**) (*Gunnar shaved him*).

að fá sér eitthvað (*to get yourself something*)

The expression **að fá sér eitthvað** means literally *to get yourself something*. This expression is used for example about a person getting or having something to eat (e.g. **Hann fékk sér epli** – *He had an apple*; **Viltu ekki fá þér meira?** – *Don't you want some more?*). The reflexive pronoun following the verb **að fá** is used in the dative form.

	dative
ég fæ	mér
þú færð	þér
hann / hún / það fær	sér
við fáum	okkur
þið fáið	ykkur
þeir / þær / þau fá	sér

Past participles used as adjectives

Past participles of verbs are often used as adjectives, and then their form slightly changes. The formation of past participles to adjectives is described below.

Past participles of verbs from Group 1 of regular verbs have the following endings as adjectives:

	m.	**f.**	**n.**
byrja (*begin*)			
(*past part.* **byrjað**)	byrja**ður**	byrj**uð**	byrja**ð**
sofna (*fall asleep*)			
(*past part.* **sofnað**)	sofna**ður**	sofn**uð**	sofna**ð**
rugla (*confuse*)			
(*past part.* **ruglað**)	rugla**ður**	rugl**uð**	rugla**ð**

Past participles of Group 2 regular verbs have the following endings as adjectives, depending on the endings they have in the past tense:

gleyma (*forget*)			
(*past part.* **gleymt**)	gleym**dur**	gleym**d**	gleym**t**
(*past tense* **gleymdi**)			
þekkja (*know*)			
(*past part.* **þekkt**)	þekk**tur**	þekk**t**	þekk**t**
(*past tense* **þekkti**)			

Past participles of strong verbs have the following endings as adjectives:

deyja (*to die*)			
(*past part.* **dáið**)	dá**inn**	dá**in**	dá**ið**
verða (*become*)			
(*past part.* **orðið**)	orð**inn**	orð**in**	orð**ið**

These past participle adjectives behave like normal adjectives, i.e. their form (masculine, feminine or neuter) depends on the form of the noun they're describing.

hann er orðinn (*masc.*) saddur	*he's (become) full*
hún er orðin (*fem.*) södd	*she's (become) full*
barnið er orðið (*neut.*) satt	*the child has (become) full*
hann er gleymdur (*masc.*)	*he's been forgotten*
hún er gleymd (*fem.*)	*she's been forgotten*
það er gleymt (*neut.*)	*it's been forgotten*
hann er vel þekktur (*masc.*)	*he's well known*
hún er vel þekkt (*fem.*)	*she's well known*
það er vel þekkt (*neut.*)	*it's well known*

Note – In English you often use the perfect tense where you use a past participle adjective in Icelandic.

Hún er **farin** heim.	*She has gone home.*
Hann er **byrjaður**.	*He has started.*
Hún er **sofnuð**.	*She has fallen asleep.*

Plural of neuter nouns

We have already learnt the declensions of neuter nouns in the singular (see Unit 11). Now we will learn the forms of neuter nouns in the plural, first of weak neuter nouns and then of strong neuter nouns.

Weak neuter nouns

Weak neuter nouns end in -**a** in the nominative singular. In the plural the following endings are added to the stem: -**u** in the nominative, -**u** in the accusative, -**um** in the dative and -**na** in the genitive.

	(singular)	plural	(singular)	plural
nom.	(aug**a**) *eye*	aug**u**	(hjart**a**) *heart*	hjört**u**
acc.		aug**u**		hjört**u**
dat.		aug**um**		hjört**um**
gen.		aug**na**		hjart**na**

Note – Remember the **a** to **ö** sound change rule (u-umlaut rule).

Strong neuter nouns

All neuter nouns that do not end in -**a** in the nominative singular are strong neuter nouns. In the plural strong neuter nouns do not have any ending in the nominative or accusative; in the dative they have the ending -**um** and in the genitive they have the ending -**a**.

	(sing.)	plural	(sing.)	plural	(sing.)	plural	(sing.)	plural
nom.	(ber)	ber	(hús)	hús	(barn)	börn	(land)	lönd
	berry		*house*		*child*		*country*	
acc.		ber		hús		börn		lönd
dat.		berjum		húsum		börnum		löndum
gen.		berja		húsa		barna		landa

Language notes

• Note that in words which have **a** as a stem vowel the **a** changes to **ö** in the nominative and accusative plural, although no ending beginning with **u** is added. This is for historical reasons: there used to be a **u** ending in these case forms.

• In some words that have **e** as a stem vowel, a **j** is inserted before the endings in the dative and genitive plural.

Some strong neuter nouns have an irregular declension in the plural:

	(singular)		plural
nom.	(hundrað)	*hundred*	hundruð
acc.			hundruð
dat.			hundruðum
gen.			hundraða

Declension of the neuter plural definite article

We've learnt the declension of the definite article in the neuter singular (see Unit 11). Now we will learn the forms of the definite article in the neuter plural.

nominative	-(i)n
accusative	-(i)n
dative	-num
genitive	-nna

Note that the **i** in the nominative and accusative is dropped when preceded by a vowel.

Weak neuter nouns

nominative	augun	*the eyes*
accusative	augun	
dative	augunum	
genitive	augnanna	

Strong neuter nouns

nominative	hús**in**	*the houses*	börn**in**	*the children*
accusative	hús**in**		börn**in**	
dative	húsu**num**		börnu**num**	
genitive	húsa**nna**		barna**nna**	

Language notes

- As with feminine and masculine nouns in the plural, the **m** in the ending of the noun in the dative is dropped before the article is added, e.g. augu<u>m</u> → augu + num; húsu<u>m</u> → húsu + num.

Pronunciation

- As with the definite feminine and masculine nouns in the plural, the **u** in the ending of the neuter noun in the dative plural normally changes in speech to **o** before the article, so **augunum** is pronounced in everyday speech **aug<u>o</u>num**, **húsunum** is pronounced **hús<u>o</u>num** etc. This is never written.

Tip

- Mnemonic help: the dative and genitive forms of the definite article are the same in the feminine, masculine and neuter.

Declension of numbers

The numbers *one, two, three* and *four* change their form according to the gender (masculine, feminine or neuter) and case (nominative, accusative, dative, genitive) of the noun they describe. We've learnt these numbers in the nominative singular in all genders (see Unit 6). Now we will look at the other case forms.

	m.	f.	n.
nominative	einn (maður)	ein (kona)	eitt (barn)
accusative	einn	eina	eitt
dative	einum	einni	einu
genitive	eins	einnar	eins

	m.	f.	n.	m.	f.	n.	m.	f.	n.
nominative	tveir	tvær	tvö	þrír	þrjár	þrjú	fjórir	fjórar	fjögur
accusative	tvo	tvær	tvö	þrjá	þrjár	þrjú	fjóra	fjórar	fjögur
dative		tveim(ur)			þrem(ur)			fjórum	
genitive		tveggja			þriggja			fjögurra	

Tip

- **Einn** (masculine) is declined like **hann**: nom. **hann**, acc. **hann**, dat. **honum**, gen. **hans**.
- **Ein** (feminine) is declined like **hún**: nom. **hún**, acc. **hana**, dat. **henni**, gen. **hennar**.
- The declension of **tveir**, **þrír** and **fjórir** is similar to the declension of **þeir**, the declension of **tvær**, **þrjár** and **fjórar** is similar to the declension of **þær** and the declension of **tvö**, **þrjú** and **fjögur** is similar to the declension of **þau**.

Practice

1   Translate these sentences into Icelandic using reflexive pronouns (**mig, þig, sig …**).

   a Ólafur is practising reading Russian.
   b What did you have to eat? (*lit.* What did you get yourself to eat?)
   c I had a sandwich with butter and apples. (*lit.* I got myself … .)
   d He shaved this morning (*lit.* He shaved himself.)

2   Match the questions with the answers.

   a Hvað hefurðu farið til margra stórborga?
   b Hvað hefurðu farið til margra landa?
   c Hvað lastu margar bækur í fyrra?
   d Hvað áttu margar vinkonur?
   e Áttu börn?
   f Áttu systur?
   g Áttu bræður?
   h Áttu bíl?

   i   Ég á þrjár vinkonur.
   ii Ég hef farið til Englands, Hollands, Frakklands og Þýskalands.
   iii Já, ég á bíl.
   iv Ég hef farið til þriggja stórborga: London, New York og Amsterdam.
   v   Ég las fjórar bækur í fyrra.
   vi Já, ég á tvo bræður.
   vii Já, ég á tvö börn.
   viii Já, ég á tvær systur.

---

stórborg (f.)   *big city*
margra, margar, mörg, marga   *many*

▶ 3 What would you say in Icelandic in the following situations?

a Ask if you can have a glass of water.
b You're sitting at a dinner table. Ask somebody politely if they can pass you the butter.
c You've just had a meal that somebody else cooked. (i) What do you say when you leave the table? (ii) What would the cook's response be?

4 Answer these questions, using whole sentences.

a Borðarðu oft epli? (Use **oft** in your answer.) En appelsínur? (Use **mjög sjaldan** in your answer.)
b Færðu þér stundum ís með jarðarberjum? (Use **oft** in your answer.)
c Hefurðu smakkað ís með bláberjum? (Use **aldrei** in your answer.)
d Borðarðu oft grænmeti? (Use **mjög oft** in your answer.)
e Hvaða grænmeti borðarðu oftast?

sjaldan *seldom*		**stundum** *sometimes*	
smakka (+ acc., Group 1) *taste*		**oftast** *most often*	

▶ 5 Fill in the correct forms of the past participle adjectives (the verb is given in brackets).

a Hann er _____ (byrja) að kenna ensku.
b Er hún _____ (sofna)?
c Hann er vel _____ (þekkja) maður.
d Er Anna hérna? Nei, hún er _____ (fara) heim.
e Það er _____ (gleyma).

15

ertu til í að koma í bíó?
do you want to go to the cinema?

In this unit you will learn
- about making plans
- about going to the cinema

Language points
- the verb **að langa** (*to want*) in the present and in the past tense
- the declension of adjectives
- the declension of the indefinite pronoun **einhver** (*somebody, some*)

▶ Ertu til í að koma í bíó? *Do you want to go to the cinema?*

Björn hringir í Gunnar, besta vin sinn.

Gunnar	Halló?
Björn	Blessaður!
Gunnar	Blessaður!
Björn	Ætlarðu að gera eitthvað í kvöld?
Gunnar	Nei, ekkert sérstakt – bara slappa af og horfa á sjónvarpið.
Björn	Við Christof ætlum að fara í bíó – ertu til í að koma með?
Gunnar	Já, á hvaða mynd ætlið þið að fara?
Björn	Við erum ekki búnir að ákveða það. Það eru margar góðar myndir í bíó núna.
Gunnar	Já, nýja spennumyndin í Háskólabíói er örugglega mjög góð.
Björn	Já, svo er líka komin ný mynd með Keanu Reeves – hún er örugglega rosalega góð.

vera til í að gera eitthvað   *be up for doing something*
bíó (acc., n.)   *cinema*
ekkert   *nothing*
sérstakt (n., from **sérstakur**)   *special*
slappa af (Group 1)   *relax*
horfa á (+ acc. Group 2 (**ð**))   *watch (something)*
sjónvarpið (acc. from **sjónvarp**, n.)   *television*
við Christof   *Christof and I*
fara í bíó   *go to the cinema*
koma með   *come with (us)*
á hvaða mynd ætlið þið að fara?   *which film are you going to see? (lit. on which film plan you to go to?)*
mynd (acc., f.)   *film* (short for **bíómynd**)
við erum ekki búnir að ákveða það   *we haven't decided*
ákveða (+ acc.)   *decide*
margar   *many*
nýja   *new*
spennumynd (f.)   *action film, thriller*
Háskólabíó (n.)   *the university cinema*
örugglega   *most likely, probably*
svo er líka komin ný mynd   *then there's also a new film out* (lit. *then has also come new film*)
kominn   *(has) come, arrived*
rosalega   *very, extremely*

▶ Förum á spennumyndina *Let's go and see the action film*

Christof Ertu búinn að tala við Gunnar?
Björn Já, hann er til í að koma í bíó.
Christof Á hvaða mynd eigum við að fara?
Björn Gunnar langaði að sjá nýju spennmyndina í Háskólabíói.
Christof Já, ég var einmitt að lesa um hana í Mogganum í dag – hún er örugglega góð.
Björn Ókei, förum á hana.
Christof Ætlaði Guðrún að koma með okkur?
Björn Ég ætla að hringja í hana og gá hvað hún er að gera.

---

langaði (from **langa**) *wanted*
sjá (+ acc.) *see*
einmitt *just*
Mogganum (dat. from **Moggi**, m.) short for **Morgunblaðið** – one of Iceland's main newspapers
gá (Group 2 (ð)) *check*

▶ Við komum eftir hálftíma *We'll come in half an hour*

Björn Hæ!
Guðrún Hæ, hvað segirðu?
Björn Allt fínt. Hvað ertu að gera?
Guðrún Ekkert sérstakt – bara að hlusta á útvarpið og taka aðeins til.
Björn Ég ætla að fara í bíó með Christof og Gunnari núna á eftir. Viltu koma með okkur?
Guðrún Já, á hvaða mynd ætlið þið?
Björn Nýju spennmyndina í Háskólabíói.
Guðrún Já, ókei.
Björn Við getum komið og náð í þig. Ertu tilbúin núna?
Guðrún Já, ég verð tilbúin eftir tuttugu mínútur.
Björn Ókei, við komum eftir svona hálftíma að ná í þig.

---

hálftíma (acc. from **hálftími**, m.) *half an hour*
hlusta á útvarpið (acc. from **útvarp**, n.) *listen to the radio*
taka til *tidy up*
aðeins *a little bit*
á eftir *later, later on*
ég verð tilbúin *I'll be ready*
svona *about*

Grammar

The irregular verb *að langa* (*to want*) in the present and past tenses

The verb **að langa** is an impersonal verb, which always takes a subject in the accusative. Remember that impersonal verbs have only **one form** for all persons in the present tense, and one form in the past tense.

að langa *to want*		
accusative	*present*	*past*
mig	langar	langaði
þig	langar	langaði
hann / hana / það	langar	langaði
okkur	langar	langaði
ykkur	langar	langaði
þá / þær / þau	langar	langaði
past participle: langa**ð**		

Declension of adjectives

Adjectives change their gender (masculine, feminine or neuter), number (singular or plural) and case (nominative, accusative, dative or genitive) according to the form of the noun they describe or qualify. There are two kinds of declension of adjectives – weak and strong declension.

Weak declension

The adjective is weak when it is used:

1 with a definite noun or a proper name.
    gamli maður<u>inn</u>   *the old man*
    <u>Guðrún</u> litla   *young Guðrún,*
                    lit. *small Guðrún*

2 with a demonstrative pronoun.
    <u>þessi</u> gamli maður   *this old man*

The declension of the weak adjectives is shown in the table at the top of page 153. The endings (in bold) are added to the stem.

good	masculine	feminine	neuter
singular nom.	góði	góða	góða
acc.	góða	góðu	góða
dat.	góða	góðu	góða
gen.	góða	góðu	góða
plural nom.	góðu	góðu	góðu
acc.	góðu	góðu	góðu
dat.	góðu	góðu	góðu
gen.	góðu	góðu	góðu

Language notes

- Note that the **a** to **ö** sound change rule (u-umlaut rule) also applies to adjectives.
- Remember that in adjectives ending in -(l)l (such as **gamall**), the last l is an ending and the first l is part of the stem; similarly in adjectives ending in -(n)n (such as **brúnn**) the last **n** is an ending and the first **n** is part of the stem (see Unit 4). Notice also that in the adjective **gamall** the second **a** is dropped before an ending beginning with a vowel is added (e.g. **gamli** (masc. nom. sing.), **gamla** (masc. acc. sing.), **gömlu** (masc. nom. pl.)). Remember that for all words ending in -(al)l the **a** is dropped before an ending beginning with a vowel is added (see **gaffall** (*fork*) in Unit 13).

Tip – In the singular the masculine endings are the same as for weak masculine nouns, the feminine endings are the same as for weak feminine nouns and the neuter endings are the same as for weak neuter nouns.

Strong declension

The adjective is strong when it is used:

1 with an indefinite noun.

Þetta er góð**ur** ostur.   *This is good cheese.*

2 after the verb **að vera**.

Maðurinn <u>er</u> ljóshærð**ur**.   *The man is blond.*

Here we will only look at the strong declension of adjectives ending in **-ur** in the masculine nominative singular, and of adjectives which are without an ending in the masculine nominative singular (stems ending in **-r** or **-s**). They are declined as follows:

English		masculine	feminine	neuter
singular	nom.	enskur	ensk	enskt
	acc.	enskan	enska	enskt
	dat.	enskum	enskri	ensku
	gen.	ensks	enskrar	ensks
plural	nom.	enskir	enskar	ensk
	acc.	enska	enskar	ensk
	dat.	enskum	enskum	enskum
	gen.	enskra	enskra	enskra

Language notes

- Adjectives which have no ending in the masculine nominative singular are, for example, **stór** (*big*), **kurteis** (*polite*), **hress** (*fun*), **vitlaus** (*stupid*), **dýr** (*expensive*).

thin		masculine	feminine	neuter
singular	nom.	grannur	grönn	grannt
	acc.	grannan	granna	grannt
	dat.	grönnum	grannri	grönnu
	gen.	granns	grannrar	granns
plural	nom.	grannir	grannar	grönn
	acc.	granna	grannar	grönn
	dat.	grönnum	grönnum	grönnum
	gen.	grannra	grannra	grannra

- The **u-umlaut sound change rule** applies here: **a** in the stressed syllable changes to **ö**. The u-umlaut rule always applies when an ending beginning with **u** is added, and also in the feminine singular nominative and neuter plural nominative and accusative for historical reasons – these forms used to have a **u** ending.

- Adjectives with a stem ending in -**ð** have irregular forms in the neuter nominative and accusative singular: the **ð** of the stem changes to **t** before the ending **t** is added, and the adjective therefore ends in -**tt** (see underlined words in the table below).

good		masculine	feminine	neuter
singular	nom.	góður	góð	<u>gott</u>
	acc.	góðan	góða	<u>gott</u>
	dat.	góðum	góðri	góðu
	gen.	góðs	góðrar	góðs

plural	nom.	góðir	góðar	góð
	acc.	góða	góðar	góð
	dat.	góðum	góðum	góðum
	gen.	góðra	góðra	góðra

- Examples of other adjectives with a stem ending in -ð are **síður** (*long*), **rauður** (*red*).

Declension of past participle adjectives

The weak and strong declension patterns also apply to past participle adjectives ending in -ur, such as **ruglaður** (*confused*), **sofnaður** (*fallen asleep*), **byrjaður** (*begun*). However, some of the past participle adjectives are not used in a weak declension and are only used in the nominative in the strong declension (such as **byrjaður** (*begun*): maðurinn er byrjaður, konan er byrjuð, barnið er byrjað, mennirnir eru byrjaðir, konurnar eru byrjaðar, börnin eru byrjuð).

Weak declension

confused		**masculine**	**feminine**	**neuter**
singular	nom.	ruglaði	rugluða	rugluða
	acc.	rugluða	rugluðu	rugluða
	dat.	rugluða	rugluðu	rugluða
	gen.	rugluða	rugluðu	rugluða
plural	nom.	rugluðu	rugluðu	rugluðu
	acc.	rugluðu	rugluðu	rugluðu
	dat.	rugluðu	rugluðu	rugluðu
	gen.	rugluðu	rugluðu	rugluðu

Note – Remember the **u-umlaut sound change rule:** a changes to u in unstressed syllables when an ending beginning with u is added (see Unit 4).

Strong declension

confused		**masculine**	**feminine**	**neuter**
singular	nom.	ruglaður	rugluð	ruglað
	acc.	ruglaðan	rugluða	ruglað
	dat.	rugluðum	ruglaðri	rugluðu
	gen.	ruglaðs	ruglaðrar	ruglaðs

plural	nom.	ruglaðir	ruglaðar	rugluð
	acc.	rugluða	ruglaðar	rugluð
	dat.	rugluðum	rugluðum	rugluðum
	gen.	ruglaðra	ruglaðra	ruglaðra

Language notes

- Here the u-umlaut rule is also at work: **a** changes to **u** in unstressed syllables before an ending beginning with u, and in the feminine singular nominative and neuter plural nominative and accusative for historical reasons – these forms used to have a **u** ending.
- Note that the ending -**t** is not added in the neuter nominative and accusative singular.

Declension of *einhver* (*somebody, some*)

The indefinite pronoun **einhver** means *somebody, some* and the form **eitthvað** means *something, some*. It is declined as follows:

		masculine	feminine	neuter
singular nom.		einhver	einhver	eitthvað
		somebody, some		*something, some*
	acc.	einhvern	einhverja	eitthvað
	dat.	einhverjum	einhverri	einhverju
	gen.	einhvers	einhverrar	einhvers
plural	nom.	einhverjir	einhverjar	einhver
	acc.	einhverja	einhverjar	einhver
	dat.	einhverjum	einhverjum	einhverjum
	gen.	einhverra	einhverra	einhverra

Language note

The endings are the same as for strong adjectives ending in -**ur** in the masculine nominative singular (except that in the masculine accusative singular the ending is -**n** instead of -**an**, and in the neuter nominative and accusative singular the ending -**t** is not added).

Practice

1   a   Ask your friend if he / she is doing something this evening.
    b   Ask your friend if he / she wants to go to the cinema.
    c   Let's assume that he / she says 'yes'. Ask which film you should see.

2 Look back at the dialogues in this unit and try to answer these questions.

a Hringir Björn í Gunnar?
b Langar Gunnar að fara í bíó?
c Í hvaða bíói er myndin sem Gunnar vill sjá?
d Hvernig mynd er það?
e Hvað heitir aðalleikarinn í myndinni sem Björn nefnir?
f Vill Guðrún líka fara í bíó?
g Ætla strákarnir að ná í hana?

---

aðal- *main*
nefna (Group 2, **d**) *name, mention*
strákarnir *the guys*

▶ **3** Fill in the correct forms of the adjectives in brackets.

a Fiskibollurnar voru rosalega _____ (góður).
b Kennararnir voru mjög _____ (góður).
c Þekkirðu _____ (enskur) strákana?
d Talaðirðu við _____ (ítalskur) konuna?
e Hún hitti mjög _____ (hress) stráka.
f Þetta voru rosalega _____ (stór) bílar.
g Konurnar voru svo _____ (vitlaus).
h Ég skrifaði _____ (danskur) manninum bréf.

▶ **4** Try to work out what the questions might have been that prompted the following answers. (Use different forms of **einhver**.)

a **A** _____
  B Í kvöld? Já, ég ætla að fara í bíó.

b **A** _____
  B Já, það eru margar góðar myndir í bíó núna. Það er til dæmis (*for example*) ný spennumynd með Harrison Ford í Háskólabíói.

16

Guðrún á afmæli

it's Guðrún's birthday

In this unit you will learn
- to say how old you are
- to say when your birthday is
- how to wish somebody a happy birthday
- the names of the months, seasons, high days and holidays
- to say what date it is

Language points
- the irregular verb **að þurfa** (*to need, have to*) in the present and the past tense
- more about declension of adjectives
- the declension of possessive pronouns
- ordinal numbers and their declension

▶ Guðrún á afmæli á morgun *It's*
Guðrún's birthday tomorrow

Björn og Christof eru að tala saman.

Björn   Guðrún á afmæli á morgun.
Christof Já, er það? Hvað verður hún gömul?
Björn   27 ára. Hún ætlar að bjóða okkur og nokkrum vinum sínum í mat annað kvöld.
Christof Já, flott. Ég þarf þá að kaupa handa henni afmælisgjöf í dag. Veistu hvað hún vill fá í afmælisgjöf?
Björn   Kannski geisladisk eða einhverja bók. Ég skal tala við hana á eftir og komast að því hvað hún vill.
Christof Hvað ætlar þú að gefa henni?
Björn   Ég ætla að gefa henni peysu og eyrnalokka.

---

afmæli (n.)   *birthday*
Hvað verður hún gömul?   *How old will she be?* (lit. *what will be she old?*)
27 ára (gen. pl. from **ár**, n.)   *27 years old* (lit. *27 years*)
að bjóða (+ dat. and + acc.)   *invite*
nokkrum vinum sínum   *a few of her friends*
í mat   *to dinner*
þarf (from **þurfa**)   *need*
þá   *then*
handa henni (**handa** + dat.)   *for her*
afmælisgjöf (f., acc.)   *birthday present*
veistu (from **vita**)   *do you know*
fá í afmælisgjöf   *get as a birthday present, get for one's birthday*
geisladisk (acc. from **geisladiskur**, m.)   *CD*
á eftir   *later on*
komast að því (**komast að** + dat.)   *find it out*
gefa (+ dat. and + acc.)   *give*
peysu (acc. from **peysa**, f.)   *sweater, jumper*
eyrnalokka (acc. pl. from **eyrnalokkur**, m.)   *earrings*

Language notes

• Note that you use the verb **að eiga** (*to own*, *have*) with **afmæli**, as in **einhver á afmæli** (*it's somebody's birthday*, lit. *somebody has a birthday*).

- The verb **að gefa** is one of the verbs which take two objects, one in the dative and one in the accusative.

Ég ætla að gefa henni (dat.) bók (acc.).	*I'm going to give her a book.*
Við ætlum að gefa Guðmundi (dat.) hund (acc.).	*We're going to give Guðmundur a dog.*

▶ Til hamingju með afmælið! *Happy birthday!*

Ásta kemur í heimsókn til Guðrúnar með pakka.

Ásta   Til hamingju með afmælið!
Guðrún   Takk!
Ásta   Hérna er smá pakki frá mér og mömmu og pabba.
Guðrún   Takk!
Ásta   Ertu búin að fá margar afmælisgjafir?
Guðrún   Já, ég fékk skó frá mömmu og pabba, bók frá Gísla bróður, trefil og vettlinga frá Önnu vinkonu …
Ásta   Hvað fékkstu frá Birni?
Guðrún   Peysu og silfureyrnalokka. Eyrnalokkarnir eru rosalega flottir!

9. sept.

Þú átt
afmæli í dag

Elsku Guðrún,
Innilegar
hamingjuóskir
með afmælið.

Ásta

til hamingju   *congratulations*
smá   *a little*
pakki (m.)   *present, parcel*
margar   *many*
skó (acc. pl. from **skór**, m.)   *shoes*
trefil (acc. from **trefill**, m.)   *winter scarf*
vettlinga (acc. pl. from **vettlingur**, m.)   *mittens*
silfureyrnalokka (acc. pl. from **silfureyrnalokkur**, m.)   *silver earrings*
flottir (from **flottur**)   *beautiful, great, cool*
elsku   *dear*
innilegar (from **innilegur**)   *warm, hearty*
hamingjuóskir (pl. from **hamingjuósk**, f.)   *congratulations*
  (lit. *wishes of happiness*)

Language notes

- Note that you can use **til hamingju** in many situations, for example if somebody gets a promotion, a scholarship, passes their driving test, etc.
- Note that the word **elsku** is used with names (such as **elsku Guðrún, elsku Björn**) if there is a close relationship between the two people. It is more affectionate than English *dear*.

▶ Hvað eru þau gömul og hvenær eiga þau afmæli? *How old are they and when are their birthdays?*

Hvað eru þau gömul?

Guðrún er 27 ára gömul.
Björn er 26 ára gamall.
Christof er líka 26 ára gamall.
Kristín, systir Björns, er 38 ára gömul.
Þór, maður Kristínar, er 42 ára gamall.
Ásta, dóttir þeirra, er 14 ára. Hún verður 15 ára eftir þrjá mánuði.
Inga, mamma Björns og Kristínar, er 62 ára.

Hvenær eiga þau afmæli?

Guðrún á afmæli 9. september.
Björn á afmæli 20. maí.
Christof á afmæli 2. mars.
Kristín á afmæli 25. janúar.
Þór á afmæli 10. júlí.
Ásta á afmæli 4. desember.

Inga á afmæli 24. febrúar.

Ástu finnst ekki gaman að eiga afmæli að vetri til. Í byrjun desember er hún líka alltaf að lesa fyrir próf, og hefur því ekki tíma til að halda upp á afmælið sitt.

Hvað eru þau gömul?   *How old are they?*, (lit. *What are they old?*)
27 ára gömul   *27 years old*
september   *September*
maí   *May*
mars   *March*
janúar   *January*
júlí   *July*
desember   *December*
febrúar   *February*
finnst ekki gaman   *doesn't like* (lit. *thinks it is not nice*)
að vetri til   *in the winter*
í byrjun (from **byrjun**, f.)   *at / in the beginning*
lesa fyrir próf (from **próf**, acc. pl., n.)   *read for exams*
því   *therefore*
hefur ekki tíma   *hasn't got time*
tíma (acc. from **tími**, m.)   *time*
til að   *to*
halda upp á afmælið sitt   *celebrate her birthday*

Note – In everyday language you would leave out **gamall / gömul** and just say **Hann / Hún er 27 (ára)**.

Grammar

The irregular verb *að þurfa* (*to need, have to*) in the present tense and the past tense

að þurfa	to need	
	present	*past*
ég	þarf	þurfti
þú	þarft	þurftir
hann	þarf	þurfti
við	þurf**um**	þurft**um**
þið	þurf**ið**	þurft**uð**
þeir	þurf**a**	þurft**u**
past participle: þurft		

Note – The plural present tense is regular as for all verbs (there are a few exceptions). The past tense is regular: stem + ending from Group 2 of regular verbs.

More about the declension of adjectives

We've learnt the weak declension of all adjectives and the strong declension of adjectives ending in **-ur** in the masculine nominative singular (like **enskur** – *English*) and of adjectives which are without an ending in the masculine nominative singular (stems ending in **-r** or **-s**, like **stór** – *big*; **kurteis** – *polite*) (see Unit 15). Now we will learn the strong declension of all other adjectives (ending in **-r**, **-n**, **-l**, **-inn** in the masculine nominative singular).

Strong adjectives ending in **-r** in the masculine nominative singular are declined as follows:

blue		masculine	feminine	neuter
singular	**nom.**	blár	blá	blá**tt**
	acc.	blá**an**	blá**a**	blá**tt**
	dat.	blá**um**	blá**rr**i	blá**u**
	gen.	blá**s**	blá**rr**ar	blá**s**
plural	**nom.**	blá**ir**	blá**ar**	blá
	acc.	blá**a**	blá**ar**	blá
	dat.	blá**um**	blá**um**	blá**um**
	gen.	blá**rr**a	blá**rr**a	blá**rr**a

Language notes

- Note that adjectives ending in **-r** in the masculine nominative singular are declined like adjectives ending in **-ur** and adjectives without an ending in the masculine nominative singular except that an extra **r** is added before endings beginning with an **r** and an extra **t** before the neuter singular ending **-t**. In the list above the endings in bold are the same for adjectives ending in **-r** and adjectives ending in **-ur** / adjectives without an ending. The **r** and **t** which are added here before the endings are underlined.

- Other adjectives which are declined like **blár** are: **hár** (*tall*), **grár** (*grey*), **opinskár** (*outspoken, frank*), **mjór** (*thin*).

Strong adjectives ending in **-n** in the masculine nominative singular are declined as follows. Remember that adjectives which have the ending **-n** in the masculine nominative singular always have another **n** immediately preceding the ending **n** (the first **n** belongs to the stem).

brown		masculine	feminine	neuter
singular	**nom.**	brúnn	brún	brúnt
	acc.	brúnan	brúna	brúnt
	dat.	brúnum	brún<u>n</u>i	brúnu
	gen.	brúns	brún<u>n</u>ar	brúns
plural	**nom.**	brúnir	brúnar	brún
	acc.	brúna	brúnar	brún
	dat.	brúnum	brúnum	brúnum
	gen.	brún<u>n</u>a	brún<u>n</u>a	brún<u>n</u>a

Pronunciation

Remember that the letters **nn** are pronounced as **dn** when preceded by a letter with a superscript mark (**í, ý, é, á, ú, ó**) or by a diphthong (**æ, ei, ey, au**). **Brúnn** is therefore pronounced as if it were spelt **brúdn**. Similarly, **brúnni, brúnnar** and **brúnna** are pronounced **brúdni, brúdnar** and **brúdna**.

Language notes

- Adjectives ending in -**n** in the masculine nominative singular are declined like adjectives ending in -**ur** / adjectives without an ending in the masculine nominative singular except that if the ending begins with an **r**, it is replaced by **n**. Again in the list above, the endings in bold are the same for all adjectives (those ending in -**r**, -**ur** or with no ending in the masculine nominative singular) and the cases where **n** replaces **r** in the endings are underlined.

Strong adjectives ending in -**l** in the masculine nominative singular are declined as follows. Remember that adjectives which have the ending -**l** in the masculine nominative singular always have another **l** immediately preceding the ending **l** (the first **l** belongs to the stem).

old		masculine	feminine	neuter
singular	**nom.**	gamall	gömul	gamalt
	acc.	gaml**an***	gaml**a***	gamalt
	dat.	gömlum	gamal<u>l</u>i	gömlu
	gen.	gamals	gamal<u>l</u>ar	gamals
plural	**nom.**	gaml**ir***	gaml**ar***	gömul
	acc.	gaml**a***	gaml**ar**	gömul
	dat.	gömlum	gömlum*	gömlum*
	gen.	gamal<u>l</u>a	gamal<u>l</u>a	gamal<u>l</u>a

Here the **u-umlaut sound change rule** applies: a in the unstressed syllable changes to **u** and a in the stressed syllable changes to **ö**. Remember that the u-umlaut rule applies in the feminine singular nominative and neuter plural nominative and accusative for historical reasons – these forms used to have a **u** ending. Remember also that for all words ending in -(al)l the a in -(al)l is dropped before an ending beginning with a vowel is added (see Units 13 and 15); e.g. in **gamlan** in the masculine singular accusative the a is dropped because the ending (-**an**) begins with a vowel (**gamal** + -**an** becomes **gamlan**) – this is marked with a * in the table above. The adjective **gamall** has regular endings, except that when the ending begins with r, it is replaced by l (in the same way as r at the beginning of the ending is replaced by n in the declension of **brúnn**). The cases where l replaces r in the endings are underlined above.

Strong adjectives ending in -**inn** in the masculine nominative singular are declined as follows (note that the ending is really -**n** and the -**in**- belongs to the stem: the stem of **feiminn** is for example **feimin**):

shy	**masculine**	**feminine**	**neuter**
singular nom.	feim**inn**	feim**in**	feim**ið**
acc.	feim**inn**	feim**na**	feim**ið**
dat.	feim**num**	feim**inni**	feim**nu**
gen.	feim**ins**	feim**innar**	feim**ins**
plural nom.	feim**nir**	feim**nar**	feim**in**
acc.	feim**na**	feim**nar**	feim**in**
dat.	feim**num**	feim**num**	feim**num**
gen.	feim**inna**	feim**inna**	feim**inna**

Language notes

• The endings in the masculine are the same as for the definite article in the masculine, the endings in the feminine are the same as for the definite article in the feminine and the endings in the neuter are the same as for the definite article in the neuter (exceptions: in the genitive plural the ending is -**inna** instead of -**nna** as for the definite article, and sometimes the initial i in the ending is left off (although there is no vowel preceding)).

• Note that this strong declension pattern for adjectives ending in -**inn** in the masculine nominative singular also applies to past participle adjectives ending in -**inn**, such as **orðinn** (*become*), **búinn** (*finished*) (**búinn** in the verb construction vera búinn að gera eitthvað is a past participle adjective), dáinn (*died*). Note that these past participle adjectives are not used in a weak declension, and some of them (such as orðinn, búinn) are only used in the nominative in the strong declension.

Adjectives ending in -*andi*

Some adjectives end in -andi and they are not declined, i.e. they do not change their form according to gender, number or case.

Konan er aðlaðandi.	*The woman is attractive.*
Maðurinn er heillandi.	*The man is charming.*
Ég hitti mjög aðlaðandi konu.	*I met a very attractive woman.*
Ég hitti mjög heillandi mann.	*I met a very charming man.*

Declension of possessive pronouns

The possessive pronouns minn (*my*) and þinn (*your*) are declined in the same way.

		masculine	feminine	neuter
singular	**nom.**	minn	mín	mitt
	acc.	minn	mína	mitt
	dat.	mínum	minni	mínu
	gen.	míns	minnar	míns
plural	**nom.**	mínir	mínar	mín
	acc.	mína	mínar	mín
	dat.	mínum	mínum	mínum
	gen.	minna	minna	minna

Note – These are like strong adjectives ending in -**n** in the masculine nominative singular, except for the masculine accusative singular (minn) and neuter nominative and accusative singular (mitt) forms (underlined above).

In the first person singular you use the possessive pronoun minn (*my, mine*) and in the second person singular you use the possessive pronoun þinn (*your, yours*). The gender of the possessive pronoun depends on the gender of what is owned:

Ég kom með manninum (*masc.*) mínum (*masc.*) / þínum (*masc.*).	*I came with my / your husband.*
Hittirðu konuna (*fem.*) mína (*fem.*) / þína (*fem.*)?	*Did you meet my / your wife?*

Er þetta glasið (*neut.*) **mitt** (*neut.*) /   *Is this my / your*
þitt (*neut.*)?   *glass?*

For other persons there are no specific possessive pronouns, so the genitive forms of the relevant personal pronoun are used (and they are then indeclinable):

third person singular	**hans** (*his*)
	hennar (*her, hers*)
	þess (*its*) – seldom used
first person plural	**okkar** (*our, ours*)
second person plural	**ykkar** (*your, yours*)
third person plural	**þeirra** (*their, theirs*)

Bíllinn **hans** er flottur.   *His car is great.*
Hittirðu konuna **hans**?   *Did you meet his wife?*
Barnið **hans** er 3 ára.   *His child is 3 years old.*

Pabbi **okkar** heitir Einar.   *Our father's name is Einar.*
Þekkirðu mömmu **okkar**?   *Do you know our mother?*
Húsið **okkar** er grátt.   *Our house is grey.*

There is also a reflexive possessive pronoun in Icelandic, **sinn**, which refers to the subject of the sentence and can be translated as 'his own, her own'. It is declined like **minn** and **þinn**, and its gender depends on the gender of what is owned:

Anna hringdi í pabba **sinn**.   *Anne rang her father.*
Hún talaði við mömmu **sína**.   *She spoke to her mother.*
Hún fór með barninu **sínu**.   *She went with her child.*

Notice the difference in meaning between **Anna talaði við mömmu hennar** (not *Anna's mum*) and **Anna talaði við mömmu sína** (*Anna's mum*).

Remember that we've already learnt the reflexive pronoun **sig**, which also refers to the subject of the sentence (see Unit 14). The difference between the two is that **sinn** is a possessive pronoun and is used when you're talking about somebody owning something.

▶ Giving somebody's age

The genitive forms of numerals are used to give somebody's age. Note however that only the numbers 1, 2, 3 and 4 have genitive forms, so you only have to think about putting the number in the genitive form when the person is 1, 2, 3 or 4 years old, or if the number ends in 1, 2, 3 or 4 (such as 21, 32 ...). We've already learnt the genitive forms of 1, 2, 3 and 4 (see Unit 14) but they are repeated here for convenience:

	masculine	**feminine**	**neuter**
genitive	eins	einnar	eins

tveggja
þriggja
fjögurra

For the number 1 there are three forms for the three genders and here you use the neuter form **eins**, because the noun **ár** is neuter. Note also that if the number ends in 1 then you use the genitive singular form of **ár** – **árs**, but otherwise the genitive plural form of **ár** – **ára**.

Hann er **fimmtíu og eins**   *He is 51 years old.*
   árs gamall.
Hún er **tuttugu og þriggja**   *She is 23 years old.*
   ára gömul.
Barnið er **tveggja ára** gamalt. *The child is two years old.*
Hann er **fimmtíu og fimm**   *He is 55 years old.*
   ára gamall.

Note that for masculine nouns / pronouns you use the masculine form of the adjective **gamall**, for feminine nouns / pronouns you use the feminine form (**gömul**), and for neuter nouns / pronouns you use the neuter form (**gamalt**).

Summary of the production steps

1 If the year ends in 1, 2, 3 or 4, then put the number in the genitive (**eins, tveggja, þriggja, fjögurra**).
2 Put the year in the genitive (either **árs** (if the number ends in 1) or **ára**).
3 Use the right gender of the adjective: **gamall** (m.), **gömul** (f.), **gamalt** (n.) (note that **gamalt** is seldom used when talking about age – it's normally only used with **barn** (*child*)).

To say that someone is *twenty years old*, you can use the adjective **tvítug(ur)**, i.e. you can say either **Hann er tuttugu ára** or **Hann er tvítugur**. Similarly there are adjectives for *thirty years old*, *forty years old* etc.:

20 ára = tvítug(ur)   60 ára = sextug(ur)
30 ára = þrítug(ur)   70 ára = sjötug(ur)
40 ára = fertug(ur)   80 ára = áttræð(ur)
50 ára = fimmtug(ur)   90 ára = níræð(ur)

These adjectives are declined like normal adjectives ending in -**ur**:

Ég hitti þrítugan mann.   *I met a thirty-year-old man.*

Ordinal numbers and their declension

The ordinal numbers in English are *first, second, third* etc. They are in Icelandic:

1. fyrsti	11. ellefti	30. þrítugasti
2. annar	12. tólfti	40. fertugasti
3. þriðji	13. þrettándi	50. fimmtugasti
4. fjórði	14. fjórtándi	60. sextugasti
5. fimmti	15. fimmtándi	70. sjötugasti
6. sjötti	16. sextándi	80. áttugasti
7. sjöundi	17. sautjándi	90. nítugasti
8. áttundi	18. átjándi	100. hundraðasti
9. níundi	19. nítjándi	101. hundraðasti
10. tíundi	20. tuttugasti	og fyrsti
	21. tuttugasti	1000. þúsundasti
	og fyrsti	1001. þúsundasti
		og fyrsti

Ordinal numbers are declined exactly like weak adjectives (see Unit 15). There is one exception though, **annar** (*second*), which is declined as follows:

second	masculine	feminine	neuter
singular nom.	annar	önnur	annað
acc.	annan	aðra	annað
dat.	öðrum	annarri	öðru
gen.	annars	annarrar	annars
plural nom.	aðrir	aðrar	önnur
acc.	aðra	aðrar	önnur
dat.	öðrum	öðrum	öðrum
gen.	annarra	annarra	annarra

Note – Most of the endings are the same as for strong adjectives ending in -**ur** / adjectives with no ending in the masculine nominative singular, but what comes before the endings is irregular.

Months, seasons, high days and holidays
▶ Months

janúar	*January*	júlí	*July*
febrúar	*February*	ágúst	*August*
mars	*March*	september	*September*
apríl	*April*	október	*October*
maí	*May*	nóvember	*November*
júní	*June*	desember	*December*

Note – The names of the months are written without a capital letter.

mánuður (m.) *month*

í hvaða mánuði *in which month*
í mánuðinum *in this month*

Í hvaða mánuði hittirðu hana?

(In) Which month did you meet her?

Ætlarðu að heimsækja hana í mánuðinum?

Are you going to visit her this month?

High days and holidays

jól (n., pl.) *Christmas*

Gleðileg jól! *Merry Christmas!*
Jólin eru í desember
Jólin – þau eru ...

gamlárskvöld (n.)
  New Year's Eve

nýársdagur (m.)
  New Year's Day

Gleðilegt nýtt ár! Gleðilegt ár!
  Happy New Year!

páskar (m., pl.) *Easter*

Gleðilega páska! *Happy Easter!*
Páskarnir eru í mars eða apríl.
Páskarnir – þeir eru ...

▶ Seasons

vor (n.) *spring*
sumar (n.) *summer*
haust (n.) *autumn*
vetur (m.) *winter*

í vor *this / last spring*
í sumar *this / last summer*
í haust *this / last autumn*
í vetur *this / last winter*

Í vor fór ég til Þýskalands.

In the spring I went to Germany.

Í vor ætla ég að fara til Þýskalands.

In the spring I'm going to Germany.

Dates

Dates are used in either the nominative or the accusative. You use the nominative when you answer questions such as:

Hvaða mánaðardagur er í dag? — *What day of the month is it today?*

Í dag er 2. (annar) september. — *Today is the 2nd of September.*

Í gær var 1. (fyrsti) september. — *Yesterday was the 1st of September.*

Á morgun er 3. (þriðji) september. — *Tomorrow is the 3rd of September.*

You use the accusative when you're saying when something happened:

Ég á afmæli 2. (annan) ágúst. — *My birthday is on the 2nd of August.*

Við förum til Svíþjóðar 10. (tíunda) maí. — *We went to Sweden on the 10th of May.*

Hún kom til Reykjavíkur 3. (þriðja) mars. — *She came to Reykjavik on the 3rd of March.*

Practice

▶ 1 Work out what the questions were that prompted these answers. If you have the recording, try to answer the questions without looking at the book.

a Ég á afmæli tólfta september.
b Mamma á afmæli tuttugasta og fjórða febrúar. Pabbi á afmæli tíunda júlí.
c Já, einn – vinur minn á afmæli annan janúar.
d Ég er þrjátíu og sjö.
e Mamma er fimmtíu og sex en pabbi er sextíu og þriggja.
f Besti vinur minn er þrjátíu og fjögurra.
g Í dag er tuttugasti og annar febrúar.
h Í gær var tuttugasti og fyrsti febrúar. Í fyrradag var tuttugasti febrúar.
i Ég byrjaði að læra íslensku fjórða mars.
j Þau eru í desember.
k Þeir eru í mars eða apríl.

2 Look back at the dialogues in this unit and see if you can answer the following questions.

a Fékk Guðrún afmælisgjöf frá Ástu?
b Hvað fékk hún í afmælisgjöf frá Birni?
c Hvað fékk hún frá mömmu sinni og pabba?
d Ætlaði Christof að gefa henni eitthvað í afmælisgjöf?
e Hvenær á Christof afmæli? En Inga?

▶ 3 Say in Icelandic how old the following people are. If you have the recording, try this as a number dictation exercise.

a Gunnar is 52 years old.
b Anna is 40 years old.
c Þór is 23 years old.
d Ragnar is 19 years old.
e Kristín is 3 years old.
f Magnús is 74 years old.

▶ 4 Fill in the correct forms of the verb að þurfa.

a Hvað _____ (*present tense*) þú að gera á morgun?
b Ég _____ (*past tense*) að fara heim klukkan níu.
c Við _____ (*present tense*) að kaupa afmælisgjöf handa Önnu.

▶ 5 Fill in the correct forms of the possessive pronouns in brackets.

a Þetta er húsið _____ (minn).
b Hún var að tala við vinkonu _____ (sinn).
c Náðirðu í bílinn _____ (minn)?
d Hún ætlar að heimsækja ömmu _____ (sinn) á morgun.
e Borðaðirðu súkkulaðið _____ (minn)?
f Ég hitti kennarann _____ (þinn).

Congratulations on completing *Teach Yourself Icelandic*

I hope you have enjoyed working your way through the course. I am always keen to receive feedback from people who have used my course, so why not contact me and let me know your reactions? I'll be pleased to receive your praise, but I should also like to know if you think things could be improved. I always welcome comments and suggestions and I do my best to incorporate constructive suggestions into later editions.

You can contact me through the publishers at:

Teach Yourself Books, Hodder Headline, 338 Euston Road, London NW1 3BH.

I hope you will want to build up your knowledge of Icelandic and have made a few suggestions to help you do this in the section entitled **Taking it further** on pages 174–6.

All the best!

Hildur Jónsdóttir

taking it further

Books

These two books are written by experienced teachers of Icelandic for foreigners (and they are all native speakers of Icelandic).

- *Learning Icelandic* by Auður Einarsdóttir, Guðrún Theodórsdóttir, María Garðarsdóttir and Sigríður Þorvaldsdóttir, 2001, Mál og menning, Reykjavik. ISBN 9 979 31919 4 (comes with a CD-ROM).

- *Af stað – kennslubók í íslensku fyrir byrjendur* by Birna Arnbjörnsdóttir, Ingibjörg Hafstað and Helga Guðrún Loftsdóttir, 2003, Fjölmenning, Reykjavik. ISBN 9 979 95670 4.

A very good grammar book is:

- *Íslenska fyrir útlendinga – kennslubók í málfræði* by Ásta Svavarsdóttir and Margrét Jónsdóttir, 1998, Málvísindastofnun Háskóla Íslands, Reykjavik. ISBN 9 979 85341 7.

This book is written by experienced native Icelandic teachers of Icelandic to foreigners. It is written in Icelandic, and might therefore be difficult for beginners, but it is essential for more advanced students.

CD-ROMs

Scholars at *Stofnun Sigurðar Nordals* are also preparing teaching material, a CD-ROM, which will be available in shops soon (it is called *Small is beautiful*; see **www.nordals.hi.is** for further information). This material might also appear on the web later on.

Dictionaries

A very good and detailed English–Icelandic dictionary is:

• *Ensk-íslensk orðabók með alfræðilegu ívafi*, Jóhann S. Hannesson (ed.), 1984, Mál og menning, Reykjavik. ISBN 9 979 31651 9.

Another English–Icelandic dictionary which is very good, but not as thorough as the one above, is:

• *Ensk–íslensk skólaorðabók*, Jón Skaptason (ed.), 1998, Mál og menning, Reykjavik. ISBN 9 979 31699 3.

Two good Icelandic–English dictionaries are:

• *Íslensk–ensk orðabók*, Arngrímur Sigurðsson, 1994, Mál og menning, Reykjavik. ISBN 9 979 30688 2.

• *Íslensk–ensk orðabók*, Sverrir Hólmarsson, 1989, Iðunn, Reykjavik. ISBN 9 979 10049 4.

Quite good bilingual dictionaries (Icelandic to and from other European languages) are also available.

Websites

Orðabók Háskólans (**www.lexis.hi.is**) has on its homepage a database where the usage of Icelandic words is shown (this database is still under construction, but will in the future show the usage of all Icelandic words). *Íslensk málstöð* (**www.ismal.hi.is**) has on its homepage terminology glossaries. For more advanced students it is useful to know that you can also ring *Orðabók Háskólans* or *Íslensk málstöð* to ask about the meaning of words or their declension / conjugation.

There is some material for learning Icelandic on the web, but not all of it is good. Material developed for teaching Icelandic to foreigners is called *Bragi* (see **www.bragi.org**). Scholars from Háskóli Íslands are at the moment developing teaching material for Icelandic which will appear on the web (see **www.icelandic.hi.is** for further information).

Stofnun Sigurðar Nordals (see web address above) organizes summer courses in Icelandic for foreigners each year. *Náms-flokkar Reykjavíkur* (**www.namsflokkar.is**) and Endurmenntunar-stofnun Háskola Íslands (**www.endurmenntun.hi.is**) also organize Icelandic courses throughout the year.

You can order books from abroad from *Bóksala stúdenta* (**www.boksala.is**), Edda (**www.edda.is**) and Penninn (**www.penninn.is**).

You can listen to the following Icelandic radio stations on line: *Rás 1* (see **www.ruv.is**), *Rás 2* (see **www.ruv.is**), *Bylgjan* (see **www.bylgjan.is**) and *Fm 95.7* (see **www.fm957.is**). You can watch two Icelandic TV channels online: *Ríkissjónvarpið* (see **www.ruv.is**) and *Stöð 2* (see **www.stod2.is**).

Some books in Icelandic (such as Icelandic novels, Icelandic folk tales, the Bible, etc.) can be found on the web; see **www.snerpa.is/net**.

The following Icelandic newspapers are available on the web:

- *Morgunblaðið* (**www.mbl.is**)
- *Fréttablaðið* and *Dagblaðið Vísir* (**www.visir.is**)

www.onlinenewspapers.com/iceland.htm gives an up-to-date list of newspapers available online.

key to the exercises

Unit 1

1 Góðan dag! / Ég er frá Englandi. / Ég heiti Suzanna. En þú?
2 a Við heitum Jon og Markus. **b** Nei, við erum frá Svíþjóð.
3 Þýskaland (*Germany*), Sviss (*Switzerland*), Noregur (*Norway*), Pólland (*Polland*), Finnland (*Finland*), Svíþjóð (*Sweden*). **4** Chantal er frá Frakklandi. Pierre er frá Kanada. Rosario er frá Mexíkó. Timur er frá Tyrklandi. Sanjay er frá Indlandi. Atsuko er frá Japan. Tanya og Vadim eru frá Rússlandi. Inga er frá Íslandi.

Unit 2

1 Fyrirgefðu, talar þú / talarðu ensku? / Ég tala líka dönsku!
2 a Hann talar þýsku sem móðurmál, og hann talar líka ensku, spænsku og ítölsku – og svolitla íslensku. **b** Hún talar hollensku sem móðurmál, og hún talar líka ensku, þýsku og rússnesku – og svolitla íslensku, eins og Christof. **3** Góðan dag! Hvaðan ertu?; Hvaða tungumál talarðu? / Ég er frá Svíþjóð. Ég tala sænsku, norsku, dönsku, íslensku og ensku. *I am from Sweden. I speak Swedish, Norwegian, Danish, Icelandic and English.* **4 a** Hann talar íslensku, dönsku og sænsku. **b** Þau (þeir / þær) tala ekki ensku. **c** Hvaða tungumál talar hann? **d** Þau (þeir / þær) tala bara frönsku. **e** Talar Anna líka íslensku?

Unit 3

1 a Hún / Mamma mín heitir Marion. **b** Hann / Pabbi minn heitir Desmond. **c** Hún / Amma mín heitir Gladys. Hann / Afi minn heitir Terry. **d** Hann / Bróðir minn heitir Sean. Hún / Systir mín heitir Tracy. **2 a** iii **b** v **c** i **d** iv **e** ii **3 a** Gunnar er frá Íslandi. **b** Hann talar íslensku. **c** Foreldrar hans heita Sigríður og Magnús. **d** Hvað heitir amma hans? **e** Systir Björns, Kristín, er gift. **f** Maðurinn hennar heitir Þór.

Unit 4

1 (*possible answers*) **a** Konan er hávaxin, dökkhærð og frekar alvarleg. **b** Konan er lágvaxin, svolítið þybbin og með ljóst hár. Hún er ung og hamingjusöm. **c** Maðurinn er lágvaxinn og sköllóttur. Hann er reiður. **d** Strákurinn er hár og grannur. Hann er með sítt, ljóst hár. 2 **a** fyndin, leiðinleg, svart **b** rólegur, traustur **c** sæt, þybbin **d** mjó **e** latur, þrjóskur, kurteis 3 **a** Hún er Atladóttir. **b** Hún er Ingadóttir. **c** Hún er Einarsdóttir. **d** Hún er Karlsdóttir. **e** Hann er Snorrason. **f** Hann er Albertsson. **g** Hann er Jóhannsson. **h** Hann er Guðmundsson.

Unit 5

1 **a** Ég er að lesa bók. / Þeir eru að tala saman um Reykjavík. / Hann er í Reykjavík. 2 What are you reading? 3 **a** Anna og Inga eru að tala saman. **b** Hvað heitir bókin? **c** Hún heitir *Ísland á morgun.* **d** Hvar er listasafnið? **e** Það er í Reykjavík. **f** Hvað ertu að lesa? **g** Ég er að lesa bók um Ítalíu.

Unit 6

1 **a** Klukkan er tólf. **b** Klukkan er tvö. **c** Klukkan er fjögur. **d** Klukkan er þrjú. **e** Klukkan er sjö. **f** Klukkan er eitt. 2 **a** Tveir plús þrír eru fimm. **b** Fjórir mínus einn eru þrír. **c** Einn plús tólf eru þrettán. **d** Þrír plús fjórtán eru sautján. **e** Fimm plús fimmtán eru tuttugu. **f** Tveir plús sextán eru átján. **g** Tveir plús þrettán eru fimmtán. **h** Fjórir plús fimmtán eru nítján. **i** Átján mínus átta eru tíu. **j** Tíu mínus átta eru tveir. 3 **a** Nítján hundruð og þrjátíu – 1930. **b** Tvö þúsund og eitt – 2001. **c** Nítján hundruð sjötíu og þrjú – 1973. **d** Fimmtán hundruð fimmtíu og eitt – 1551. **e** Fjórtán hundruð þrjátíu og sjö – 1437. 4 **a** Símanúmerið hjá Önnu er fimm, sex, fjórir, þrír, núll, fimm, sex. **b** Símanúmerið hjá Ingu er fjórir, þrír, einn, átta, níu, fjórir, einn. **c** Síminn hjá Ástu er fimm, fimm, núll, tveir, núll, þrír, einn. **d** Síminn hjá Kára er fjórir, fimm, þrír, níu, fjórir, sjö, átta. **e** Síminn hjá Atla er fimm, sex, fjórir, þrír, tveir, tveir, þrír. 5 Eitt þúsund níu hundruð og níutíu krónur. / Nítján hundruð og níutíu krónur. Tvö þúsund níu hundruð og níutíu krónur. Þrjú þúsund níu hundruð og níutíu krónur. Níu þúsund, níu hundruð og níutíu krónur. Fimm þúsund níu hundruð og níutíu krónur. 6 **a** Ég bý í London. **b** Hún býr á Akureyri. **c** Hann býr í Reykjavík. **d** Hann býr í Berlín. **e** Hún býr í München. **f** Þau búa á Ísafirði. 7 **a** Kringlunni eitt, hundrað og þrjú Reykjavík. Sími: fimm, sex, níu, einn, einn, núll, núll / fimm, sex, níu, ellefu, núll, núll / fimm, sextíu og níu, ellefu, núll, núll / fimm, sextíu og níu, ellefu hundruð / fimm, sex, níu, ellefu hundruð. Símbréf:

fimm, sex, níu, einn, þrír, tveir, níu / fimm, sex, níu, þrettán, tuttugu og níu / fimm, sextíu og níu, þrettán, tuttugu og níu. **b** Stórhöfði þrjátíu og þrjú. Sími: fimm, sjö, sjö, fjórir, einn, núll, núll / fimm, sjö, sjö, fjörutíu og einn, núll, núll / fimm, sjötíu og sjö, fjörutíu og einn núll núll. Fax: fimm, sjö, sjö, fjórir, einn, núll, einn / fimm, sjö, sjö, fjörutíu og einn, núll, einn / fimm, sjötíu og sjö, fjörutíu og einn, núll, einn. **c** Opið á sunnudag frá klukkan þrettán til sextán / frá klukkan eitt til fjögur. Bæjarlind sex, tvö hundruð Kópavogi. Sími: fimm, fimm, fjórir, sex, þrír, núll, núll / fimm, fimm fjórir, sextíu og þrír, núll, núll / fimm, fimmtíu og fjórir, sextíu og þrír, núll, núll. **d** Klapparstíg fjörutíu og fjögur. Sími: fimm, sex, tveir, þrír, sex, einn, fjórir / fimm, sex, tveir, þrjátíu og sex, fjórtán / fimm, sextíu og tveir, þrjátíu og sex, fjórtán. **e** Sími: fimm, sex, níu, fimm, einn, núll, núll / fimm, sex, níu, fimmtíu og einn, núll, núll / fimm, sextíu og níu, fimmtíu og einn, núll, núll. Fax: fimm, sex, níu, fimm, tveir, fimm, einn / fimm, sex, níu, fimmtíu og tveir, fimmtíu og einn / fimm, sextíu og níu, fimmtíu og tveir, fimmtíu og einn.

Unit 7

1 a Ég ætla að hitta Önnu annað kvöld. **b** Ég ætla að hitta Erlu á morgun. **c** Ég ætla að hringja í Láru á föstudaginn. **d** Ég ætla að fara til Íslands á mánudaginn **e** Þeir (Tónleikarnir) byrja klukkan hálfníu. **f** Ég ætla að fara á morgun klukkan korter yfir þrjú. **g** Ég ætla að hitta Dóru klukkan tuttugu mínútur yfir níu. **h** Við ætlum að fara klukkan korter í níu. **2 a** á morgun = *tomorrow*, annaðkvöld = *tomorrow evening*, sunnudagskvöldið = *Sunday evening*; í dag = *today*, laugardaginn 19. = *Saturday 19th* **b** í kvöld = *tonight, this evening*, föstudag = *Friday*, laugardag = *Saturday* **c** í dag = *today*, fimmtudag = *Thursday*, á morgun = *tomorrow*, föstudag = *Friday* **d** mán. – fim. = *Mondays – Thursdays*, föst. = *Fridays*, laug. og sun. = *Saturdays and Sundays*, mán. – mið. = *Mondays – Wednesdays*, þri. – föst. = *Tuesdays – Fridays*, mán. – fös. = *Mondays – Fridays*, lau. = *Saturdays*. **3 a** Miðvikudagur. / Í dag er miðvikudagur. **b** þriðjudagur. / Í gær var þriðjudagur. **c** Mánudagur. / Í fyrradag var mánudagur. **d** Fimmtudagur. / Á morgun er fimmtudagur. **4** Ég er að lesa bók um Ítalíu. / Hún heitir *Italía á morgun*. / Jú, ég er líka að lesa bók um Ísland – hún heitir *Ísland í dag*. / Ég fer snemma, klukkan níu í fyrramálið. **5 a** Hvaða dagur er í dag? Það er sunnudagur. **b** Fyrirgefðu, hvað er klukkan? Hún er hálfþrjú. **6 b** Hún byrjar klukkan tuttugu og sex mínútur yfir níu. (09.26). **c** Hún byrjar klukkan sjö mínútur í tíu. (09.53). **d** Það byrjar klukkan tíu mínútur yfir ellefu. (11.10). **e** Hann byrjar klukkan tuttugu og fimm mínútur yfir eitt. (13.25). **f** Það byrjar klukkan tíu mínútur í fjögur. (15.50). **g** Það byrjar klukkan tuttugu mínútur í átta. (19.40). **h** Hún byrjar klukkan tuttugu og fimm mínútur yfir átta. (20.25). **i** Hún byrjar klukkan hálf ellefu. (22.30). **j** Hann byrjar klukkan átta. (08.00). **k** Hún byrjar klukkan tuttugu mínútur í sex. (17.40). **l** Það byrjar klukkan fimm mínútur í sjö. (18.55). **m** Það byrjar klukkan sjö. (19.00). **n** Hún byrjar klukkan hálftvö. (01.30)

Unit 8

1 a kenni **b** gerir **c** gera **d** þekkir **e** ætlaði **f** ætluðum **g** kenndum **h** hittu **2** Hún er viðskiptafræðingur og vinnur hjá Landsbanka Íslands. / Nei, hann er að læra læknisfræði. / Nei, hann er lögfræðingur. / Nei, hún er fiðluleikari. / Nei, hún vinnur hjá (*or* á) fasteignasölu. / Nei, hann er dósent í sagnfræði. **3** leikkona, leikari, lögfræðingur, kennari, þjónn, tölvufræðingur, sálfræðingur, fiðluleikari, sagnfræðingur, líffræðingur, læknir, þýðandi, smiður, kokkur, ritari.

Unit 9

1 a hann **b** hans **c** hana **d** hennar **e** mig **f** þig **g** hann **h** það **i** þær **j** ykkur **k** þá **l** þau **m** okkur. **2 a** Já, hann var búinn að hitta Erlu. **b** Já, hann var búinn að skoða hús Davíðs Stefánssonar. **c** Já, hann var búinn að fara í Akureyrarkirkju. **d** Nei, hann var ekki búinn að heimsækja Snorra. **e** Já, hann var búinn að fara í sund. **f** Já, hann var búinn að skoða Lystigarðinn. **3** Sæl! / Mjög vel. / Já, ég hitti Erlu í gær og ég ætla að heimsækja Snorra á morgun. / Nei, hún er í Reykjavík núna. / Já, ég fór að skoða það í gær. / **4 a** Have you met Kári yet? / Yes, we met on Tuesday. / Did you like him? / Yes, very much!

Unit 10

1 a kem **b** komum **c** Kemur **d** komst **e** kom **2** kom – fyrradag – mjög – heimsækja – vinkonu – mánudaginn – bráðum **3 a** Hæ! Gaman að sjá þig! **b** Hafðirðu það ekki gott? **c** Hvenær kemurðu aftur heim? **4** Lárétt: 1 Kristján 4 Páls 6 skólann 7 Gunnar 9 Ólafi 11 mann 13 Ísafirði 17 bróður 18 Finns 21 Birni 22 kennarans **Lóðrétt:** 2 sellóleikarann 3 jeppann 5 lækninn 8 skólanum 10 Arnar 12 Ísleif 14 afa 15 Ingólfs 16 ritarann 19 Ingvari 20 bílinn

Unit 11

1 Góðan daginn. / Já, ég ætla að fá samloku með smjöri, hangikjöti og salati. / Já, eina flösku af sódavatni. / Já, takk. / Takk! **2 a** Rétt. **b** Rétt. **c** Rétt. **d** Rangt. **e** Rangt. **f** Rétt. **g** Rangt. **h** Rétt. **i** Rétt. **3 b** Björn vildi koma við í sjoppu á leiðinni heim, af því að hann var rosalega svangur. **c** Anna vildi líka fá eitthvað að borða. **d** Björn vildi fá samloku með osti og grænmeti. **e** Björn vildi ekki fá poka. **f** Björn og mamma hans voru að tala saman. **g** Það vantaði bara smjör og hangikjöt. **h** Björn ætlaði að fara út í búð. **i** Mamma Björns skrifaði lista. **4 a** talað **b** skrifað **c** farið **d** komið **e** get

Unit 12

1 a Áttu **b** Eiga **c** Eigið **d** á **e** næ **2** Eigum við ekki að kaupa perur og gulrætur? / Eigum við ekki líka að kaupa fisk? / Ég ætla að ná í nammið. Getur þú náð í ísinn? **3 a** Já, þau keyptu grænmeti. **b** Já, þau keyptu appelsínur. **c** Nei, þau keyptu ekki hangikjöt. **d** Já, þau keyptu brauð. **e** Nei, þau keyptu ekki pylsur. **f** Nei, þau keyptu ekki kjötbollur. **g** Nei, þau keyptu ekki samlokur. **4 a** Talaðu við hann! **b** Náðu í bílinn! **c** Kauptu bókina! **d** Kallaðu á hann! **e** Farðu með honum! **f** Hringdu í Ingu!

Unit 13

1 Já, mér finnst fiskur góður. / Nei, mér finnst fiskibollur ekki góðar. / Já, mér finnst brauð með smjöri og osti gott. / Já, mér finnst sælgæti rosalega gott. / Nei, mér finnst grænmeti ekki gott. **2 a** Já, ég hef lesið bók/bækur eftir Halldór Laxness. / Nei, ég hef aldrei lesið bók eftir Halldór Laxness. **b** Já, ég hef oft farið til Þýskalands. / Nei, ég hef aldrei farið Þýsklands. **c** Já, ég hef oft komið til Íslands. / Nei, ég hef aldrei komið til Íslands. **d** Já, ég hef oft hitt Íslendinga. / Nei, ég hef aldrei hitt Íslendinga. **e** Já, ég hef lesið bók um Ísland / Nei, ég hef aldrei lesið bók um Ísland. **3 a** Þeir **b** Þeir **c** Þær **d** þá **e** þær **f** þá **4 a** kennarana **b** hnífa **c** strákana **d** mennina **e** læknana **f** bílana **g** lögfræðingana

Unit 14

1 a Ólafur er að æfa sig að lesa rússnesku. **b** Hvað fékkstu þér að borða? **c** Ég fékk mér samloku með smjöri og eplum. **d** Hann rakaði sig í morgun. **2 a** iv **b** ii **c** v **d** i **e** vii **f** viii **g** vi **h** iii **3 a** Get ég (nokkuð) fengið vatnsglas? **b** Geturðu nokkuð rétt mér smjörið? **c i** Takk fyrir mig. **ii** Verði þér að góðu. **4 a** Já, ég borða oft epli. Nei, ég borða mjög sjaldan appelsínur. **b** Já, ég fæ mér oft ís með jarðarberjum. **c** Nei, ég hef aldrei smakkað ís með bláberjum. **d** Já, ég borða mjög oft grænmeti. **e** Ég borða oftast gulrætur. **5 a** byrjaður **b** sofnuð **c** þekktur **d** farin **e** gleymt

Unit 15

1 a Ætlarðu að gera eitthvað í kvöld? b Viltu koma í bíó? / Ertu til í að koma í bíó? / Langar þig að koma í bíó? c Á hvaða mynd eigum við að fara? / Hvaða mynd eigum við að sjá? 2 a Já, Björn (hann) hringir í Gunnar. b Já, Gunnar (hann) langar að fara í bíó. c Hún er í Háskólabíói. d Það er spennumynd. e Hann heitir Keanu Reeves. f Já, hún vill líka fara í bíó. g Já, þeir ætla að ná í hana. 3 a góðar b góðir c ensku d ítölsku e hressa f stórir g vitlausar h danska 4 a A Ætlarðu að gera eitthvað í kvöld? / b Eru einhverjar góðar myndir í bíó núna?

Unit 16

1 a Hvenær áttu afmæli? b Hvenær á mamma þín afmæli? En pabbi þinn? c Þekkirðu einhvern sem á afmæli í janúar? d Hvað ertu gamall (/gömul)? e Hvað eru mamma þín og pabbi gömul? f Hvað er besti vinur þinn gamall? g Hvaða mánaðardagur er í dag? h Hvaða mánaðardagur var í gær? En í fyrradag? i Hvenær byrjaðirðu að læra íslensku? j Í hvaða mánuði eru jólin? k Í hvaða mánuði eru páskarnir? 2 a Já, hún fékk afmælisgjöf frá Ástu (og foreldrum hennar / mömmu hennar og pabba). b Hún fékk peysu og silfureyrnalokka. c Hún fékk skó. d Já, hann ætlaði að gefa henni eitthvað í afmælisgjöf. e Hann / Christof á afmæli annan mars. Hún / Inga á afmæli tuttugasta og fjórða febrúar. 3 a Gunnar er fimmtíu og tveggja ára (gamall). b Anna er fertug / fjörutíu ára (gömul). c Þór er tuttugu og þriggja ára (gamall). d Ragnar er nítján ára (gamall). e Kristín er þriggja ára (gömul). f Magnús er sjötíu og fjögurra ára (gamall). 4 a þarft b þurfti c þurfum 5 a mitt b sína c minn d sína e mitt f þinn

Symbols in square brackets are IPA (International Phonetic Alphabet) symbols except for the following, which are commonly used in Icelandic phonetics books:

Icelandic	IPA
[þ]	[θ]
[ö]	[œ]

Vowels

a 1) [a] like French / German / Italian / Spanish *a* – similar to *a* in English *father*. Example: **sandur** (*sand*)
   2) [au] before the letters *ng* and *nk*, like *ow* in English *down*. Example: **ganga** (*walk*)

á [au] see description above. Example: **ást** (*love*)

e 1) [ɛ] like *e* in English *bed*. Example: **senda** (*send*)
   2) [ɛi] before the letters *ng, nk, gi* and *gj*, like *a* in English *came*. Examples: **England** (*England*), **skenkja** (*pour*), **feginn** (*relieved*), **segja** (*say*)

é [jɛ] like *ye* in English *yes*. Example: **ég** (*I*)

i 1) [ɪ] like *i* in English *hid, bid*. Example: **listi** (*a list*)
   2) [i] before the letters *ng, nk* and *gi*, like *ea* in English *heat*. Examples: **Inga** (a woman's name), **sink** (*zinc*), **stigi** (*stairs, ladder*)

í [i] see description above. Example: **sími** (*telephone*)

o 1) [ɔ] like *aw* in English *law, bawd*. Example: **loft** (*air*)
   2) [ɔi] before the letters *gi*, like *oy* in English *Boyd*. Example: **logi** (*flame*)

ó [ɔu] very similar to the exclamation *oh* in English. Example: **bóndi** (*farmer*)

u 1) [ʏ] This sound does not occur in English. It is produced by trying to pronounce [ɪ] (as in Icelandic *listi* or English *hid*) with rounded lips. This sound appears in German short *ü*, as in *fünf, küssen*. Example: **hundur** (*dog*)
2) [u] before the letters *ng* and *nk*, like *o* in English *who*. Examples: **ungur** (*young*), **bunki** (*pile*)
3) [ʏi] before the letters *gi* (*ugi* is not a very common combination!); see description of [ʏ] and [i] above. Example: **Huginn** (a man's name)

ú [u] see description above. Example: **Rússi** (*a Russian*)

y [ɪ] see description above. Example: **synda** (*swim*)

ý [i] see description above. Example: **sýna** (*show*)

æ [ai] like *i* in English *hide*. Example: **læsa** (*lock*)

ö [ö] This sound does not occur in English. It is produced by trying to pronounce [e] (as in Icelandic *senda* or English *bed*) with rounded lips. It is quite similar to the *i* in English *bird* and *ea* in English *heard*. This sound appears in German ö, as in *plötzlich* and in French *eu*, as in *neuf*. Example: **hönd** (*hand*)

ei [ei] see description above. Example: **neisti** (*spark*)

ey [ei] see description above. Example: **keyra** (*drive*)

au [öy] see description of [ö] above – [y] is pronounced like [i], except that it is rounded. The sound [y] only appears in this combination [öy] in Icelandic. Example: **haust** (*autumn*)

Consonants

b [b̥] like English [b], except voiceless; like *p* in English *spin*. Example: **bær** (*town*)

d [d̥] like English [d], except voiceless; like *t* in English *stop*. Example: **draumur** (*dream*)

ð 1) [ð] like *th* in English *father, Sutherland*. Example: **eða** (*or*)
2) [þ] before voiceless sounds, like *th* in English *thriller, heath*. Examples: **iðka** (*practise*)

f 1) [f] like *f* in English *father*. Example: **fá** (*get*)
2) [v] between voiced sounds, like *v* in English *very*. Examples: **lifa** (*live*), **hafði** (*had*)

3) [b̥] between a vowel and the letters *n* or *l*, see description above. Examples: **sofna** (*fall asleep*), **Keflavík** (Icelandic town; site of international airport)

g 1) [ǥ] at the beginning of words before the letters *a, á, o, ó, u, ú, ö* or consonants; before the letters *n, l*; after consonants; and before the letters *a, u*; and at the end of words after consonants, like English [g], except voiceless; like *k* in English *skip*. Occurs anywhere except in the positions listed in (2–5). Examples: **gata** (*street*), **grár** (*grey*), **vegna** (*because of*), **sigla** (*sail*), **bjarga** (*rescue*), **borg** (*city*)

2) [ɟ] before the letters *e, i, í, y, ý, æ, ei, ey* or *j*, like *g* in English *geese*; you can think of it as [gj]. Examples: **gefa** (*give*), **Helgi** (a man's name)

3) [x] before the letters *t* or *s*. This sound does not occur in English. It appears in German *ch*, as in *ach*, in Spanish *j*, as in *jota* and in Scottish *ch*, as in *loch*. *g* before *s* can also be pronounced [ǥ] (common amongst younger people). Examples: **hægt** (*possible*), **hugsa** (*think*)

4) [ɣ] between two vowels, when the latter one is not *i*; between a vowel and *ð* and *r*; and at the end of a word after a vowel. This sound does not occur in English. It appears in Spanish *g*, as in *Tarragona*. Examples: **saga** (*story*), **sagði** (*said*), **sigra** (*win*), **lag** (*song*)

5) [j] between a vowel and the letter *i* or *j*, like *y* in English *yes*. Examples: **stigi** (*stairs, ladder*), **segja** (*say*)

h 1) [h] like *h* in English *he*. Example: **hundur** (*dog*)

2) [kʰ] when followed by the letter *v*, like *k* in English *kick*. Example: **hvað** (*what*)

3) The letters *hj* are pronounced [ç]. This sound does not occur in English, but it is quite similar to the *h* in English *huge*. It appears in German *ch*, as in *ich*. Example: **hjón** (*couple*)

4) The letters *hé* are pronounced [çɛ]; see description of [ç] and [ɛ] above. Example: **hér** (*here*)

5) The letters *hr* are pronounced [r̥]. This is a voiceless r-sound, which does not occur in English. It occurs in Welsh, like *rh* in *rhan*. The voiced [r] in Icelandic is a trill, i.e. it is rolled. This sound also does not appear in English, but it appears in Spanish *rr*, as in *Tarragona*, and it is very similar to [r] in Scottish. Now say this rolled voiced [r] and then try to let more air out of your mouth while pronouncing the voiced [r], and you should get the voiceless r-sound. Example: **hrópa** (*yell*)

6) The letters *hl* are pronounced [ḷ]. This is a voiceless l-sound, which does not occur in English, but it appears in Welsh, like *ll* in *Lloyd*. The voiced [l] in Icelandic is pronounced like *l* in English *land*. Use the same method as when producing voiceless [r]: say normal [l] (i.e. voiced [l]) and then, while you are saying the [l], try to let more air out of your mouth. Example: **hlusta** (*listen*)

7) The letters *hn* are pronounced as [n̥]. This is a voiceless n-sound, which does not occur in English. The voiced [n] in Icelandic is pronounced like *n* in English *nature*. To produce the voiceless n-sound, say a voiced [n] and then at the same time let the air out of your nose, and the sound will become voiceless. Example: **hnútur** (*knot*)

j 1) [j] see description above. Example: **já** (*yes*)

2) The letters *hj* are pronounced as [ç]; see description above. Example: **hjón** (*couple*)

k 1) [kʰ] at the beginning of words before the letters *a, á, o, ó, u, ú, ö* or consonants; see description above. Examples: **kasta** (*throw*), **króna** (unit of money used in Iceland)

2) [cʰ] at the beginning of words before the letters *e, i, í, y, ý, æ, ei, ey* or *j*, like *k* in English *keen*; you can think of it as [kj]. Example: **kenna** (*teach*)

3) [ɡ̊] medially (i.e. inside words) before the letters *a, á, o, ó, u, ú, ö* and at the end of words, see description above. Examples: **taka** (*take*), **tak** (*hold*)

4) [ɟ̊] medially before the letters *e, i, í, y, ý, æ, ei, ey* or *j*; see description above. Example: **poki** (*bag*)

5) [x] before the letters *t* or *s*; see description above. *k* before *s* can also be pronounced [ɡ̊] (common amongst younger people). Example: **rakt** (*damp*)

l 1) [l] see description above. Example: **lás** (*lock*)

2) [ḷ] at the beginning of words which are written with *hl*, before the letters *p, t, k* and at the end of words after voiceless sounds; see description above. Examples: **hlusta** (*listen*), **sulta** (*jam*), **skafl** (*snow drift*)

m 1) [m] like *m* in English *mother*. Example: **mála** (*paint*)

2) [m̥] before the letters *p, t, k* and at the end of words. This is a voiceless m-sound, which does not occur in English. To produce this sound, say a voiced [m] and then let the air out of your nose, and the sound will become voiceless. Examples: **lampi** (*lamp*), **stam** (*stuttering*)

n 1) [n] like *n* in English *night*. Example: **nú** (*now*)
2) [n̥] at the beginning of words which are written with *hn*, before the letters *p, t, k* and at the end of words after voiceless sounds; see description above. Examples: **hnútur** (*knot*), **vanta** (*need*), **vagn** (*wagon*)

3) [n] before the sound [ɟ], when there is *g* in the spelling. This is pronounced as [n], but a bit further back in the mouth (but not as far as [ŋ], see below). Example: **enginn** (*nobody*)
4) [ɲ] before the sound [ɟ], when there is *k* in the spelling; same method as before: say [n] and then let the air out of your nose. Example: **banki** (*bank*)
5) [ŋ] before the sound [ǥ], when there is *g* in the spelling; like *n* in English *finger*. Example: **fingur** (*finger*)
6) [ŋ̊] before the sound [ǥ], when there is *k* in the spelling; again the same method: say [ŋ] and then let the air out of your nose. Example: **banka** (*knock*)

p 1) [pʰ] at the beginning of words; like *p* in English *pen*. Example: **penni** (*pen*)
2) [b̥] see description above. Examples: **tapa** (*lose*), **tap** (*loss*)
3) [f] before the letters *t, k* or *s*; see description above. Examples: **skipta** (*divide*), **dýpka** (*deepen*), **skips** (*ship, genitive*)

r 1) [r] see description above. Example: **rós** (*rose*)
2) [r̥] at the beginning of words which are written with *hr*, before the letters *p, t, k* or *s*; see description above. Examples: **hrópa** (*yell*), **orka** (*energy*)

s [s] like s in English *sea*. Example: **sól** (*sun*)

t 1) [tʰ] at the beginning of words, like *t* in English *time*. Example: **taska** (*handbag, suitcase*)
2) [d̥] see description above. Example: **gata** (*street*)

v [v] see description above. Example: **vasi** (*pocket*)

x [xs] or [ǥs] It is optional whether you pronounce the letter *x* as [xs] or [ǥs]. The pronunciation [ǥs] is more common amongst younger people. See description of [x], [s] and [ǥ] above. Example: **buxur** (*trousers*)

þ [þ] see description above. Example: **þurfa** (*need*)

Other rules

The letters *ll* are pronounced as [d̥l/d̥l̥]. Examples: **fjall** (*mountain*), **hóll** (*hill*), **kjóll** (*dress*), **galli** (*flaw*), **hellir** (*cave*),

stóll (*chair*). In a few loanwords and in nicknames, however, *ll* is pronounced as long [l]: in nicknames: **Kalli, Palli, Solla, Ella,** in loanwords: **galli** (*clothes, overall*), **gallabuxur** (*jeans*), **halló** (*hello*), **Holland** (*the Netherlands*), **ball** (*ball, dance*).

The letters *nn* are pronounced [d̥n] / [d̥n̥] when preceded by a letter with a superscript mark (*í, ý, é, á, ú, ó*) or by a diphthong (*æ, ei, ey, au*). Examples: **brúnn** (*brown*), **steinn** (*stone*), **Spánn** (*Spain*). Otherwise *nn* is pronounced as long [n]. Examples: **inni** (*inside*), **tunna** (*barrel*). There is, however, an exception to this rule: if *nn* is part of the definite article it is always pronounced as long [n]. Examples: **brúnni** (*the bridge, dative*), **kránni** (*the pub, dative*).

The letters *rn* are pronounced as [rd̥n] / [rd̥n̥]. Examples: **fornöld** (*ancient times*). The r-sound can often be dropped, so the letters *rn* are then just pronounced [d̥n]/[d̥n̥]. This is can be done (1) in very common words (**Björn** (a man's name), **Bjarni** (a man's name), **þarna** (*there*), **hérna** (*here*), **barn** (*child*)) and (2) when the *n* belongs to the definite article (**afarnir** (*the grandfathers, definite*)). Note that the dropping of the [r] is optional: **Björn** can be pronounced [b̥jördn̥] or [b̥jödn̥]. In everyday speech it is very common, however, though to drop the [r] in these cases.

When the letters *pp, tt, kk; pl, tl, kl; pn, tn, kn* appear between vowels, they are **preaspirated**, i.e. an [h] sound is pronounced before them, and the following stop ([b̥, d̥, g̊, ɟ̊]) is then short. The [h] sound is (normally) a clear, ordinary h sound, like the one in **hús** (*house*). It is helpful to imagine a false boundary between the [h] sound and the stop ([b̥, d̥, g̊, ɟ̊]); then you have an [h] sound at the end of the first part, and it is easier to pronounce an [h] at the end than in the middle of a word. So when you say the word **uppi**, say it in two steps: [ʏh – b̥ɪ]. Examples: **uppi** (*upstairs*), **köttur** (*cat*), **ekki** (*not*), **epli** (*apple*), **fatlaður** (*handicapped*), **hekla** (*crochet*), **opna** (*open*), **vatn** (*water*), **sakna** (*miss*).

Icelandic–English vocabulary

The words are listed according to the Icelandic alphabet:

a á b d ð e é f g h i í j k l m
n o ó p r s t u ú v x y ý þ æ ö

að *that, to*
aðal- *main*
aðallega *mainly*
aðeins *a little bit; only*
aðlaðandi *attractive*
aðstoða *help, assist*
af *of, from*
af því að *because*
afgreiðslumaður *shop assistant* (male)
afgreiðslukona *shop assistant* (female)
afi *grandfather*
afmæli *birthday*
  ég á afmæli *it's my birthday*
  til hamingju með afmælið *happy birthday*
afmælisgjöf *birthday present*
  fá í afmælisgjöf *get as a birthday present*
aftur *again*
alast upp *grow up*
aldeilis, það er aldeilis! *that's impressive*
aldrei *never*
  aldrei (...) áður *never (...) before*
allir *everybody*
allt *everything*
  allt í lagi *OK, all right*

alltaf *always*
alvarlegur *serious*
alveg *just, absolutely*
Alþingi *the Icelandic parliament*
Alþingishúsið *the Icelandic parliament* (building)
Ameríka *America*
Ameríkani *American*
amerískur *American* (adj.)
amma *grandmother*
annar *(the) second*
ansi *quite, rather*
appelsína *orange*
appelsínusafi *orange juice*
apríl *April*
Argentína *Argentina*
argentínskur *Argentine* (adj.)
Argentínumaður *Argentine*
athyglisverður *interesting*
auðvitað *of course*
austur *east*
austur- *eastern*
austurhluti *the eastern part*
Austurland *the eastern part of Iceland*
Austurríki *Austria*
Austurríkismaður *Austrian*
austurrískur *Austrian* (adj.)

á   *at, on, in, onto, into*
á eftir   *later, later on*
á meðan   *while*
áður   *before, earlier*
áður en   *before*
ágúst   *August*
ákveða   *decide*
ár   *year*
ást   *love*
Ástrali   *Australian*
Ástralía   *Australia*
ástralskur   *Australian* (adj.)
átján   *eighteen*
átjándi   *(the) eighteenth*
átta   *eight*
áttatíu   *eighty*
áttugasti   *(the) eightieth*
áttundi   *(the) eighth*
ávaxtaskál   *fruit bowl*
ávöxtur   *fruit*

bakpoki   *backpack*
banani   *banana*
Bandaríkin   *United States*
Bandaríkjamaður   *American*
bandarískur   *American* (adj.)
banki   *bank*
bara   *just, only*
barn   *child*
Belgi   *Belgian*
Belgía   *Belgium*
belgískur   *Belgian* (adj.)
Belgíumaður   *Belgian*
ber   *berry*
bestur   *the best*
bið   *wait*
bíða   *wait* (verb)
biðja   *ask, request*
biðröð   *queue*
bilaður   *broken (down)*
bílasala   *car sale*
bíll   *car*
bílstjóri   *driver*
bíó   *cinema*
bjóða   *offer, invite*
blað   *paper, newspaper*
bláber   *blueberry*
blár   *blue*
bless   *goodbye, bye*
blessaður/blessuð   *hello, hi;*

goodbye, bye
bolla   *ball, bun*
bolur   *top, T-shirt*
borð   *table*
borða   *eat*
borg   *city*
bók   *book*
bóndabær   *farm*
bóndi   *farmer*
bragð   *taste*
Brasilía   *Brazil*
brasilískur   *Brazilian* (adj.)
Brasilíumaður   *Brazilian*
brauð   *bread*
bráðum   *soon*
breskur   *British*
Breti   *Briton*
Bretland   *Britain*
bréf   *letter*
bróðir   *brother*
brúnn   *brown*
buxur   *trousers*
búa   *live*
búð   *shop*
búinn   *(has) finished*
   vera búinn að gera eitthvað
      *have finished doing
      something, have done
      something*
Búlgari   *Bulgarian*
Búlgaría   *Bulgaria*
búlgarska   *Bulgarian (language)*
búlgarskur   *Bulgarian (adj.)*
byrja   *start*
byrjaður (*from* byrja)   *(has)
   started*
byrjun   *beginning*
   í byrjun   *at/in the beginning
      (of)*
bæ   *bye*
bæði   *both*
   bæði ... og   *both ... and*
bær   *town*

dagur   *day*
   í dag   *today*
Dani   *Dane*
Danmörk   *Denmark*
danska   *Danish (language)*
danskur   *Danish (adj.)*

dáinn *dead*
desember *December*
deyja *die*
diskur *plate; disc*
dós *can, tin*
dósent *senior lecturer*
dóttir *daughter*
drekka *drink*
draumur *dream*
duglegur *hard working, efficient*
dýr *expensive*
dökkhærður *dark-haired*

eða *or*
ef *if*
eftir *after, in*
  á eftir *later on, afterwards*
eftirmatur *dessert*
eiga *have, own, be supposed to,
  shall*
eiginkona *wife* (formal)
eiginmaður *husband* (formal)
ein *one* (fem.)
einhver *someone, some*
einhvern tíma *sometime, some
  day; ever*
einhvers staðar *somewhere*
einmitt *exactly; just*
einn *one* (masc.)
eins og *like, as*
Eisti *Estonian*
Eistland *Estonia*
Eistlendingur *Estonian*
eistneska *Estonian* (language)
eistneskur *Estonian* (adj.)
eitt *one* (neut.)
eitthvað *something*
ekkert *nothing*
  ekkert mál *no problem*
eldhús *kitchen*
ellefti *(the) eleventh*
ellefu *eleven*
elska *love*
  elskan mín *my love, my dear*
  elsku Anna *dear Anna, Anna
    my love*
e-mail *e-mail*
en *but; how about; than*
endilega *by all means*

England *England*
Englendingur *Englishman*
enska *English* (language)
enskur *English* (adj.)
eplasafi *apple juice*
epli *apple*
eyra *ear*
eyri *sandbank, sand spit*
eyrnalokkur *earring*

faðir *father*
fallegur *beautiful*
fangi *prisoner*
fara *go, leave*
  fara á kaffihús *go to a café*
  fara á safn *go to a museum*
  fara á tónleika *go to a concert*
  fara í bíó *go to the cinema*
  fara í sund *go swimming*
  fara út að borða *go out for
    dinner*
farinn (*from* fara) *(has) gone*
farsími *mobile phone*
fasta *fast*
fasteignasala *estate agency*
fax *fax*
fá *get*
  fá sér *have, lit. get oneself
    (something)*
febrúar *February*
feiminn *shy*
feitur *fat*
fertugasti *(the) fortieth*
fé *money*
fiðla *violin*
fiðluleikari *violinist*
fimm *five*
fimmtán *fifteen*
fimmtándi *(the) fifteenth*
fimmti *(the) fifth*
fimmtíu *fifty*
fimmtudagur *Thursday*
fimmtugasti *(the) fiftieth*
finnast *think, feel*
fingur *finger*
Finni *Finn*
Finnland *Finland*
finnska *Finnish* (language)
finnskur *Finnish* (adj.)

fiskibolla *fishcake*
fiskur *fish*
fínn *fine, good*
fínt! *great!*
fjórar *four* (fem.)
fjórði *(the) fourth*
fjórir *four* (masc.)
fjórtán *fourteen*
fjórtándi *fourteenth*
fjögur *four* (neut.)
fjölskylda *family*
fjörður *fjord*
fjörutíu *forty*
flaska *bottle*
fleira *more*
fljótur *quick*
flott! *great!*
flottur *beautiful, great, smart*
flug *flight*
flugfélag *airline*
flugvél *aeroplane*
flugvöllur *airport*
foreldrar *parents*
fótbolti *football*
Frakki *Frenchman*
Frakkland *France*
framhaldsskóli *secondary
    school, high school*
frami *distinction; career*
franska *French* (language)
franskur *French* (adj.)
frá *from*
frábær *great, fantastic*
frábært! *great!*
frekar *rather, a bit*
frændi *nephew, uncle, cousin,
    male relative*
frænka *niece, aunt, cousin,
    female relative*
fullur *full*
fyndinn *funny*
fyrir *for*
fyrir utan *outside*
fyrirgefa e-m *forgive somebody*
fyrirgefðu *sorry, excuse me*
í fyrra *last year*
í fyrradag *the day before yesterday*
í fyrramálið *tomorrow morning*
fyrsti *(the) first*

fyrstur *first*
fæddur *born*
föstudagur *Friday*

gaffall *fork*
gamall *old*
gaman *nice, pleasant, enjoyable,
    fun*
    mér finnst það gaman *I enjoy
    / like it*
gamlárskvöld *New Year's Eve*
garður *park, garden*
gata *street, road*
gá *check*
gáfaður *intelligent*
gefa *give*
geisladiskur *CD*
geisli *beam, ray*
gemsi *mobile phone*
gera *do*
gestrisinn *hospitable*
geta *can, be able to*
gift / giftur *married*
giska *make a guess, guess*
gjöf *present*
gjöra *do* (old form of *gera*)
    gjörðu svo vel (*sing.*) / gjörið þið
    svo vel (*pl.*) *here you are;
    please go ahead* (an invitation to
    come to the table (lit. *do so well*)
glas *glass*
gleyma *forget*
gleymdur *forgotten*
góður *good*
grannur *thin*
gráhærður *grey-haired*
grár *grey*
grein *article*
Grikki *Greek*
Grikkland *Greece*
gríska *Greek* (language)
grískur *Greek* (adj.)
grunnskóli *primary school,
    secondary school* (6–16 yrs.)
grunnur *foundation, base*
Grænland *Greenland*
Grænlendingur *Greenlander*
grænlenska *Greenlandic*
    (language)

grænlenskur   *Greenlander* (adj.)
grænmeti   *vegetables*
gsm-sími   *mobile phone*
gulrót   *carrot*
gulur   *yellow*
gúrka   *cucumber*
í gær   *yesterday*
í gærkvöldi   *last night*

hafa   *have*
  hafa samband við   *contact*
  hafa það gott   *have a nice time*
    (when speaking about
    holidays / time off from work)
halda   *hold*
halda áfram   *continue*
  halda áfram að gera eitthvað
    continue doing something
halda upp á eitthvað   *celebrate*
    something
hamingja   *happiness*
  til hamingju   *congratulations*
hamingjusamur   *happy*
hamingjuóskir   *congratulations,*
    lit. *wishes of happiness*
handa   *for*
handbolti   *handball*
hangikjöt   *smoked meat*
hans   *his, (to) him*
haust   *autumn*
há-   *high*
hádegi   *midday, noon*
hádegismatur   *lunch*
hálftími   *half an hour*
hálfur   *half*
hár   *hair*
hár   *tall, high*
hárgreiðslukona   *hairdresser*
    (female)
hárgreiðslumaður   *hairdresser*
    (male)
háskóli   *university*
hávaxinn   *tall*
hefna sín   *avenge oneself*
heiðarlegur   *honest*
heillandi   *charming, fascinating*
heim   *home*
heima   *at home*
heimasíða   *home page*

heimasími   *home telephone*
    number
heimilisfang   *address*
heimspeki   *philosophy*
heimsækja   *visit*
heita   *be called*
helgi   *weekend*
helst   *most*
hennar   *her, hers, (to) her*
hér   *here*
hérna   *here*
himinn   *sky*
hiti   *heat, warmth*
hitta   *meet*
hittast   *meet,* lit. *meet each other*
hjá   *by, at, with*
hjálpa   *help*
hjón   *married couple*
hjúkrunarfræði   *nursing*
hjúkrunarfræðingur   *nurse*
hljómsveit   *orchestra, band*
hlusta   *listen*
hluti   *part*
hneta   *nut*
hnífur   *knife*
Holland   *Holland*
Hollendingur   *Dutchman*
hollenska   *Dutch* (language)
hollenskur   *Dutch* (adj.)
horfa   *watch*
  horfa á eitthvað   *watch*
    something
hress   *fun, lively*
hringja   *ring, phone*
hugsa   *think*
hundrað   *hundred*
hundraðasti   *(the) hundredth*
hundur   *dog*
hús   *house*
hvað   *what*
hvaða   *which*
hvaðan   *where from*
hvar   *where*
hve margir / margar / mörg (*from*
    margur)   *how many*
hvenær   *when*
hver   *who*
hvernig   *how*
hvers   *whose*

hæ *hi*
hægt *possible*
hætta *stop, quit*
höfn *harbour*
höfuð *head*
höfuðborg *capital*
höfuðborgarsvæðið *the capital area*
hönd *hand* (noun)

illska *evil*
Indland *India*
Indverji *Indian*
indverskur *Indian (adj.)*
inn (*movement*) *inside*
  inn í *into*
inni (*position*) *inside*
  inni í (*position*) *inside (of)*
innilegur *warm, hearty*

í *in, to, into*
Íri *Irishman*
Írland *Ireland*
írska *Irish (language)*
írskur *Irish* (adj.)
ís *ice, ice cream*
Ísland *Iceland*
Íslandsmót *Icelandic championship*
Íslendingur *Icelander*
íslenska *Icelandic (language)*
íslenskur *Icelandic (adj.)*
Ísrael *Israel*
Ítali *Italian*
Ítalía *Italy*
ítalska *Italian (language)*
ítalskur *Italian (adj.)*

janúar *January*
Japan *Japan*
Japani *Japanese*
japanska *Japanese (language)*
japanskur *Japanese (adj.)*
jarðarber *strawberry*
já *yes*
  já takk *yes, please*
jeppi *jeep*
jól *Christmas*
  Gleðileg jól! *Merry Christmas!*
jú *yes (to a negative question)*

jú takk *yes, please* (to a negative question)
júlí *July*
júní *June*
jæja *well*

kaffi *coffee*
kaffihús *café*
kafli *chapter*
kall *slang for* **krónur**, cf. *quid, bucks*
kalla *call, shout*
Kanada *Canada*
Kanadabúi *Canadian*
kanadískur *Canadian* (adj.)
kannski *maybe*
karfa *basket*
kartafla *potato*
kassi *till, checkout*
kasta *throw*
kastljós *spotlight*
kaupa *buy*
kálhaus *cabbage*
kápa *(woman's) coat*
kenna *teach*
kennari *teacher*
kerra *shopping trolley*
keyra *drive*
kirkja *church*
kíkja *have a look*
Kína *China*
Kínverji *Chinese*
kínverska *Chinese (language)*
kínverskur *Chinese* (adj.)
kjöt *meat*
klukka *clock*
  klukkan er 5 *it's five o'clock*
  klukkan 5 *at five o'clock*
  klukkan hvað? *(at) what time?*
kokkur *cook*
koma *come, arrive*
  koma við í / á *stop at*
komast að *find out*
kominn (*from* koma) *(has) come, arrived*
kona *woman, wife*
kort *map*
korter *quarter*
kók *coke*
kór *choir*

Kórea   Korea

kóreska   Korean (language)
kóreskur   Korean (adj.)
Kóreubúi   Korean
krani   tap
krá   pub
króna   Icelandic currency
kurteis   polite
kveðja   regards, greetings
kvæntur   married (used about a man)
kvöld   evening
  í kvöld   this evening, tonight
  annað kvöld   tomorrow evening
kvöldmatur   dinner
kær   dear, beloved
kærasta   girlfriend
kærasti   boyfriend
kærlega   dearly

labba   walk
lag   song
lakkrís   liquorice
land   country, land
langa   want
langafi   great-grandfather
langamma   great-grandmother
latur   lazy
laug   hot spring
laugardagskvöld   Saturday evening
laugardagur   Saturday
lágvaxinn   short
lás   lock (noun)
láta   let
leggja   lay, put
  leggja á borðið   lay the table, set the table
  leggja af stað   go, start a journey
leið   way, route
leiðinlegur   boring
leigubíll   taxi
leigubílstjóri   taxi driver
leika   act, perform; play
leikari   actor
leikhús   theatre
leikkona   actress

leikskóli   kindergarten
lesa   read
Letti   Latvian
Lettland   Latvia
lettneska   Latvian (language)
lettneskur   Latvian (adj.)
léttmjólk   semi-skimmed milk
list   art
listasafn   art gallery
listi   list
líf   life
líffræði   biology
líffræðingur   biologist
líka   also
líka (verb)   like
lítri   litre
ljós   fair, blond, light
ljóst hár   blond hair
ljóshærður   blond
ljótur   ugly
loft   air
lottó   lottery
lystigarður   park, botanic garden
læknir   doctor
læknisfræði   medicine
læra   learn, study
læsa   lock (verb)
lög   law
lögfræði   law, jurisprudence
lögfræðingur   lawyer

maður   man, husband
maí   May
mamma   mother, mum
margir (from margur)   many people
margt (from margur)   many things
margur   many, a lot
mars   March
matur   food
mál   speech; matter, concern
mála   paint
mánaðardagur   date
máni   moon (no longer in use)
mánudagur   Monday
mánuður   month
með   with
mega   can, may

meira *more*
mennta *educate*
menntaskóli *secondary school,
high school*
Mexíkani *Mexican*
mexíkanskur *Mexican* (adj.)
Mexíkó *Mexico*
Mexíkói *Mexican*
Mexíkóskur *Mexican* (adj.)
mið- *middle*
miðbær *city centre, town centre*
miðvikudagur *Wednesday*
milljón *million*
minjar *relics*
minn *my, mine*
mínus *minus*
mínúta *minute*
mjólk *milk*
mjór *thin*
mjög *very*
mold *earth, soil*
morgunn *morning*
  í morgun *this morning*
  á morgun *tomorrow*
móðir *mother*
móðurmál *mother tongue,
native language*
mussa *blouse, top*
mynd *film*
myndlistarkona *painter, artist*
  (female)
myndlistarmaður *painter, artist*
  (male)
mæða *distress, trouble*
mæta *show up, turn up*
mörg *many*
mörk *field, wood*

nafn *name*
nammi *sweets*
ná *get, reach*
ná í *get, fetch, pick up*
nám *study, studying*
  vera í námi *study*
nefna *mention*
nei *no*
neisti *spark*
nema *except*
netfang *e-mail address*

niðri *down (by)*
niður *down*
  niður að *down to*
nítján *nineteen*
nítjándi *(the) nineteenth*
nítugasti *(the) ninetieth*
níu *nine*
níundi *(the) ninth*
níutíu *ninety*
nokkrir *a few (people)*
norðaustur *north-east*
Norðmaður *Norwegian*
norður *north*
norður- *northern*
norðurhluti *northern part*
Norðurland *the northern part of
Iceland*
norðvestur *north-west*
Noregur *Norway*
norska *Norwegian
  (language)*
norskur *Norwegian* (adj.)
nóg *enough*
nógu *enough*
nótt *night*
  í nótt *tonight, last night*
nóvember *November*
nú *now*
númer *number*
núna *now*
nýársdagur *New Year's day*
  Gleðilegt nýtt ár! Gleðilegt ár!
  Happy new year!
nýjung *newness*
nýlega *recently*
nýr *new*
næsti *next*

of *too*
ofsalega *really, extremely*
oft *often*
  oft (…) áður *often (…) before*
oftast *most often*
og *and*
okkar *our, ours; (to) us*
október *October*
opið *open*
opinskár *outspoken, frank*
orðinn *(from* verða*) (has)*

become
ostapopp *cheese popcorn*
ostur *cheese*
ókei *OK*
ósk *wish*

pabbi *father, dad*
pakki *present, parcel*
paprika *pepper*
páskar *Easter*
  Gleðilega páska! *Happy
    Easter!*
penni *pen*
pera *pear*
persónuleiki *personality*
peysa *sweater, jumper*
plús *plus*
poki *bag*
popp *popcorn*
Portúgal *Portugal*
Portúgali *Portuguese*
portúgalska *Portuguese*
  (language)
portúgalskur *Portuguese* (adj.)
Pólland *Poland*
pólska *Polish* (language)
pólskur *Polish* (adj.)
Pólverji *Pole*
póstkassi *mailbox*
próf *exam*
pylsa *hot dog*

raka *shave*
  raka sig *shave, lit. shave
    oneself*
rakt *damp*
rangur *false, incorrect*
rauður *red*
reiður *angry*
rétt hjá *near, close to*
rétta *hand* (verb)
réttur *true, right*
ritari *secretary*
rosalega *terribly, extremely, very*
rólegur *quiet*
rót *root*
rós *rose*
ruglaður *confused*
Rúmeni *Romanian*

Rúmenía *Romania*
rúmenska *Romanian* (language)
rúmenskur *Romanian* (adj.)
Rússi *Russian*
Rússland *Russia*
rússneska *Russian* (language)
rússneskur *Russian* (adj.)
rækja *shrimp*
rækjuostur *soft shrimp cheese*
röð *row*

saddur *full (have eaten enough)*
safi *juice*
safn *museum*
saga *story; history*
sagnfræði *(the science of)
  history*
sagnfræðingur *historian*
sakna *miss*
salat *salad*
saman *together*
samband *contact, connection,
  relationship*
samloka *sandwich*
samt *still, yet*
sandur *sand*
sautján *seventeen*
sautjándi *(the) seventeenth*
sálfræði *psychology*
sálfræðingur *psychologist*
segja *say*
seinna *later*
sellóleikari *cellist*
sem *as; who, which*
senda *send*
september *September*
setjast *take a seat, sit down*
sex *six*
sextán *sixteen*
sextándi *(the) sixteenth*
sextíu *sixty*
sextugasti *(the) sixtieth*
sigra *win*
sigur *victory*
silfur *silver*
silfureyrnalokkar *silver earrings*
sinfóníuhljómsveit *symphony
  orchestra*
sinn *his (own), her (own), their*

(own)

sinnep *mustard*
sía *filter*
síaður *filtered*
síður *long*
símanúmer *telephone number*
símbréf *fax*
sími *telephone*
sítróna *lemon*
sjampó *shampoo*
sjaldan *seldom*
sjá *see*
sjáumst *we'll see each other, see you*
sjoppa *kiosk*
sjónvarp *television*
sjö *seven*
sjötíu *seventy*
sjötti *(the) sixth*
sjötugasti *(the) seventieth*
sjöundi *(the) seventh*
skál *bowl*
skáld *poet*
skeið *spoon*
skemmtanalíf *nightlife (lit. entertainment life)*
skemmtilegur *fun, entertaining*
skemmtun *entertainment*
skera *cut*
skila *return*
skoða *see, look at, view; do sightseeing (in city)*
skollitað hár *dark blond hair, light brown hair*
skóli *school*
skór *shoes*
skreppa *pop (for a short time)*
skrifa *write*
skulu *shall, will*
    við skulum *let's*
sköllótur *bald*
smakka *taste (verb)*
smá *a little*
smiður *builder*
smjör *butter*
snemma *early*
sofna *fall asleep*
sofnaður *(from* sofna*)* *(has) fallen asleep*

sonur *son*
sódavatn *soda water*
sól *sun*
spaug *joke, fun*
Spánn *Spain*
Spánverji *Spaniard*
spenna *excitement, tension*
spennumynd *action film, thriller*
spítali *hospital*
springa *explode*
    ég er að springa lit. *I'm about to explode* (used when the speaker is really full)
spænska *Spanish (language)*
spænskur *Spanish (adj.)*
staður *place*
standa *stand*
    standa upp *stand up*
starfa *work*
steinn *stone*
stelpa *girl*
stig *degree*
stór *big*
stórborg *big city*
strákur *boy, guy*
stundum *sometimes*
stuttur *short*
stærstur *largest, biggest*
stöð *channel*
suðaustur *south-east*
suður *south*
suður- *southern*
Suður-Afríka *South Africa*
Suður-Afríkubúi *South African*
suður-afrískur *South African (adj.)*
suðurhluti *the southern part*
Suðurland *the southern part of Iceland*
suðvestur *south-west*
sumar *summer*
sund *swimming, swim*
sunna *sun* (no longer in use)
sunnudagur *Sunday*
súkkulaði *chocolate*
súkkulaðiís *chocolate ice cream*
svangur *hungry*
svartur *black*
Sviss *Switzerland*

Svisslendingur *Swiss*
svissneskur *Swiss* (adj.)
Svíi *Swede*
Svíþjóð *Sweden*
svo *then, so*
svolítill/svolítið *little, a little bit*
svona *such, about*
svæði *area*
synda *swim*
systir *sister*
systkini *siblings, brothers and sisters*
sýna *show*
sælgæti *sweets*
sæll / sæl *hello, hi*
sænska *Swedish* (language)
sænskur *Swedish* (adj.)
sætur *cute, good looking*
sömuleiðis *likewise*

tak *hold* (noun)
taka *take*
taka til *tidy up*
takk *thank you, thanks*
 takk fyrir *thanks*
 takk fyrir mig *thanks for the meal, lit. thanks for me*
 takk kærlega *thanks very much, thanks a lot*
tala *speak, talk*
 tala saman *talk to each other, chat*
 tala við (einhvern) *talk to (somebody)*
tap *loss*
tapa *lose*
taska *handbag; suitcase*
Tékki *Czech*
Tékkland *Czech Republic*
tékkneska *Czech* (language)
tékkneskur *Czech* (adj.)
til *to*
til að *to, in order to*
tilbúinn *ready*
tími *time; hour*
tíu *ten*
tíundi *(the) tenth*
tjörn *small lake, pond*
tólf *twelve*

tólfti *(the) twelfth*
tómatsósa *ketchup*
tómatur *tomato*
tónleikar *concert*
tónlist *music*
tónlistarskóli *music school*
tónn *tone*
trefill *winter scarf*
tryggur *loyal*
tungumál *language*
tuttugasti *(the) twentieth*
tuttugu *twenty*
tveir, tvær, tvö *two* (masc., fem., neut.)
Tyrki *Turk*
Tyrkland *Turkey*
tyrkneska *Turkish* (language)
tyrkneskur *Turkish* (adj.)
tækniskóli *polytechnic university*
Tæland *Thailand*
Tælendingur *Thai*
tælenska *Thai* (language)
tælenskur *Thai* (adj.)
tölva *computer*
tölvufræði / tölvunarfræði *computer science*
tölvufræðingur / tölvunarfræðingur *computer scientist*
tölvupóstur *e-mail*

um *about, at*
Ungverjaland *Hungary*
Ungverji *Hungarian*
ungverska *Hungarian* (language)
ungverskur *Hungarian* (adj.)
upp *up*
uppáhalds- *favourite*
uppi *above, up on*
upplýsingar *information*
uppþvottavél *dishwasher*
uppþvottur *washing up*
úr *from*
út *out*
úti *outside*
útlit *look*
útskrifast *graduate*
útvarp *radio*

vald *power*
vanta *need*
vasi *pocket; vase*
vatn *water*
vatnsglas *glass of water*
vá! *wow!*
veður *weather*
vegur *street, road*
vel *well*
velkominn *welcome*
vera *be*
  vera að gera eitthvað *be doing
    something*
  verði þér/ykkur að góðu
    *you're welcome, lit. be you to
    good*
  vera til *exist*
  vera til í að gera eitthvað *be
    up for doing sth.*
verða *have to, must; become,
  turn; will be*
verkfræði *engineering*
verkfræðingur *engineer*
verslun *shop*
Vestfirðir *Western fjords (of
  Iceland)*
vestur *west*
vestur- *western*
vesturhluti *the western part*
Vesturland *the western part of
  Iceland*
vettlingur *mitten*
vetur *winter*
vél *machine*
við *we*
við *at, by*
  við hliðina á *beside*
viðbót *addition, extra*
  í viðbót *in addition*
viðskiptafræði *business
  administration*
viðskiptafræðingur *graduate in
  business administration*
vika *week*
vilja *want*
vinkona *friend (female)*
vinna *work*
vinur *friend (male)*

vita *know*
vitlaus *stupid*
vík *cove, creek*
vín *wine*
vínber *grape*
víst *probably*
vor *spring*
völlur *field*

yfir *over*
ykkar *your, yours, (to) you –
  2nd pers. pl.*

það *it*
  Það er / eru *There is / are*
  Er það? *Really?*
þar *there*
þau *they (neut.)*
þá *then*
þegar *when*
þegja *be quiet, shut up*
þeir *they (masc.)*
þeirra *their, theirs, (to) them*
þekkja *know*
þekktur *known*
  vel þekktur *well known*
þess *its, (to) it*
þetta *this*
þið *you (pl.)*
þing *parliament*
þinn *your / yours*
þjóð *nation*
þjóðerni *nationality*
þjóðleikhús *national theatre*
þjóðminjasafn *national museum*
Þjóðverji *German*
þjónn *waiter*
þraut *hardship, trial*
þrettán *thirteen*
þrettándi *(the) thirteenth*
þriðji *(the) third*
þriðjudagur *Tuesday*
þrír *three (masc.)*
þrítugasti *(the) thirtieth*
þrjár *three (fem.)*
þrjátíu *thirty*
þrjú *three (neut.)*
þurfa *need, have to*
þú *you (sing.)*

þúsund *thousand*
því *therefore*
þvo *wash*
þvottur *washing*
þybbinn *chubby*
þýða *mean; translate*
þýðandi *translator*
þýska *German* (language)
Þýskaland *Germany*
þýskur *German* (adj.)
þægilegt *convenient*
þær *they* (fem.)

æðislegt! *great!*
æðislegur *great, really nice*
æfa *practise, train*
æi! *oh!*
ætla *be going to, intend, plan*

öflugur *great, powerful*
örugglega *most likely, probably*

English-Icelandic vocabulary

about *um; svona*
above *uppi*
absolutely *alveg*
act *leika*
action film *spennumynd*
actor *leikari*
actress *leikkona*
addition *viðbót*
  in addition *í viðbót*
address *heimilisfang*
aeroplane *flugvél*
after *eftir*
again *aftur*
air *loft*
airline *flugfélag*
airport *flugvöllur*
all right *allt í lagi*
also *líka*
always *alltaf*
America *Ameríka*
American (adj.) *amerískur,*
  bandarískur
American *Ameríkani,*
  Bandaríkjamaður
and *og*
angry *reiður*
apple *epli*
apple juice *eplasafi*
April *apríl*
area *svæði*
Argentina *Argentína*
Argentine (adj.) *argentínskur*
Argentine *Argentínumaður*
arrive *koma*
  (has) arrived *(er) kominn*

art *list*
art gallery *listasafn*
article *grein*
artist *myndlistarmaður* (male),
  myndlistarkona (female)
as *eins og; sem*
ask *biðja*
assist *aðstoða*
at *á; hjá; um; við*
attractive *aðlaðandi*
August *ágúst*
aunt *frænka*
Australia *Ástralía*
Australian *Ástrali*
Australian (adj.) *ástralskur*
Austria *Austurríki*
Austrian *Austurríkismaður*
Austrian (adj.) *austurrískur*
autumn *haust*
avenge oneself *hefna sín*

backpack *bakpoki*
bag *poki*
bald *sköllóttur*
banana *banani*
band *hljómsveit*
bank *banki*
base *grunnur*
basket *karfa*
be *vera*
  be able to *geta*
  be doing something *vera að*
    gera eitthvað
  be up for doing something
    vera til í að gera eitthvað

beam *geisli*
beautiful *fallegur, flottur*
because *af því að*
become *verða*
  (has) become *(er) orðinn*
before *áður en; áður*
beginning *byrjun*
  at/in the beginning *í byrjun*
Belgian (adj.) *belgískur*
Belgian *Belgíumaður*
Belgium *Belgía*
beloved *kær*
berry *ber*
beside *við hliðina á*
(the) best *bestur*
big *stór*
biggest *stærstur*
biologist *líffræðingur*
biology *líffræði*
birthday *afmæli*
  it's my birthday *ég á afmæli*
  happy birthday *til hamingju
    með afmælið*
birthday present *afmælisgjöf*
  get as a birthday present *fá í
    afmælisgjöf*
(a) bit *frekar*
black *svartur*
blond *ljóshærður*
  blond hair *ljóst hár*
  dark blond hair *skollitað hár*
blue *blár*
blueberry *bláber*
book *bók*
boring *leiðinlegur*
born *fæddur*
botanic garden *lystigarður*
both *bæði*
  both ... and *bæði ... og*
bottle *flaska*
bowl *skál*
boy *strákur*
boyfriend *kærasti*
Brazil *Brasilía*
Brazilian *Brasilíumaður*
Brazilian (adj.) *brasilískur*
bread *brauð*
Britain *Bretland*
British *breskur*

Briton *Breti*
broken (down) *bilaður*
brother *bróðir*
brown *brúnn*
builder *smiður*
Bulgaria *Búlgaría*
Bulgarian *Búlgari*
Bulgarian (language) *búlgarska*
Bulgarian (adj.) *búlgarskur*
business administration
  viðskiptafræði
  graduate in business
    administration
    viðskiptafræðingur
but *en*
butter *smjör*
buy *kaupa*
by *hjá; við*
  by all means *endilega*
bye *bless, bæ, blessaður /
  blessuð*

cabbage (head of) *kálhaus*
café *kaffihús*
call *kalla*
  (be) called *heita*
can *geta, mega*
can *dós*
Canada *Kanada*
Canadian (adj.) *kanadískur*
Canadian *Kanadabúi*
capital *höfuðborg*
car *bíll*
car sale *bílasala*
career *frami*
carrot *gulrót*
CD *geisladiskur*
celebrate sth. *halda upp á
  eitthvað*
cellist *sellóleikari*
channel *stöð*
chapter *kafli*
charming *heillandi*
chat *tala saman*
check *gá*
checkout *kassi*
cheese *ostur*
  cheese popcorn *ostapopp*
child *barn*

China *Kína*
Chinese *Kínverji*
Chinese (adj.) *kínverskur*
Chinese (language) *kínverska*
chocolate *súkkulaði*
chocolate ice cream *súkkulaðiís*
choir *kór*
church *kirkja*
Christmas *jól*
 Merry Christmas! *Gleðileg jól!*
chubby *þybbinn*
cinema *bíó*
city *borg*
 big city *stórborg*
city centre *miðbær*
clock *klukka*
 It's five o'clock *Klukkan er 5*
 at five o'clock *klukkan 5*
close to *rétt hjá*
coat (woman's) *kápa*
coffee *kaffi*
coke *kók*
come *koma*
 (has) come *(er) kominn*
come to the table *gjörðu svo vel*
 (sing.) / *gjörið þið svo vel* (pl.)
computer *tölva*
computer science *tölvufræði /*
 tölvunarfræði
computer scientist
 tölvufræðingur /
 tölvunarfræðingur
concern *mál*
concert *tónleikar*
confused *ruglaður*
congratulations *til hamingju,*
 hamingjuóskir
connection *samband*
contact (noun) *samband*
contact (verb) *hafa samband við*
continue *halda áfram*
 continue doing sth. *halda*
 áfram að gera eitthvað
convenient *þægilegt*
cook *kokkur*
country *land*
cousin (male) *frændi*
cousin (female) *frænka*
cove *vík*

creek *vík*
cucumber *gúrka*
cut *skera*
cute *sætur*
Czech *Tékki*
Czech (language) *tékkneska*
Czech (adj.) *tékkneskur*
Czech Republic *Tékkland*

dad *pabbi*
damp *rakt*
Dane *Dani*
Danish (adj.) *danskur*
Danish (language) *danska*
dark-haired *dökkhærður*
date *mánaðardagur*
daughter *dóttir*
day *dagur*
 the day before yesterday
 í fyrradag
dead *dáinn*
dear *kær*
 dear Anna *elsku Anna*
 my dear *elskan mín*
dearly *kærlega*
December *desember*
decide *ákveða*
degree *stig*
Denmark *Danmörk*
dessert *eftirmatur*
die *deyja*
dinner *kvöldmatur*
disc *diskur*
dishwasher *uppþvottavél*
distinction *frami*
distress *mæða*
do *gera, gjöra* (old form)
doctor *læknir*
dog *hundur*
down *niður*
 down by *niðri við*
 down to *niður að*
dream *draumur*
drink *drekka*
drive *keyra*
driver *bílstjóri*
Dutchman *Hollendingur*
Dutch (language) *hollenska*
Dutch (adj.) *hollenskur*

ear *eyra*
early *snemma*
  earlier (i.e. in the past) *áður*
earring *eyrnalokkur*
earth *mold*
east *austur*
Easter *páskar*
  Happy Easter! *Gleðilega páska!*
eastern *austur-*
  (the) eastern part *austurhluti*
  the eastern part of Iceland *Austurland*
eat *borða*
educate *mennta*
efficient *duglegur*
eight *átta*
eighteen *átján*
eighteenth *átjándi*
eighth *áttundi*
eightieth *áttugasti*
eighty *áttatíu*
eleven *ellefu*
(the) eleventh *ellefti*
e-mail *tölvupóstur, e-mail*
  e-mail address *netfang*
England *England*
Englishman *Englendingur*
English (adj.) *enskur*
English (language) *enska*
engineer *verkfræðingur*
engineering *verkfræði*
enjoy *finnast gaman*
  I enjoy it *mér finnst það gaman*
enjoyable *gaman*
enough *nóg, nógu*
entertaining *skemmtilegur*
entertainment *skemmtun*
estate agency *fasteignasala*
Estonia *Eistland*
Estonian *Eisti, Eistlendingur*
Estonian (adj.) *eistneskur*
Estonian (language) *eistneska*
evening *kvöld*
  this evening *í kvöld*
  tomorrow evening *annað kvöld*
  yesterday evening *í gærkvöldi*

ever *einhvern tíma*
everybody *allir*
everything *allt*
evil *illska*
exactly *einmitt*
exam *próf*
except *nema*
excitement *spenna*
excuse me *fyrirgefðu*
exist *vera til*
expensive *dýr*
explode *springa*
extra *viðbót*
extremely *ofsalega, rosalega*

fall asleep *sofna*
  (has) fallen asleep *er sofnaður*
false *rangur*
family *fjölskylda*
farm *bóndabær*
farmer *bóndi*
fascinating *heillandi*
fast *fasta*
fat *feitur*
father *pabbi, faðir*
favourite *uppáhalds-*
fax *fax, símbréf*
February *febrúar*
feel *finnast*
fetch *ná í*
(a) few (people) *nokkrir*
field *völlur; mörk*
fifteen *fimmtán*
(the) fifteenth *fimmtándi*
(the) fifth *fimmti*
fiftieth *fimmtugasti*
fifty *fimmtíu*
finished: (has) finished *búinn*
  have finished doing something *vera búinn að gera eitthvað*
film *mynd*
filter *sía*
filtered *síaður*
find out *komast að*
fine *fínn*
finger *fingur*
Finland *Finnland*
Finn *Finni*
Finnish (adj.) *finnskur*

Finnish (language) *finnska*
first *fyrstur*
(the) first *fyrsti*
fish *fiskur*
fishcake *fiskibolla*
five *fimm*
fjord *fjörður*
flight *flug*
food *matur*
football *fótbolti*
for *fyrir, handa*
forget *gleyma*
forgotten *gleymdur*
forgive s-b. *fyrirgefa e-m.*
fork *gaffall*
(the) fortieth *fertugasti*
forty *fjörutíu*
foundation *grunnur*
four *fjórar* (fem.), *fjórir* (masc.), *fjögur* (neut.)
fourteen *fjórtán*
fourteenth *fjórtándi*
(the) fourth *fjórði*
France *Frakkland*
frank *opinskár*
French (adj.) *franskur*
French (language) *franska*
Frenchman/woman *Frakki*
Friday *föstudagur*
friend *vinur* (male), *vinkona* (female)
from *frá; af; úr*
fruit *ávöxtur*
fruit bowl *ávaxtaskál*
full *fullur*
full (i.e. have eaten enough) *saddur*
I'm really full *ég er að springa*
fun (adj.) *hress, skemmtilegur*
fun (noun) *gaman, spaug*
funny *fyndinn*

garden *garður*
German *Þjóðverji*
German (adj.) *þýskur*
German (language) *þýska*
Germany *Þýskaland*
get *fá; ná; ná í*
get oneself (something) *fá sér*

(eitthvað)
girl *stelpa*
girlfriend *kærasta*
give *gefa*
glass *glas*
go *fara; leggja af stað*
go to a café *fara á kaffihús*
go to a museum *fara á safn*
go to a concert *fara á tónleika*
go out for dinner *fara út að borða*
go swimming *fara í sund*
go to the cinema *fara í bíó*
be going to *ætla*
(has) gone *farinn*
good *góður, fínn*
good looking *sætur*
goodbye *bless, blessaður / blessuð*
graduate *útskrifast*
grandfather *afi*
grandmother *amma*
grape *vínber*
great *flottur; öflugur*
great! *fínt!, flott!, frábært!, æðislegt!*
great-grandfather *langafi*
great-grandmother *langamma*
Greece *Grikkland*
Greek *Grikki*
Greek (adj.) *grískur*
Greek (language) *gríska*
Greenland *Grænland*
Greenlander *Grænlendingur, grænlenskur* (adj.)
Greenlandish (language) *grænlenska*
greetings *kveðja*
grey *grár*
grey-haired *gráhærður*
grow up *alast upp*
guess *giska*
make a guess *giska*
guy *strákur*

hair *hár*
hairdresser *hárgreiðslukona* (female), *hárgreiðslumaður* (male)
half *hálfur*

half an hour *hálftími*
hand (noun) *hönd*
hand (verb) *rétta*
handbag *taska*
handball *handbolti*
happiness *hamingja*
happy *hamingjusamur*
harbour *höfn*
hard working *duglegur*
hardship *þraut*
have *hafa, eiga*
   have a nice time (when speaking
      about holidays / time off from
      work) *hafa það gott*
   have a look *kíkja*
   have to *verða, þurfa*
head *höfuð*
hearty *innilegur*
heat *hiti*
hello *sæll / sæl, blessaður / blessuð*
help *hjálpa, aðstoða*
her *hennar*
   her own *sinn*
   to her *til hennar*
here *hér, hérna*
   here you are *gjörðu svo vel*
      (sing.) / *gjörið þið svo vel* (pl.)
hers *hennar*
hi *hæ, sæll / sæl, blessaður /*
   blessuð
(to) him *(til) hans*
high *há-, hár*
high school *framhaldsskóli,*
   menntaskóli
his *hans*
   his own *sinn*
historian *sagnfræðingur*
history *sagnfræði* (the science of
   history), *saga*
hold (noun) *tak*
hold (verb) *halda*
Holland *Holland*
home *heim*
   at home *heima*
home page *heimasíða*
home telephone number
   heimasími
honest *heiðarlegur*
hospitable *gestrisinn*

hospital *spítali*
hot dog *pylsa*
hour *tími, klukkutími*
house *hús*
how *hvernig*
how about *en*
how many *hve margir / margar /*
   mörg
hundred *hundrað*
(the) hundredth *hundraðasti*
Hungarian *Ungverji*
Hungarian (adj.) *ungverskur*
Hungarian (language) *ungverska*
Hungary *Ungverjaland*
hungry *svangur*
husband *maður, eiginmaður*
   (formal)

ice *ís*
ice cream *ís*
Iceland *Ísland*
Icelander *Íslendingur*
Icelandic (adj.) *íslenskur*
Icelandic (language) *íslenska*
Icelandic championship
   Íslandsmót
if *ef*
impressive: that's impressive *það*
   er aldeilis
in *í, á; eftir*
incorrect *rangur*
India *Indland*
Indian *Indverji*
Indian (adj.) *indverskur*
information *upplýsingar*
inside *inn* (movement), *inni* (position)
   inside (of) *inni í*
intelligent *gáfaður*
intend *ætla*
interesting *athyglisverður*
into *inn í, á, í*
invite *bjóða*
Ireland *Írland*
Irish (adj.) *írskur*
Irish (language) *írska*
Irishman *Íri*
Israel *Ísrael*
it *það*
   (to) it *þess*

its *þess*
Italian *Ítali*
Italian (adj.) *ítalskur*
Italian (language) *ítalska*
Italy *Ítalía*

January *janúar*
Japan *Japan*
Japanese *Japani*
Japanese (adj.) *japanskur*
Japanese (language) *japanska*
jeep *jeppi*
joke *spaug*
juice *safi*
July *júlí*
jumper *peysa*
June *júní*
jurisprudence *lögfræði*
just *alveg; bara; einmitt*

ketchup *tómatsósa*
kindergarten *leikskóli*
kiosk *sjoppa*
kitchen *eldhús*
knife *hnífur*
know *vita; þekkja*
known *þekktur*
    well known *vel þekktur*
Korea *Kórea*
Korean *Kóreubúi*
Korean (adj.) *kóreskur*
Korean (language) *kóreska*
Krona   the Icelandic currency:
    króna, kall (slang for *króna*)

(small) lake *tjörn*
land *land*
language *tungumál*
largest *stærstur*
later *seinna*
later on *á eftir*
Latvia *Lettland*
Latvian *Letti*
Latvian (adj.) *lettneskur*
Latvian (language) *lettneska*
law *lög; lögfræði*
lawyer *lögfræðingur*
lay *leggja*
    lay the table *leggja á borðið*

lazy *latur*
learn *læra*
leave *fara*
lemon *sítróna*
let *láta*
let's (let us) *við skulum*
letter *bréf*
life *líf*
like *eins og*
like (verb) *líka; finnast gaman*
    I like it *mér finnst það gaman*
likewise *sömuleiðis*
liquorice *lakkrís*
list *listi*
listen *hlusta*
litre *lítri*
little: a little bit *aðeins, smá,*
    svolítill, svolítið
live *búa*
lively *hress*
lock (verb) *læsa*
lock (noun) *lás*
long *síður*
look *útlit*
look at *skoða*
lose *tapa*
loss *tap*
lot (of), a *margur*
lottery *lottó*
love (noun) *elska; ást*
    my love *elskan mín*
loyal *tryggur*
lunch *hádegismatur*

machine *vél*
mailbox *póstkassi*
main *aðal-*
mainly *aðallega*
man *maður*
many *margur*
    many people *margir*
    many things *margt*
map *kort*
March *mars*
married *gift / giftur, kvæntur*
    (used about a man)
married couple *hjón*
matter *mál*
may *mega*

May *maí*
maybe *kannski*
mean *þýða*
meat *kjöt*
medicine *læknisfræði*
meet *hitta, hittast*
mention *nefna*
Mexican *Mexíkani, Mexíkói*
Mexican (adj.) *mexíkanskur*
Mexico *Mexíkó*
midday *hádegi*
middle *mið-*
milk *mjólk*
million *milljón*
mine *minn*
minus *mínus*
minute *mínúta*
miss *sakna*
mitten *vettlingur*
mobile phone *farsími, gemsi,*
  gsm-sími
Monday *mánudagur*
money *fé*
month *mánuður*
more *meira, fleira*
morning *morgunn*
  this morning *í morgun*
most *helst*
  most likely *örugglega*
mother *mamma, móðir*
mother tongue *móðurmál*
mum *mamma*
museum *safn*
music *tónlist*
music school *tónlistarskóli*
must *verða*
mustard *sinnep*
my *minn*

name *nafn*
nation *þjóð*
national museum *þjóðminjasafn*
national theatre *þjóðleikhús*
nationality *þjóðerni*
native language *móðurmál*
near *rétt hjá*
need *vanta; þurfa*
never *aldrei*
  never (...) before *aldrei (...)*

  áður
new *nýr*
New Year's Day *nýársdagur*
  Happy New Year! *Gleðilegt*
  nýtt ár!, Gleðilegt ár!
New Year's Eve *gamlárskvöld*
newness *nýjung*
newspaper *blað*
next *næsti*
nice *gaman*
night *nótt*
  last night *í nótt; í gærkvöldi*
nine *níu*
nineteen *nítján*
(the) nineteenth *nítjándi*
(the) ninetieth *nítugasti*
ninety *níutíu*
(the) ninth *níundi*
no *nei*
noon *hádegi*
north *norður*
north-east *norðaustur*
northern *norður-*
  northern part *norðurhluti*
  the northern part of Iceland
  Norðurland
north-west *norðvestur*
Norway *Noregur*
Norwegian *Norðmaður*
Norwegian (adj.) *norskur*
Norwegian (language) *norska*
nothing *ekkert*
November *nóvember*
now *núna, nú*
number *númer*
nurse *hjúkrunarfræðingur*
nursing *hjúkrunarfræði*
nut *hneta*

October *október*
of *af*
of course *auðvitað*
offer *bjóða*
often *oft*
  often (...) before *oft (...) áður*
  most often *oftast*
oh! *æi!*
OK *allt í lagi, ókei*
old *gamall*

on *á*
one *einn* (masc.), *ein* (fem.),
  eitt (neut.)
only *aðeins, bara*
onto *á*
open *opið*
or *eða*
orange *appelsína*
orange juice *appelsínusafi*
orchestra *hljómsveit*
(in) order to *til að*
our *okkar*
ours *okkar*
out *út*
outside *úti; fyrir utan*
outspoken *opinskár*
over *yfir*
own *eiga*

paint *mála*
painter *myndlistarmaður* (male),
  myndlistarkona (female)
paper *blað*
parcel *pakki*
parents *foreldrar*
park *garður; lystigarður*
parliament *þing*
  the Icelandic parliament *Alþingi*
  the Icelandic parliament
    building *Alþingishúsið*
part *hluti*
pear *pera*
pen *penni*
pepper *paprika*
perform *leika*
personality *persónuleiki*
philosophy *heimspeki*
phone *hringja*
pick up *ná í*
place *staður*
plan *ætla*
plate *diskur*
play *leika*
pleasant *gaman*
plus *plús*
pocket *vasi*
poet *skáld*
Poland *Pólland*
Pole *Pólverji*

Polish (adj.) *pólskur*
Polish (language) *pólska*
polite *kurteis*
polytechnic university
  tækniskóli
pond *tjörn*
pop *skjótast*
popcorn *popp*
Portugal *Portúgal*
Portuguese *Portúgali*
Portuguese (adj.) *portúgalskur*
Portuguese (language)
  portúgalska
possible *hægt*
potato *kartafla*
power *vald*
powerful *öflugur*
practise *æfa*
present *gjöf, pakki*
primary school *grunnskóli*
prisoner *fangi*
probably *örugglega; víst*
problem: no problem *ekkert mál*
psychologist *sálfræðingur*
psychology *sálfræði*
pub *krá*
put *leggja*

quarter *korter*
queue *biðröð*
quick *fljótur*
quiet *rólegur*
  (be) quiet *þegja*
quit *hætta*
quite *ansi*

radio *útvarp*
rather *frekar, ansi*
ray *geisli*
reach *ná*
read *lesa*
ready *tilbúinn*
really *ofsalega*
really? *er það?*
recently *nýlega*
red *rauður*
regards *kveðja*
relationship *samband*
relative *frændi* (male), *frænka*

(female)
relics *minjar*
request *biðja*
return *skila*
right *réttur*
ring *hringja*
road *gata, vegur*
Romania *Rúmenía*
Romanian *Rúmeni*
Romanian (adj.) *rúmenskur*
Romanian (language) *rúmenska*
root *rót*
rose *rós*
route *leið*
row *röð*
Russia *Rússland*
Russian *Rússi*
Russian (adj.) *rússneskur*
Russian (language) *rússneska*

salad *salat*
sand *sandur*
sand spit, sandbank *eyri*
sandwich *samloka*
Saturday *laugardagur*
    Saturday evening
    laugardagskvöld
say *segja*
school *skóli*
second *annar*
secondary school
    *framhaldsskóli, menntaskóli;
    grunnskóli*
secretary *ritari*
see *sjá; skoða*
    see you / we'll see each other
    sjáumst
seldom *sjaldan*
semi-skimmed milk *léttmjólk*
send *senda*
senior lecturer *dósent*
September *september*
serious *alvarlegur*
set the table *leggja á borðið*
seven *sjö*
seventeen *sautján*
(the) seventeenth *sautjándi*
(the) seventh *sjöundi*
(the) seventieth *sjötugasti*

seventy *sjötíu*
shall *eiga, skulu*
shampoo *sjampó*
shave *raka, raka sig*
shoes *skór*
shop *búð, verslun*
shop assistant *afgreiðlumaður*
    (male), *afgreiðlukona* (female)
shopping trolley *kerra*
short *lágvaxinn, stuttur*
shout *kalla*
show (verb) *sýna*
show up *mæta*
shrimp *rækja*
shut up *þegja*
shy *feiminn*
siblings *systkini*
(do) sightseeing (in a city) *skoða*
silver *silfur*
sister *systir*
sit down *setjast*
six *sex*
sixteen *sextán*
(the) sixteenth *sextándi*
(the) sixtieth *sextugasti*
(the) sixth *sjötti*
sixty *sextíu*
sky *himinn*
smart *flottur*
smoked meat *hangikjöt*
so *svo*
soda water *sódavatn*
soft shrimp cheese *rækjuostur*
soil *mold*
some day *einhvern tíma*
someone *einhver*
something *eitthvað*
sometime *einhvern tíma*
sometimes *stundum*
somewhere *einhvers staðar*
son *sonur*
song *lag*
soon *bráðum*
sorry *fyrirgefðu*
south *suður*
South Africa *Suður-Afríka*
South African *Suður-Afríkubúi,
    suður-afrískur*
south-east *suðaustur*

southern *suður-*
  the southern part *suðurhluti*
  the southern part of Iceland
    Suðurland
south-west *suðvestur*
Spain *Spánn*
Spaniard *Spánverji*
Spanish (adj.) *spænskur*
Spanish (language) *spænska*
spark *neisti*
speak *tala*
speech *mál*
spoon *skeið*
spotlight *kastljós*
spring *vor*
stand *standa*
  stand up *standa upp*
start *byrja*
  start a journey *leggja af stað*
  (has) started *byrjaður*
still *samt*
stop *hætta*
stop at *koma við í / á*
story *saga*
strawberry *jarðarber*
street *gata, vegur*
study (noun) *nám*
study (verb) *læra, vera í námi*
stupid *vitlaus*
such *svona*
summer *sumar*
sun *sól*
Sunday *sunnudagur*
be supposed to *eiga*
sweater *peysa*
Swede *Svíi*
Sweden *Svíþjóð*
Swedish (adj.) *sænskur*
Swedish (language) *sænska*
sweets *nammi, sælgæti*
swim (noun) *sund*
swim (verb) *synda*
swimming *sund*
Swiss (adj.) *svissneskur*
Swiss *Svisslendingur*
Switzerland *Sviss*
symphony orchestra
  sinfóníuhljómsveit

table *borð*
take *taka*
  take a seat *setjast*
talk *tala*
  talk to each other *tala saman*
  talk to sb. *tala við einhvern*
tall *hávaxinn, hár*
tap *krani*
taste (noun) *bragð*
taste (verb) *smakka*
taxi *leigubíll*
  taxi driver *leigubílstjóri*
teach *kenna*
teacher *kennari*
telephone *sími*
telephone number *símanúmer*
television *sjónvarp*
ten *tíu*
tension *spenna*
(the) tenth *tíundi*
terribly *rosalega*
Thai *Tælendingur*
Thai (adj.) *tælenskur*
Thai (language) *tælenska*
Thailand *Tæland*
than *en*
thank you, thanks *takk, takk
  fyrir*
  thanks very much / a lot *takk
    kærlega*
  thanks for the meal *takk fyrir
    mig*
that *að*
theatre *leikhús*
their *þeirra*
  their (own) *sinn*
theirs *þeirra*
(to) them *(til) þeirra*
then *svo; þá*
there *þar*
  There is / are *Það er / eru*
therefore *því*
they *þeir* (masc.), *þær* (fem.),
  þau (neut.)
thin *grannur, mjór*
think *hugsa, finnast*
(the) third *þriðji*
thirteen *þrettán*
(the) thirteenth *þrettándi*

(the) thirtieth *þrítugasti*
thirty *þrjátíu*
this *þetta*
thousand *þúsund*
three *þrír* (masc.), *þrjár* (fem.),
  þrjú (neut.)
thriller *spennumynd*
throw *kasta*
Thursday *fimmtudagur*
tidy up *taka til*
till *kassi*
time *tími*
  (at) what time? *klukkan hvað?*
tin *dós*
to *til, í, að, til að*
today *í dag*
together *saman*
tomato *tómatur*
tomorrow *á morgun*
  tomorrow morning *í fyrramálið*
tone *tónn*
tonight *í kvöld; í nótt*
too *of*
top (item of women's clothing)
  bolur, mussa
town *bær*
town centre *miðbær*
train *æfa*
translate *þýða*
translator *þýðandi*
trial *þraut*
trouble *mæða*
trousers *buxur*
true *réttur*
Tuesday *þriðjudagur*
Turk *Tyrki*
Turkey *Tyrkland*
Turkish (adj.) *tyrkneskur*
Turkish (language) *tyrkneska*
turn *verða*
  turn up *mæta*
(the) twelfth *tólfti*
twelve *tólf*
twentieth *tuttugasti*
twenty *tuttugu*
two *tveir* (masc.), *tvær* (fem.),
  tvö (neut.)

ugly *ljótur*

uncle *frændi*
United States *Bandaríkin*
university *háskóli*
up *upp*
up on *uppi*
us *okkur, okkar*

vase *vasi*
vegetables *grænmeti*
very *mjög, rosalega*
victory *sigur*
view *skoða*
violin *fiðla*
violinist *fiðluleikari*
visit *heimsækja*

wait (noun) *bið*
wait (verb) *bíða*
waiter *þjónn*
walk *labba*
want *langa, vilja*
warm *innilegur*
warmth *hiti*
wash *þvo*
  wash oneself *þvo sér*
wash basin *vaskur*
washing up *uppþvottur*
watch *horfa*
  watch sth. *horfa á eitthvað*
water *vatn*
  glass of water *vatnsglas*
way *leið*
we *við*
weather *veður*
Wednesday *miðvikudagur*
week *vika*
weekend *helgi*
welcome *velkominn*
  you're welcome *verði þér /*
  ykkur að góðu
well *vel; jæja*
west *vestur*
western *vestur-*
  the western fjords of Iceland
  Vestfirðir
  the western part *vesturhluti*
  the western part of Iceland
  Vesturland
what *hvað*

when   *hvenær; þegar*
where   *hvar*
where from   *hvaðan*
which   *hvaða; sem*
while   *á meðan*
who   *hver; sem*
whose   *hvers*
wife   *kona, eiginkona* (formal)
will   *skulu*
will be   *verða*
win   *sigra*
wine   *vín*
winter   *vetur*
   winter scarf   *trefill*
wish   *ósk*
with   *með; hjá*
woman   *kona*
wood   *mörk*

work   *vinna, starfa*
wow!   *vá!*
write   *skrifa*

year   *ár*
   last year   *í fyrra*
yellow   *gulur*
yes   *já, jú* (answer to a negative question)
   yes, please   *já takk, jú takk* (answer to a negative question)
yesterday   *í gær*
yet   *samt*
you   *þú* (sing.) / *þið* (pl.)
   (to) you (pl.)   *(til) ykkar*
your   *þinn* (sing.) / *ykkar* (pl.)
yours   *þinn* (sing.) / *ykkar* (pl.)

index

Numbers refer to units.